UPON A TIME

OUT
OF THE
PAST

COLLECTION EDITOR: **JENNIFER GRÜNWALD**
ASSISTANT EDITOR: **SARAH BRUNSTAD**
ASSOCIATE MANAGING EDITOR: **ALEX STARBUCK**
EDITOR, SPECIAL PROJECTS: **MARK D. BEAZLEY**
SENIOR EDITOR, SPECIAL PROJECTS: **JEFF YOUNGQUIST**
SVP PRINT, SALES & MARKETING: **DAVID GABRIEL**

EDITOR IN CHIEF: **AXEL ALONSO**
CHIEF CREATIVE OFFICER: **JOE QUESADA**
PUBLISHER: **DAN BUCKLEY**
EXECUTIVE PRODUCER: **ALAN FINE**

ONCE UPON A TIME: OUT OF THE PAST. First printing 2015. ISBN# 978-0-7851-9116-2. Published by MARVEL WORLDWIDE, INC., a subsidiary of MARVEL ENTERTAINMENT, LLC. OFFICE OF PUBLICATION: 135 West 50th Street, New York, NY 10020. Once Upon a Time © ABC Studios. All Rights Reserved. All characters featured in this issue and the distinctive names and likenesses thereof, and all related indicia are trademarks of ABC Studios. No similarity between any of the names, characters, persons, and/or institutions in this magazine with those of any living or dead person or institution is intended, and any such similarity which may exist is purely coincidental. Marvel and its logos are TM & © Marvel Characters, Inc. **Printed in the U.S.A.** ALAN FINE, EVP - Office of the President, Marvel Worldwide, Inc. and EVP & CMO Marvel Characters B.V.; DAN BUCKLEY, Publisher & President - Print, Animation & Digital Divisions; JOE QUESADA, Chief Creative Officer; TOM BREVOORT, SVP of Publishing; DAVID BOGART, SVP of Operations & Procurement, Publishing; C.B. CEBULSKI, SVP of Creator & Content Development; DAVID GABRIEL, SVP Print, Sales & Marketing; JIM O'KEEFE, VP of Operations & Logistics; DAN CARR, Executive Director of Publishing Technology; SUSAN CRESPI, Editorial Operations Manager; ALEX MORALES, Publishing Operations Manager; STAN LEE, Chairman Emeritus. For information regarding advertising in Marvel Comics or on Marvel.com, please contact Niza Disla, Director of Marvel Partnerships, at ndisla@marvel.com. For Marvel subscription inquiries, please call 800-217-919. **Manufactured between 1/23/2015 and 3/2/2015 by R.R. DONNELLEY, INC., SALEM, VA, USA.**
10 9 8 7 6 5 4 3 2 1

ONCE UPON A TIME

OUT OF THE PAST

Based on the television series *Once Upon a Time*
created by Edward Kitsis & Adam Horowitz

KALINDA VAZQUEZ
STORY

CORINNA BECHKO & KALINDA VAZQUEZ
SCRIPT

DEAD IN THE WATER
PASCAL CAMPION
ART & COLORS

TRUTH AND DAGGERS
BETSY PETERSCHMIDT
ART & COLORS

GHOSTS
VANESA DEL REY
ART
ESTHER SANZ
COLORS

TEA PARTY IN MARCH
JANET LEE
ART & COLORS

STACEY LEE
COVER ART

VC'S CLAYTON COWLES
LETTERS

EMILY SHAW
EDITOR

CHAPTER ONE

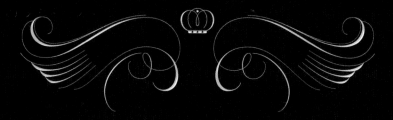

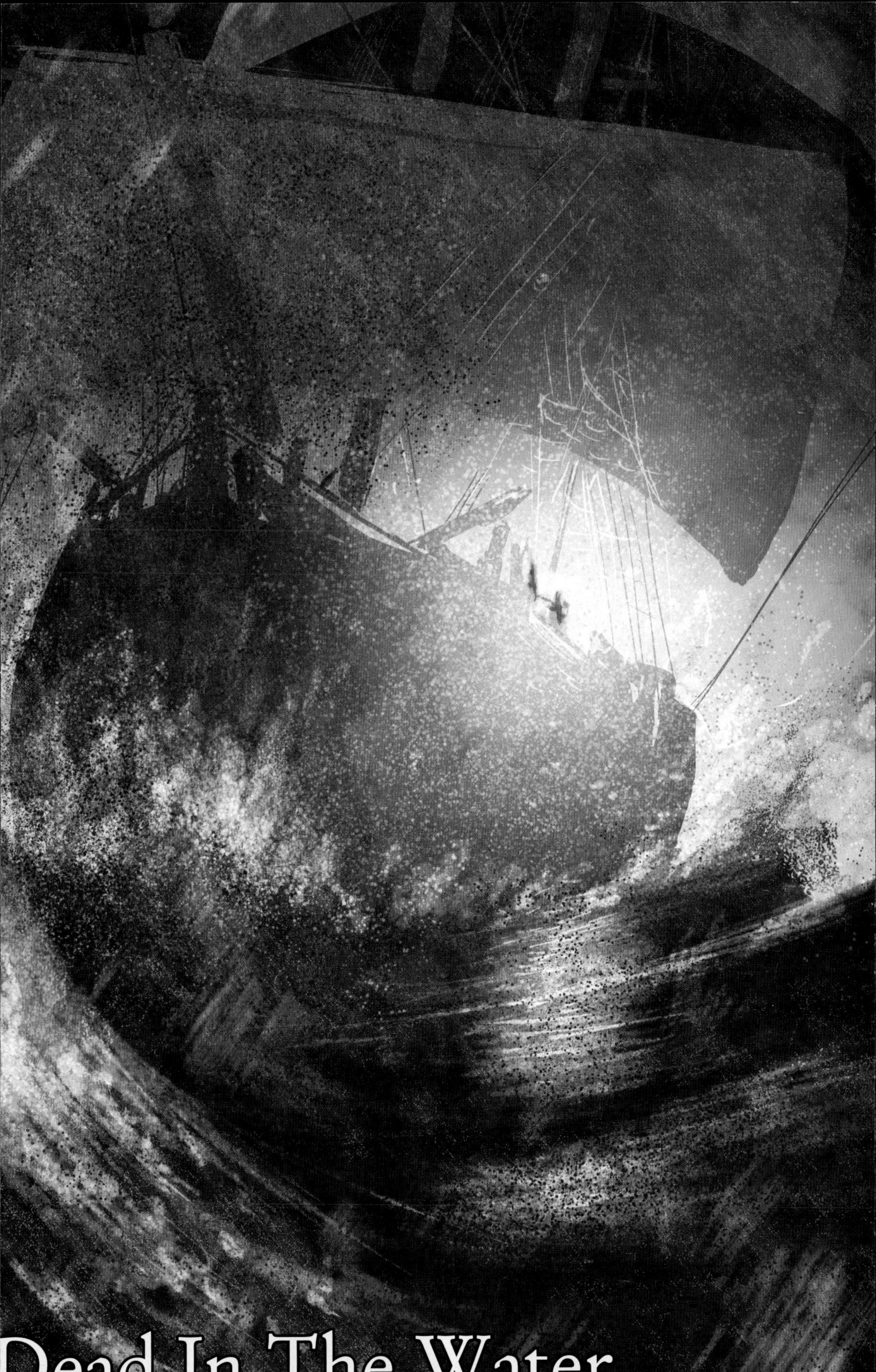

Dead In The Water

llustrated by Pascal Campion

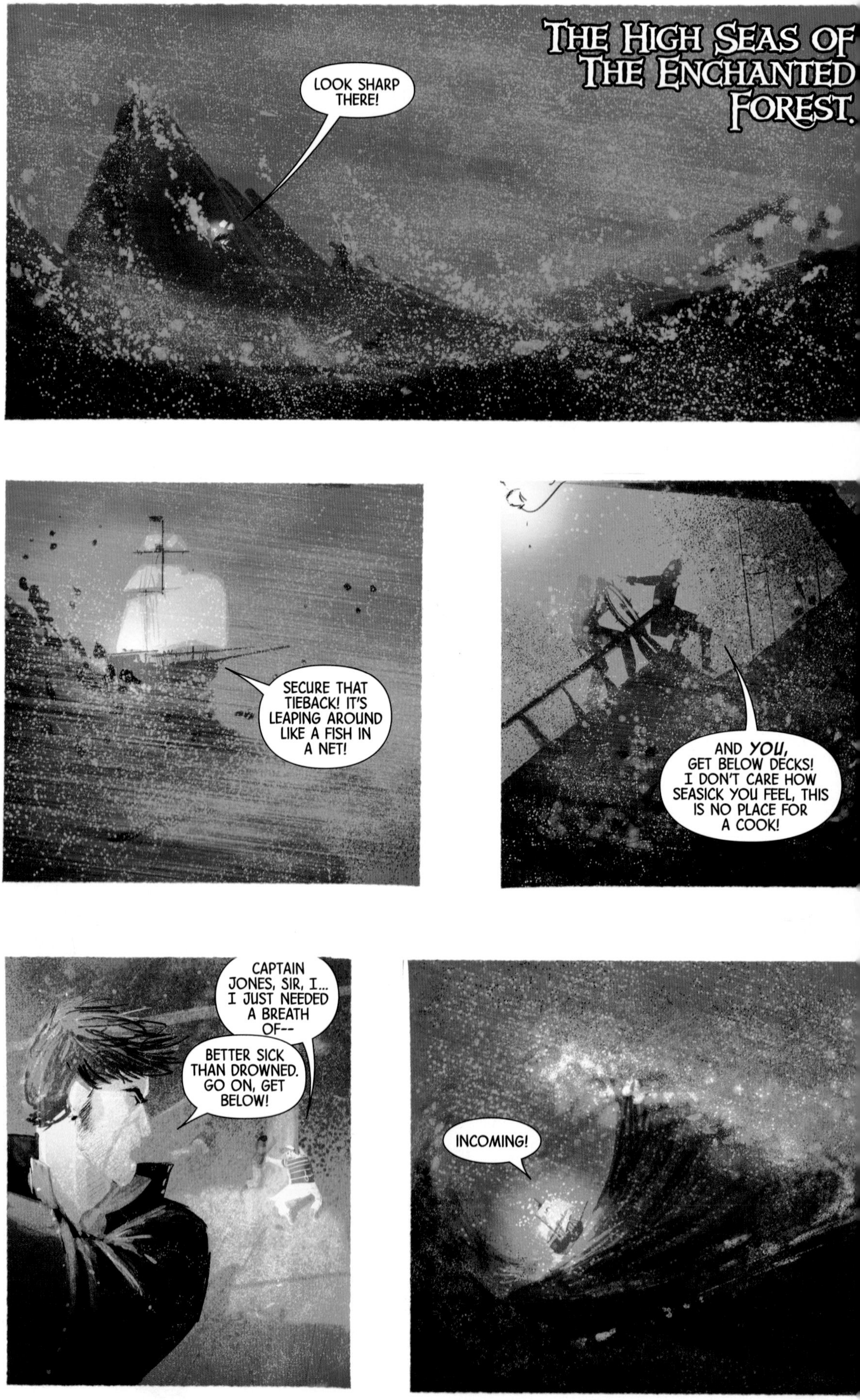
THE HIGH SEAS OF THE ENCHANTED FOREST.
LOOK SHARP THERE!
SECURE THAT TIEBACK! IT'S LEAPING AROUND LIKE A FISH IN A NET!
AND *YOU*, GET BELOW DECKS! I DON'T CARE HOW SEASICK YOU FEEL, THIS IS NO PLACE FOR A COOK!
CAPTAIN JONES, SIR, I... I JUST NEEDED A BREATH OF--
BETTER SICK THAN DROWNED. GO ON, GET BELOW!
INCOMING!

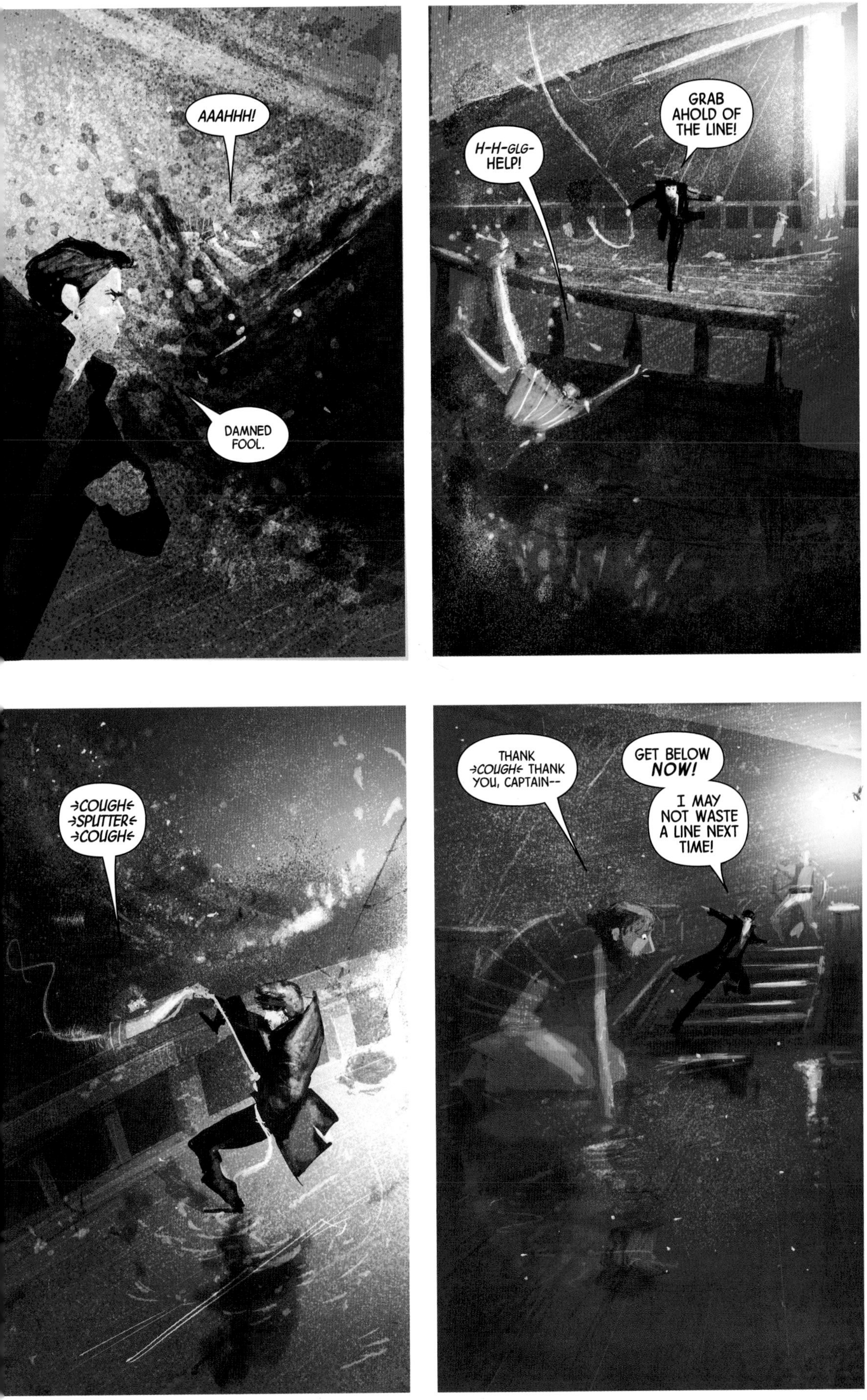
AAAHHH!
DAMNED FOOL.
H-H-GLG-HELP!
GRAB AHOLD OF THE LINE!
→COUGH← →SPUTTER← →COUGH←
THANK →COUGH← THANK YOU, CAPTAIN--
GET BELOW NOW!
I MAY NOT WASTE A LINE NEXT TIME!

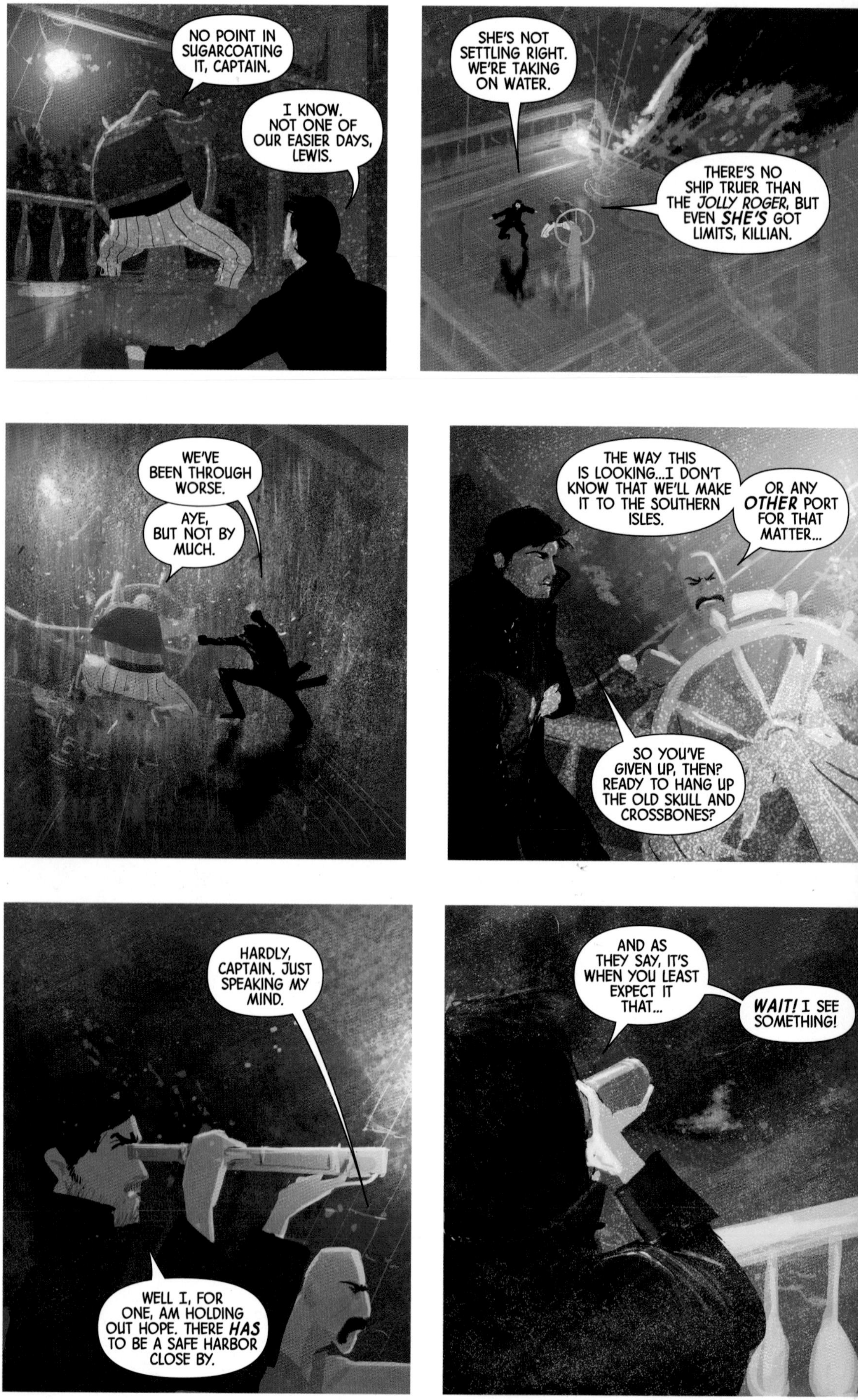
NO POINT IN SUGARCOATING IT, CAPTAIN.
I KNOW. NOT ONE OF OUR EASIER DAYS, LEWIS.
SHE'S NOT SETTLING RIGHT. WE'RE TAKING ON WATER.
THERE'S NO SHIP TRUER THAN THE *JOLLY ROGER*, BUT EVEN ***SHE'S*** GOT LIMITS, KILLIAN.
WE'VE BEEN THROUGH WORSE.
AYE, BUT NOT BY MUCH.
THE WAY THIS IS LOOKING...I DON'T KNOW THAT WE'LL MAKE IT TO THE SOUTHERN ISLES.
OR ANY ***OTHER*** PORT FOR THAT MATTER...
SO YOU'VE GIVEN UP, THEN? READY TO HANG UP THE OLD SKULL AND CROSSBONES?
HARDLY, CAPTAIN. JUST SPEAKING MY MIND.
WELL I, FOR ONE, AM HOLDING OUT HOPE. THERE ***HAS*** TO BE A SAFE HARBOR CLOSE BY.
AND AS THEY SAY, IT'S WHEN YOU LEAST EXPECT IT THAT...
WAIT! I SEE SOMETHING!

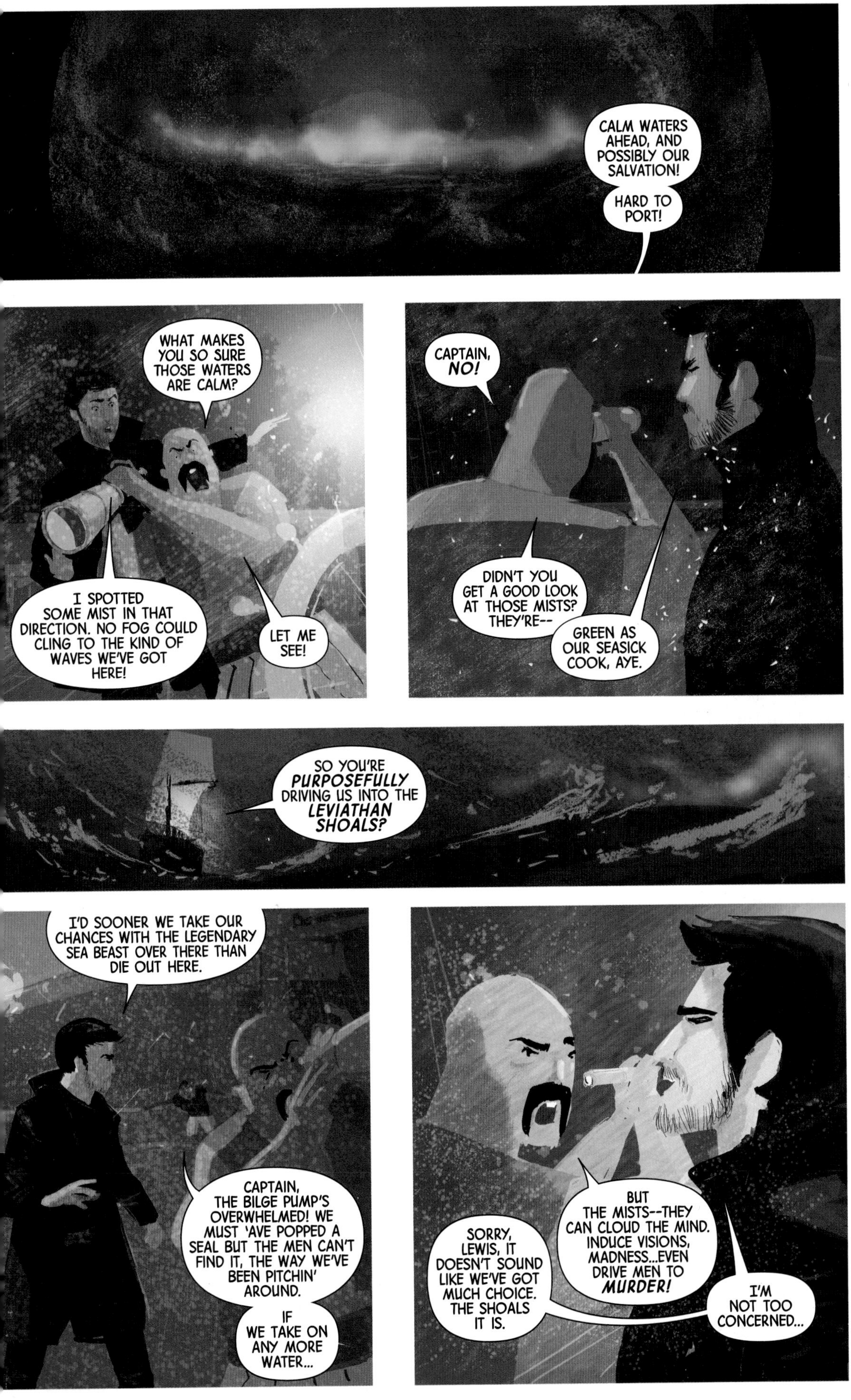
CALM WATERS AHEAD, AND POSSIBLY OUR SALVATION!
HARD TO PORT!
WHAT MAKES YOU SO SURE THOSE WATERS ARE CALM?
I SPOTTED SOME MIST IN THAT DIRECTION. NO FOG COULD CLING TO THE KIND OF WAVES WE'VE GOT HERE!
LET ME SEE!
CAPTAIN, *NO!*
DIDN'T YOU GET A GOOD LOOK AT THOSE MISTS? THEY'RE--
GREEN AS OUR SEASICK COOK, AYE.
SO YOU'RE *PURPOSEFULLY* DRIVING US INTO THE *LEVIATHAN SHOALS?*
I'D SOONER WE TAKE OUR CHANCES WITH THE LEGENDARY SEA BEAST OVER THERE THAN DIE OUT HERE.
CAPTAIN, THE BILGE PUMP'S OVERWHELMED! WE MUST 'AVE POPPED A SEAL BUT THE MEN CAN'T FIND IT, THE WAY WE'VE BEEN PITCHIN' AROUND.
IF WE TAKE ON ANY MORE WATER...
SORRY, LEWIS, IT DOESN'T SOUND LIKE WE'VE GOT MUCH CHOICE. THE SHOALS IT IS.
BUT THE MISTS--THEY CAN CLOUD THE MIND. INDUCE VISIONS, MADNESS...EVEN DRIVE MEN TO *MURDER!*
I'M NOT TOO CONCERNED...

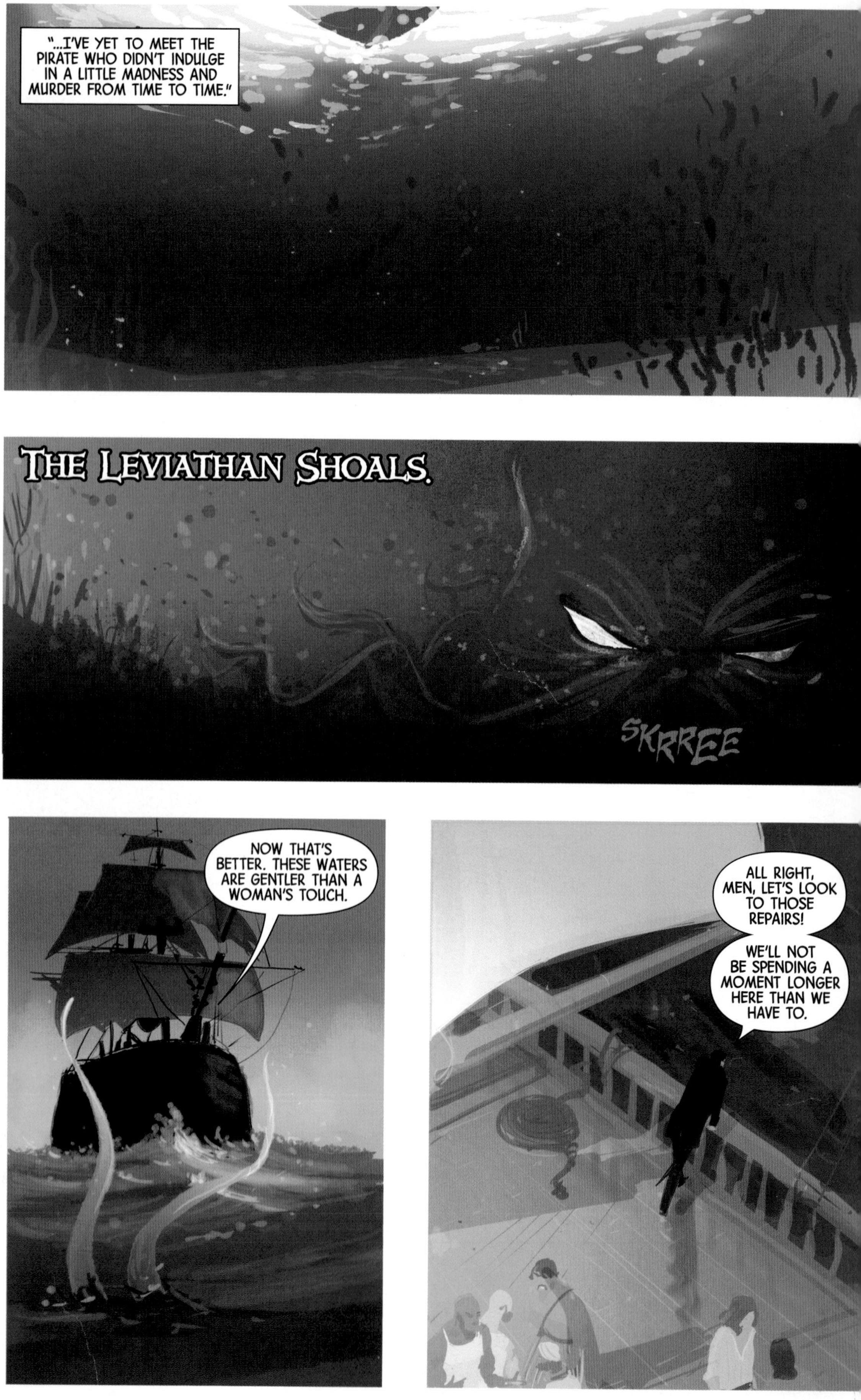
"...I'VE YET TO MEET THE PIRATE WHO DIDN'T INDULGE IN A LITTLE MADNESS AND MURDER FROM TIME TO TIME."
THE LEVIATHAN SHOALS.
SKRREE
NOW THAT'S BETTER. THESE WATERS ARE GENTLER THAN A WOMAN'S TOUCH.
ALL RIGHT, MEN, LET'S LOOK TO THOSE REPAIRS!
WE'LL NOT BE SPENDING A MOMENT LONGER HERE THAN WE HAVE TO.

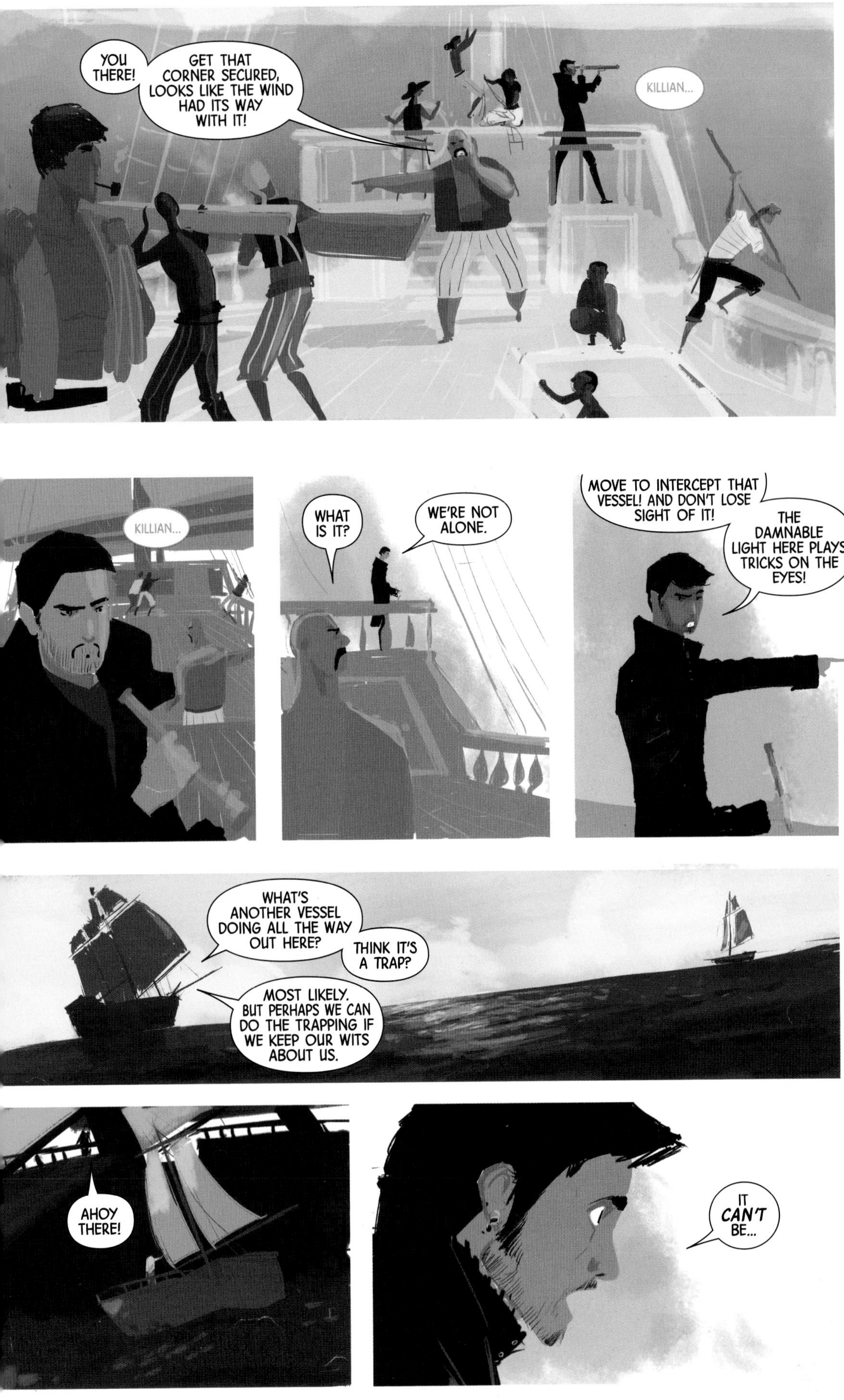
YOU THERE!
GET THAT CORNER SECURED, LOOKS LIKE THE WIND HAD ITS WAY WITH IT!
KILLIAN...
KILLIAN...
WHAT IS IT?
WE'RE NOT ALONE.
MOVE TO INTERCEPT THAT VESSEL! AND DON'T LOSE SIGHT OF IT!
THE DAMNABLE LIGHT HERE PLAYS TRICKS ON THE EYES!
WHAT'S ANOTHER VESSEL DOING ALL THE WAY OUT HERE?
THINK IT'S A TRAP?
MOST LIKELY. BUT PERHAPS WE CAN DO THE TRAPPING IF WE KEEP OUR WITS ABOUT US.
AHOY THERE!
IT *CAN'T* BE...

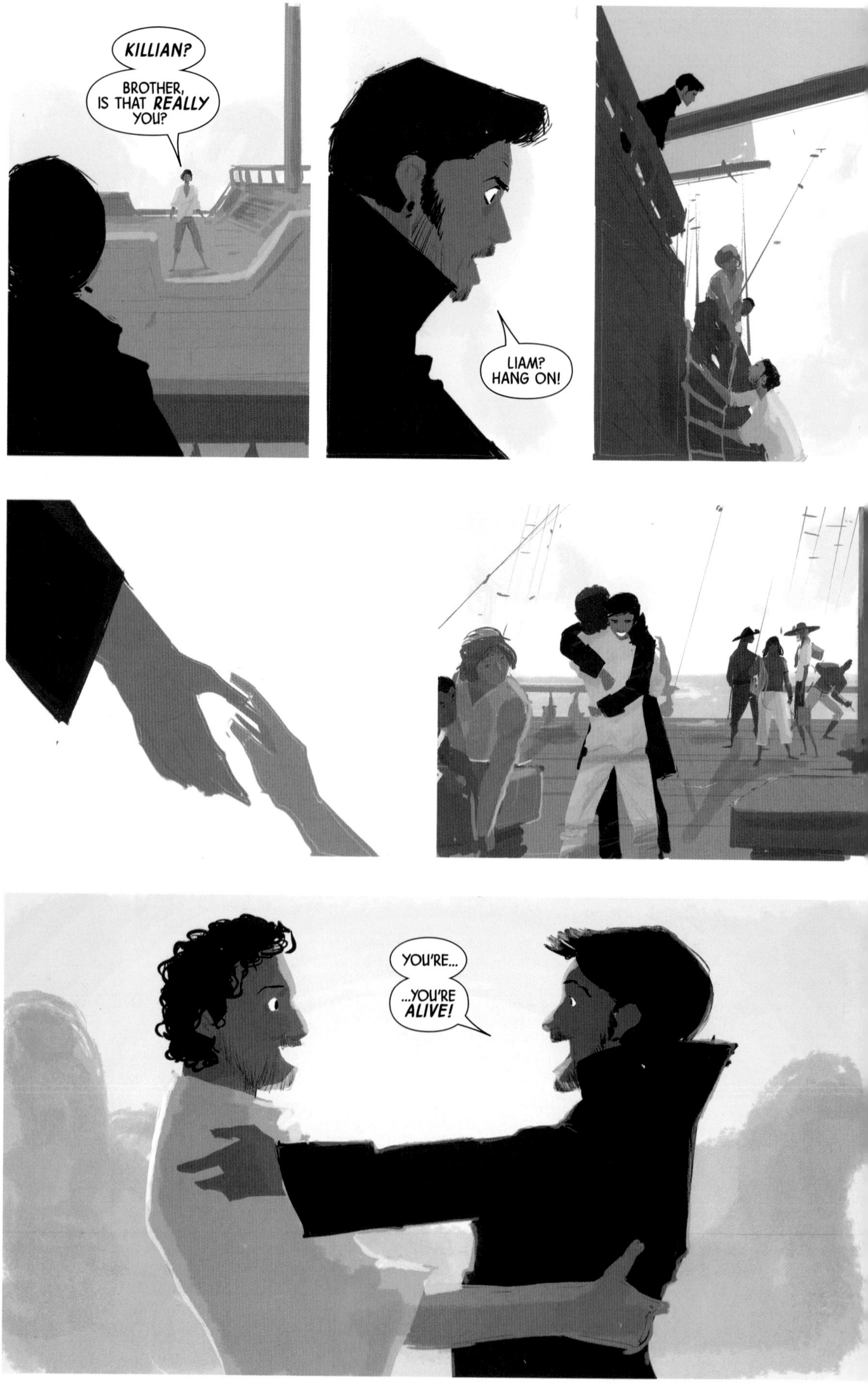
KILLIAN?
BROTHER, IS THAT REALLY YOU?
LIAM? HANG ON!
YOU'RE...
...YOU'RE ALIVE!

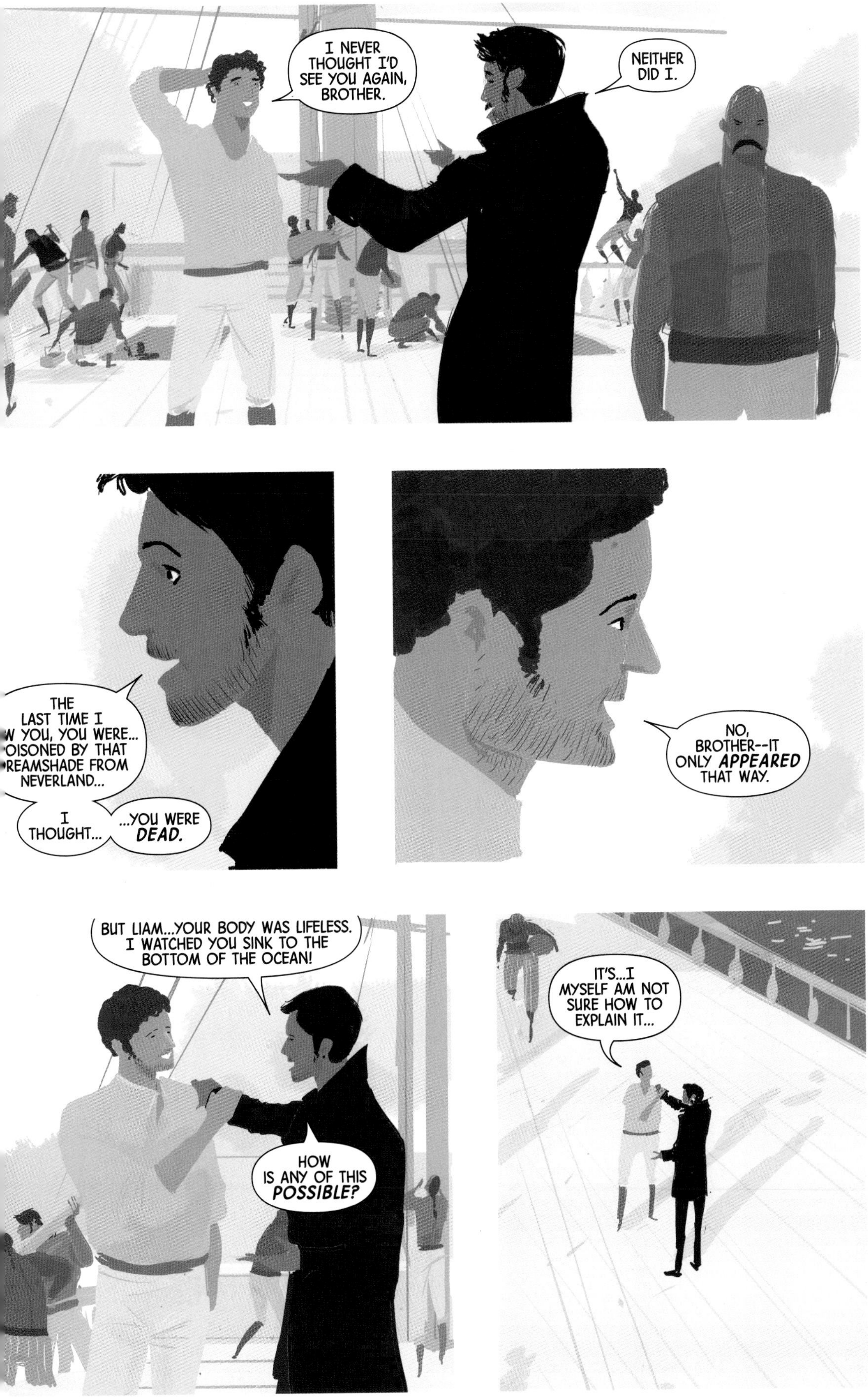
I NEVER THOUGHT I'D SEE YOU AGAIN, BROTHER.
NEITHER DID I.
THE LAST TIME I W YOU, YOU WERE... OISONED BY THAT REAMSHADE FROM NEVERLAND...
I THOUGHT...
...YOU WERE DEAD.
NO, BROTHER--IT ONLY APPEARED THAT WAY.
BUT LIAM...YOUR BODY WAS LIFELESS. I WATCHED YOU SINK TO THE BOTTOM OF THE OCEAN!
HOW IS ANY OF THIS POSSIBLE?
IT'S...I MYSELF AM NOT SURE HOW TO EXPLAIN IT...

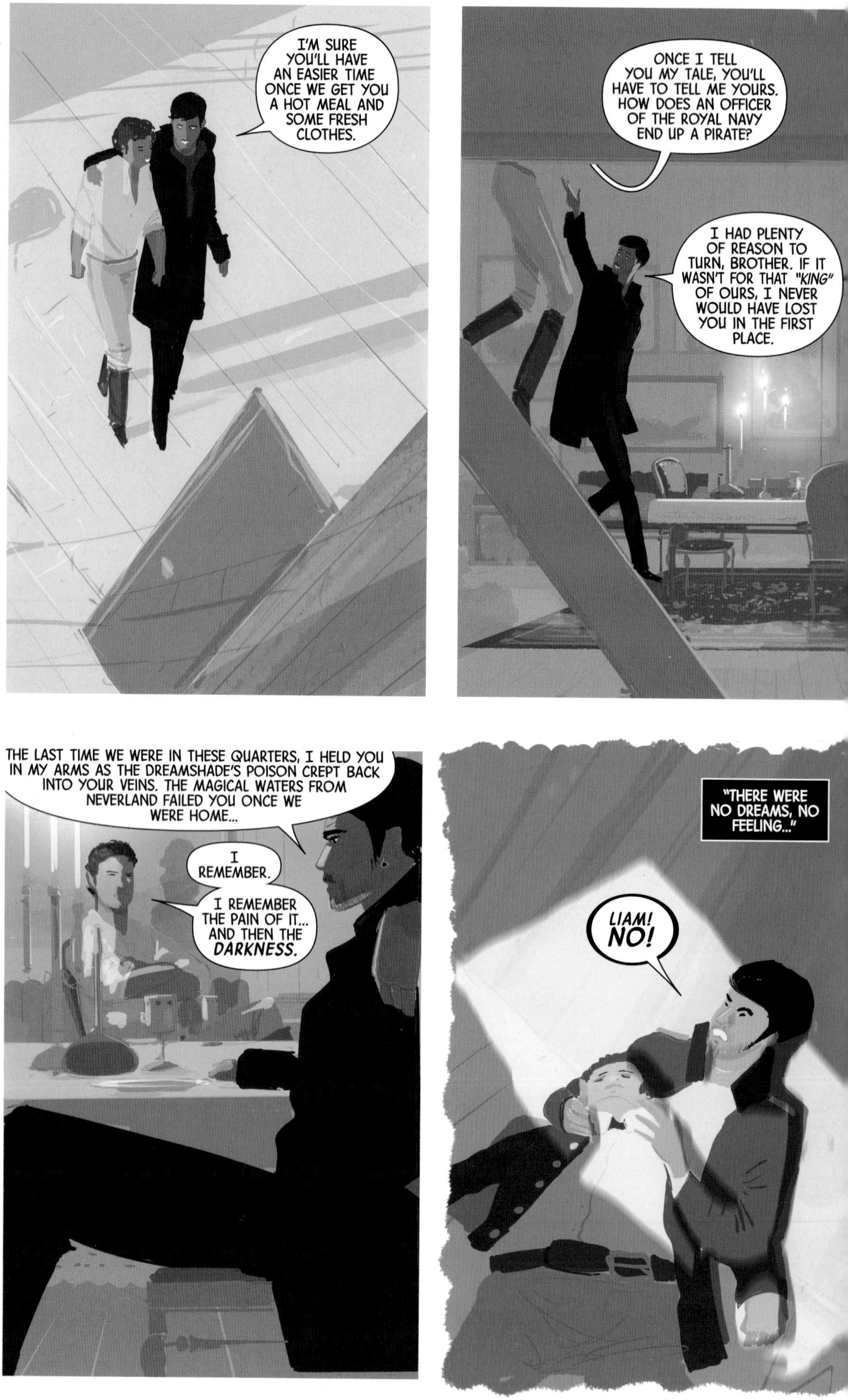
I'M SURE YOU'LL HAVE AN EASIER TIME ONCE WE GET YOU A HOT MEAL AND SOME FRESH CLOTHES.
ONCE I TELL YOU MY TALE, YOU'LL HAVE TO TELL ME YOURS. HOW DOES AN OFFICER OF THE ROYAL NAVY END UP A PIRATE?
I HAD PLENTY OF REASON TO TURN, BROTHER. IF IT WASN'T FOR THAT "KING" OF OURS, I NEVER WOULD HAVE LOST YOU IN THE FIRST PLACE.
THE LAST TIME WE WERE IN THESE QUARTERS, I HELD YOU IN MY ARMS AS THE DREAMSHADE'S POISON CREPT BACK INTO YOUR VEINS. THE MAGICAL WATERS FROM NEVERLAND FAILED YOU ONCE WE WERE HOME...
I REMEMBER.
I REMEMBER THE PAIN OF IT... AND THEN THE DARKNESS.
"THERE WERE NO DREAMS, NO FEELING..."
LIAM! NO!

"WHEN I FINALLY AWOKE, I FOUND MYSELF MAROONED ON A DESOLATE ISLAND.

"THERE WAS FRESH WATER AND ABUNDANT FISHING. BUT NO PEOPLE, NO LANDMARKS I COULD RECOGNIZE. THE LONELINESS WAS ALMOST TOO MUCH.

"I DON'T KNOW HOW LONG I WAS THERE BEFORE A BOAT ARRIVED ON THE ISLAND'S SHORES, BLOWN OFF COURSE DURING A STORM.

"I BEGGED THEM TO LET ME ON BOARD, THOUGH THEIR VESSEL WAS SMALL. THEY AGREED, AND I THOUGHT I WAS ON MY WAY BACK TO YOU, KILLIAN.

"BUT THEN A STORM BLEW UP, MORE FEROCIOUS THAN ANY I'D EVER ENCOUNTERED...

"WHEN THE WAVES SUDDENLY CALMED, WE THOUGHT WE HAD BEEN MIRACULOUSLY SPARED.

"WE GAVE THANKS TO THE GODS OF THE SEA.

"IT WAS ONLY ONCE THE MADNESS STRUCK THE CREW THAT I KNEW WITHOUT A DOUBT WHERE WE WERE.

"...THE *LEVIATHAN SHOALS.*

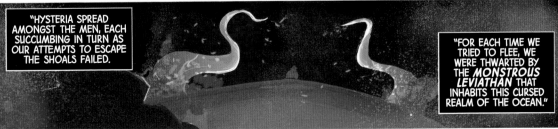

"HYSTERIA SPREAD AMONGST THE MEN, EACH SUCCUMBING IN TURN AS OUR ATTEMPTS TO ESCAPE THE SHOALS FAILED.

"FOR EACH TIME WE TRIED TO FLEE, WE WERE THWARTED BY THE *MONSTROUS LEVIATHAN* THAT INHABITS THIS CURSED REALM OF THE OCEAN."

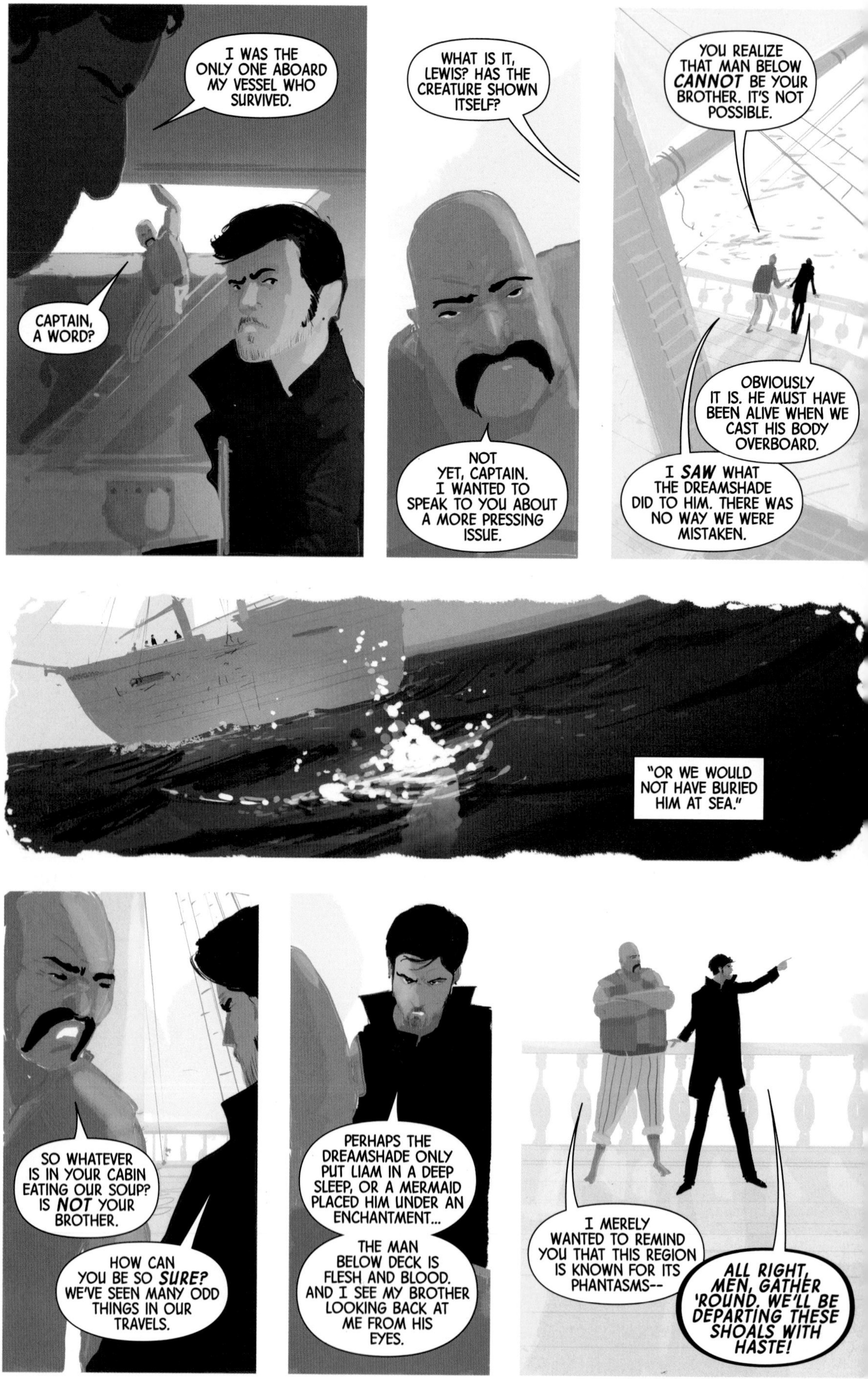
I WAS THE ONLY ONE ABOARD MY VESSEL WHO SURVIVED.
CAPTAIN, A WORD?
WHAT IS IT, LEWIS? HAS THE CREATURE SHOWN ITSELF?
NOT YET, CAPTAIN. I WANTED TO SPEAK TO YOU ABOUT A MORE PRESSING ISSUE.
YOU REALIZE THAT MAN BELOW CANNOT BE YOUR BROTHER. IT'S NOT POSSIBLE.
OBVIOUSLY IT IS. HE MUST HAVE BEEN ALIVE WHEN WE CAST HIS BODY OVERBOARD.
I SAW WHAT THE DREAMSHADE DID TO HIM. THERE WAS NO WAY WE WERE MISTAKEN.
"OR WE WOULD NOT HAVE BURIED HIM AT SEA."
SO WHATEVER IS IN YOUR CABIN EATING OUR SOUP? IS NOT YOUR BROTHER.
HOW CAN YOU BE SO SURE? WE'VE SEEN MANY ODD THINGS IN OUR TRAVELS.
PERHAPS THE DREAMSHADE ONLY PUT LIAM IN A DEEP SLEEP, OR A MERMAID PLACED HIM UNDER AN ENCHANTMENT...
THE MAN BELOW DECK IS FLESH AND BLOOD. AND I SEE MY BROTHER LOOKING BACK AT ME FROM HIS EYES.
I MERELY WANTED TO REMIND YOU THAT THIS REGION IS KNOWN FOR ITS PHANTASMS--
ALL RIGHT, MEN, GATHER 'ROUND. WE'LL BE DEPARTING THESE SHOALS WITH HASTE!

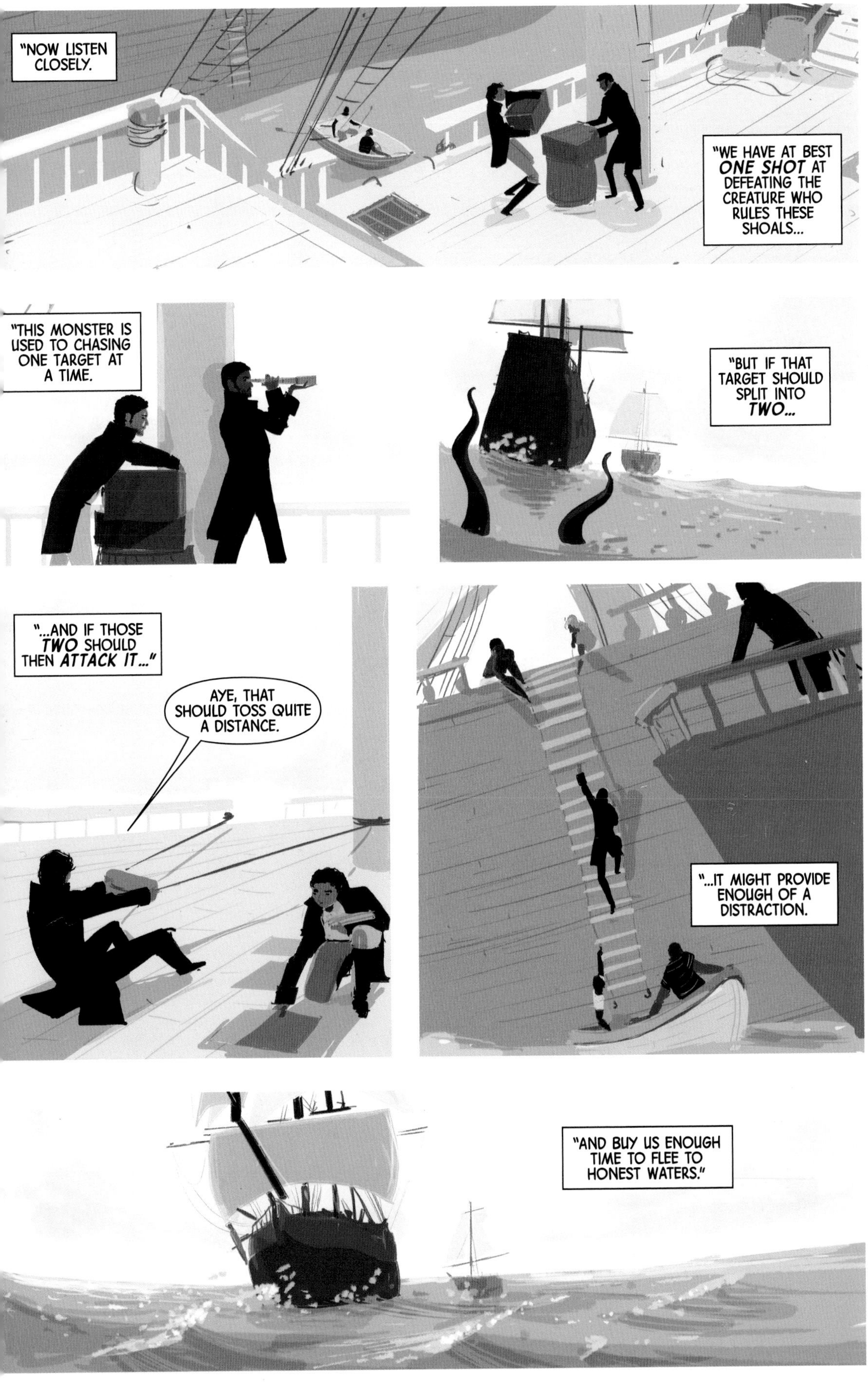
"NOW LISTEN CLOSELY.
"WE HAVE AT BEST ONE SHOT AT DEFEATING THE CREATURE WHO RULES THESE SHOALS...
"THIS MONSTER IS USED TO CHASING ONE TARGET AT A TIME.
"BUT IF THAT TARGET SHOULD SPLIT INTO TWO...
"...AND IF THOSE TWO SHOULD THEN ATTACK IT..."
AYE, THAT SHOULD TOSS QUITE A DISTANCE.
"...IT MIGHT PROVIDE ENOUGH OF A DISTRACTION.
"AND BUY US ENOUGH TIME TO FLEE TO HONEST WATERS."

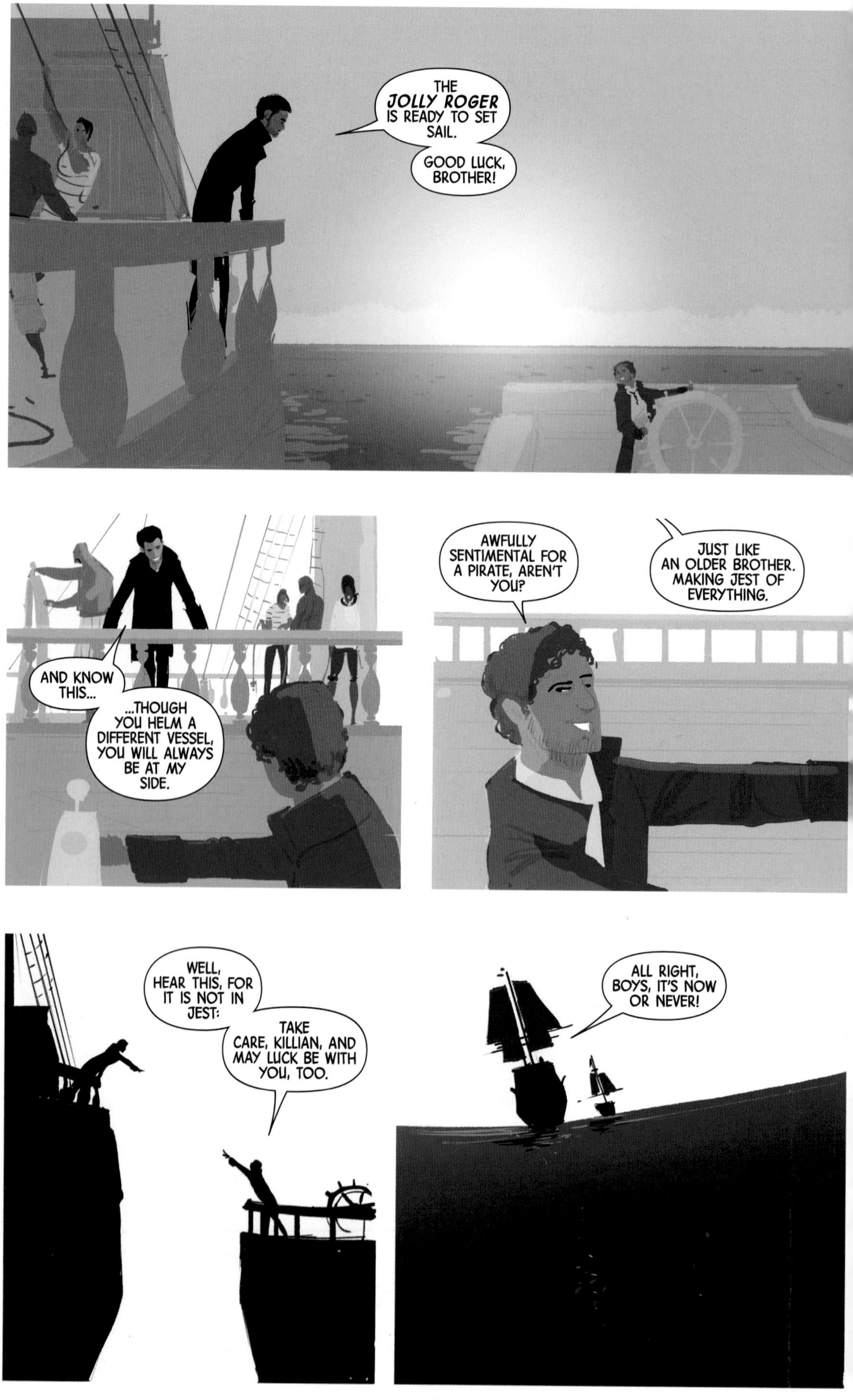
THE *JOLLY ROGER* IS READY TO SET SAIL.
GOOD LUCK, BROTHER!
AND KNOW THIS...
...THOUGH YOU HELM A DIFFERENT VESSEL, YOU WILL ALWAYS BE AT MY SIDE.
AWFULLY SENTIMENTAL FOR A PIRATE, AREN'T YOU?
JUST LIKE AN OLDER BROTHER. MAKING JEST OF EVERYTHING.
WELL, HEAR THIS, FOR IT IS NOT IN JEST:
TAKE CARE, KILLIAN, AND MAY LUCK BE WITH YOU, TOO.
ALL RIGHT, BOYS, IT'S NOW OR NEVER!

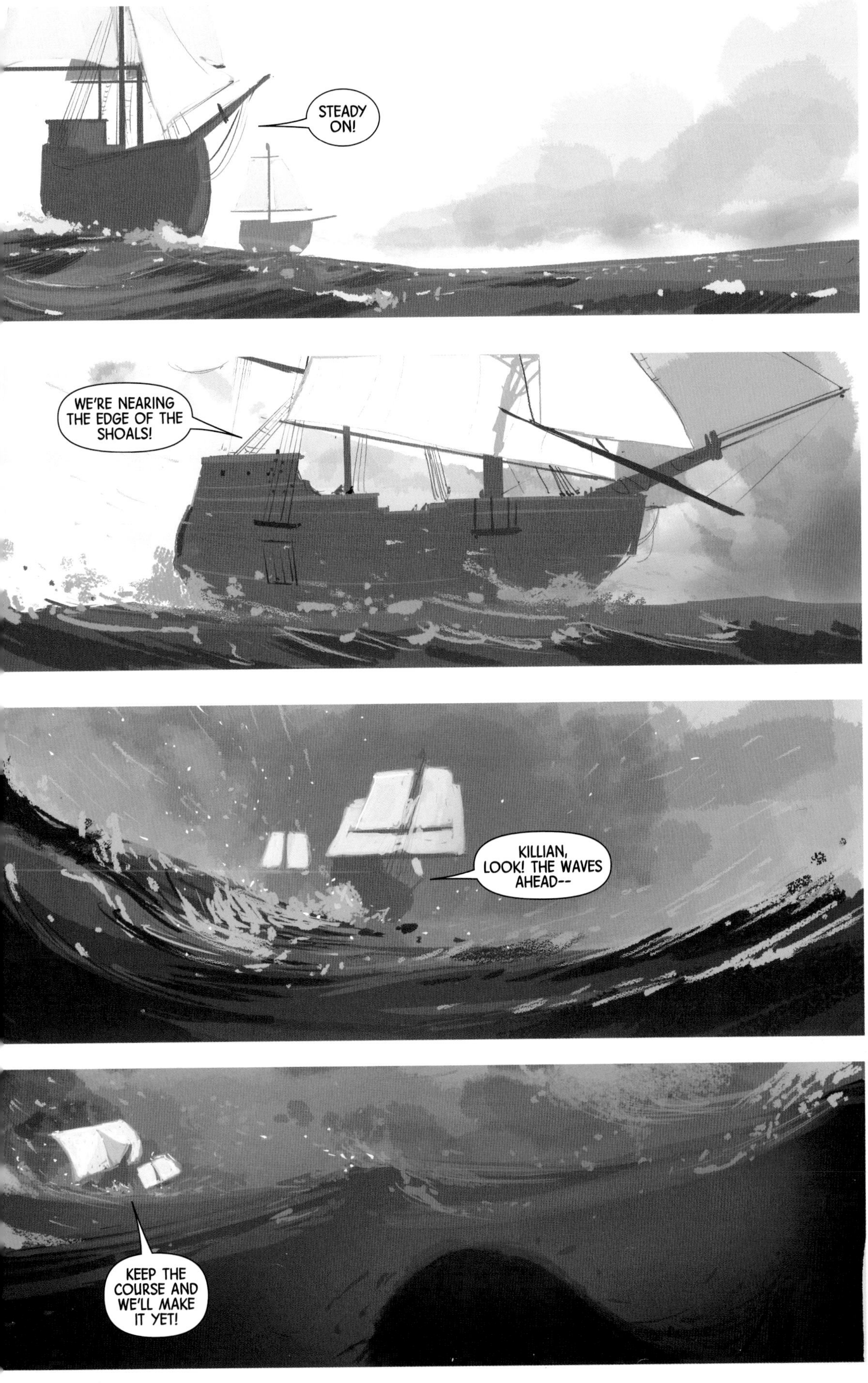
STEADY ON!
WE'RE NEARING THE EDGE OF THE SHOALS!
KILLIAN, LOOK! THE WAVES AHEAD--
KEEP THE COURSE AND WE'LL MAKE IT YET!

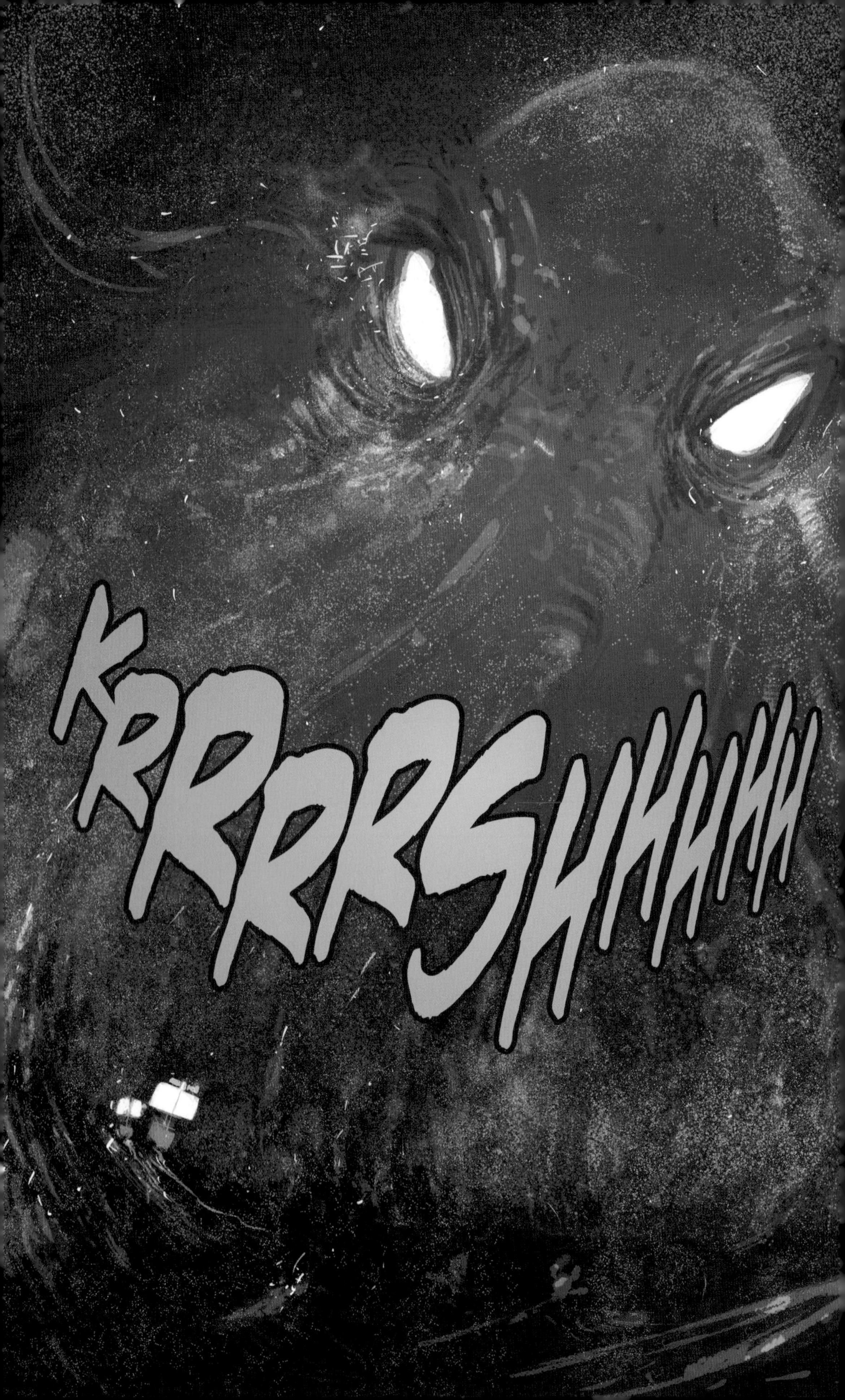
KRRRRSHHHHHH

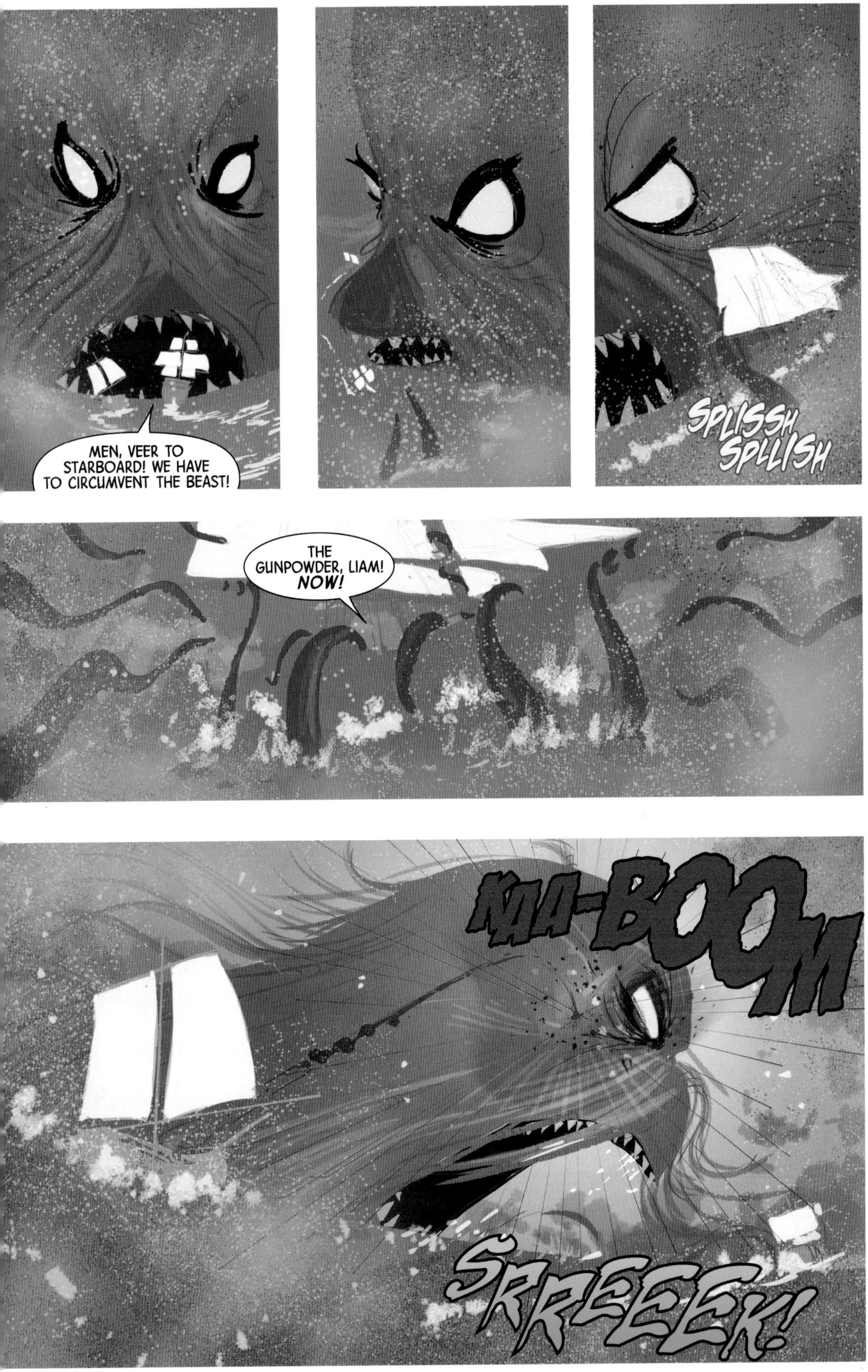
MEN, VEER TO STARBOARD! WE HAVE TO CIRCUMVENT THE BEAST!
SPLISSH SPLLISH
THE GUNPOWDER, LIAM! NOW!
KAA-BOOM
SRREEEK!

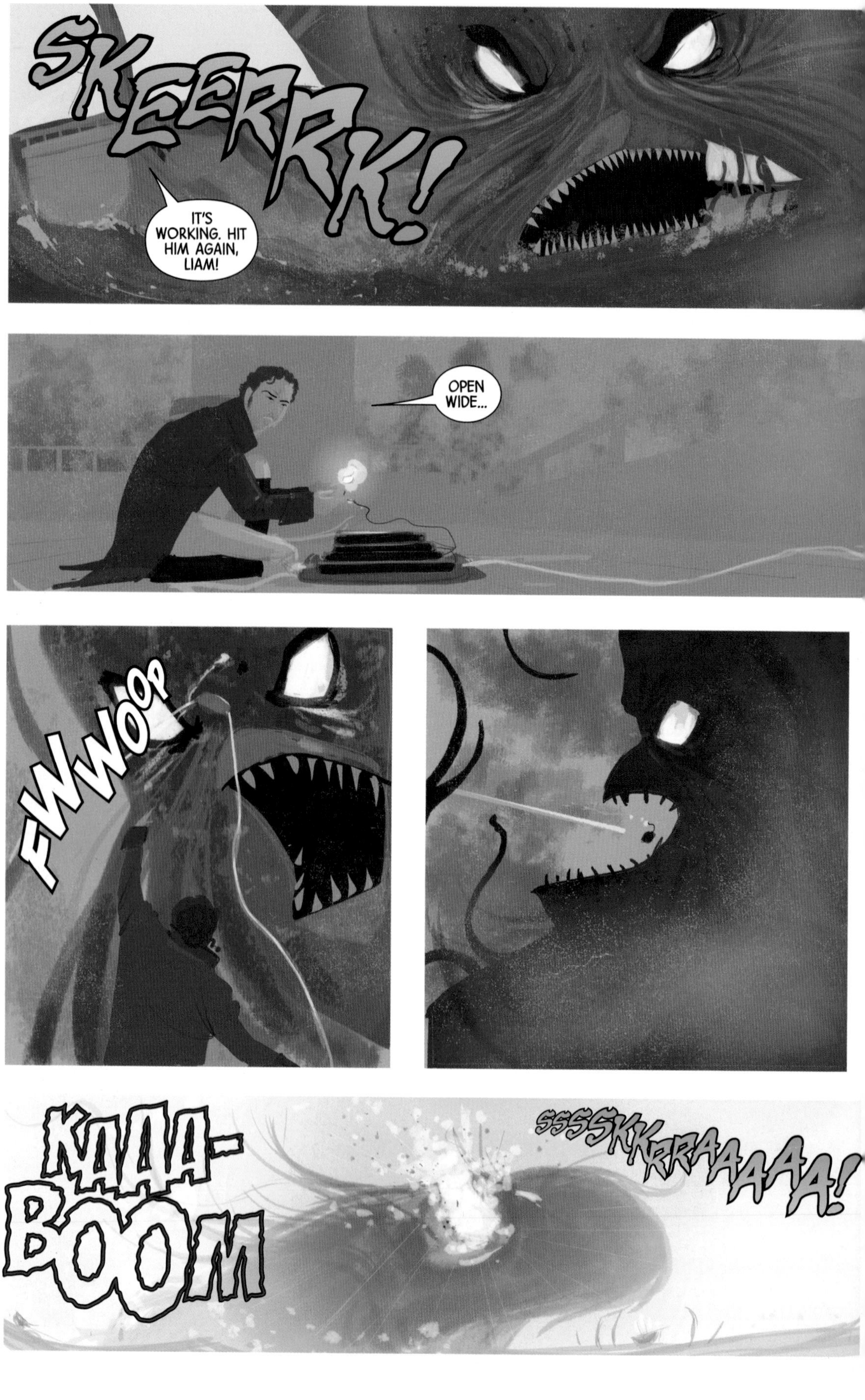
SKEERRK!
IT'S WORKING. HIT HIM AGAIN, LIAM!
OPEN WIDE...
FWWOOP
KADA-BOOM
SSSSKKRRAAAAA!

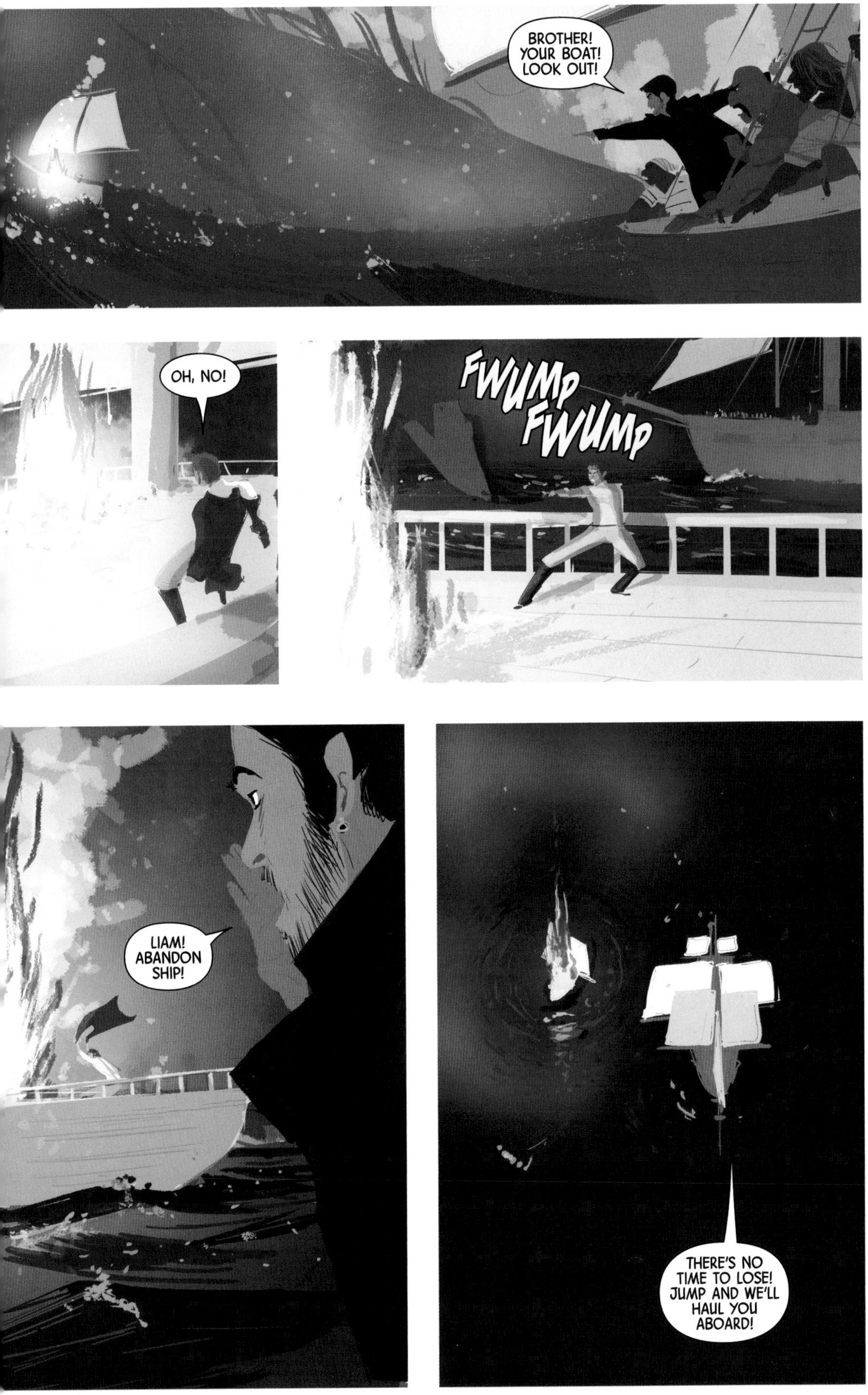
BROTHER! YOUR BOAT! LOOK OUT!
OH, NO!
FWUMP FWUMP
LIAM! ABANDON SHIP!
THERE'S NO TIME TO LOSE! JUMP AND WE'LL HAUL YOU ABOARD!

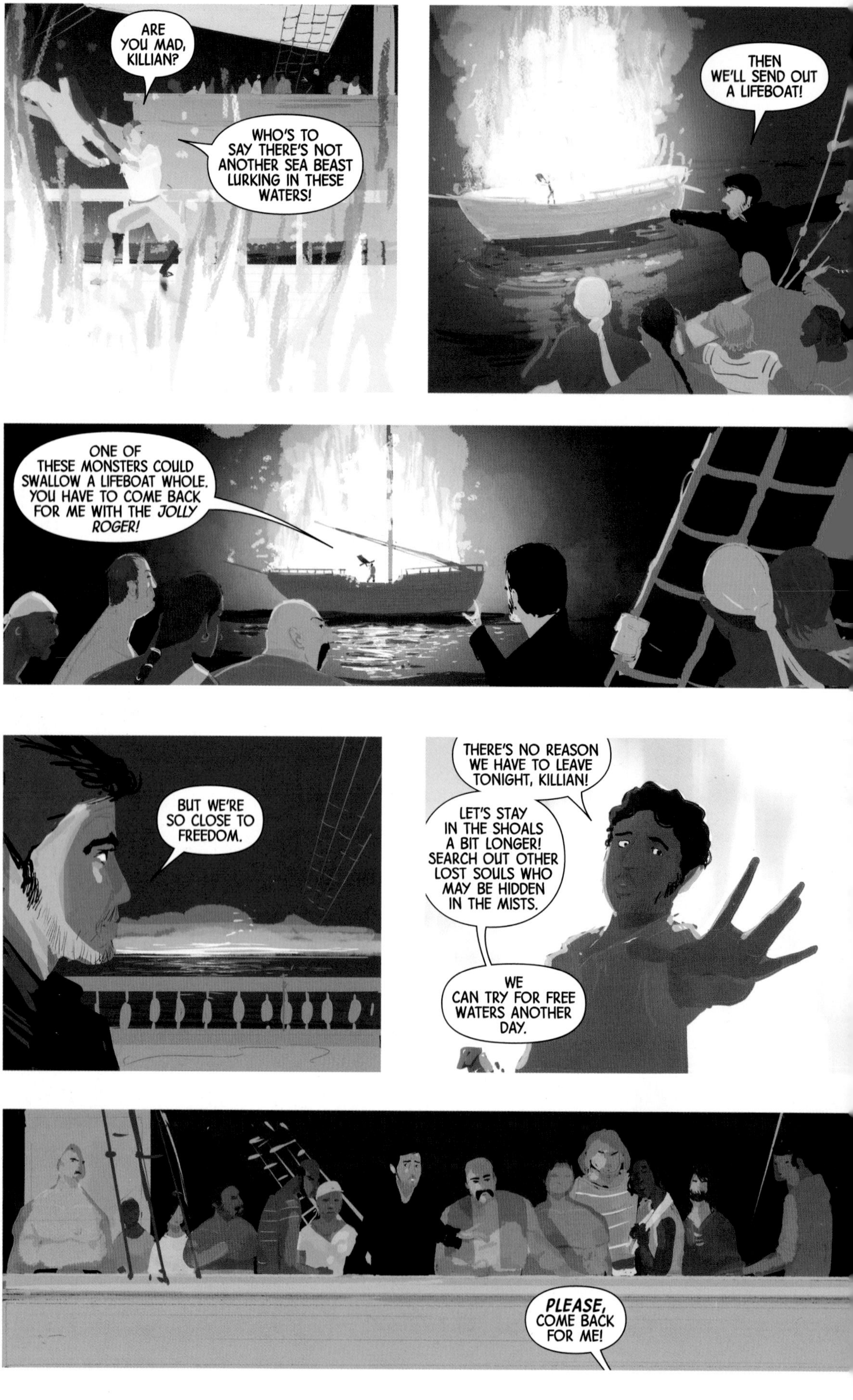
ARE YOU MAD, KILLIAN?
WHO'S TO SAY THERE'S NOT ANOTHER SEA BEAST LURKING IN THESE WATERS!
THEN WE'LL SEND OUT A LIFEBOAT!
ONE OF THESE MONSTERS COULD SWALLOW A LIFEBOAT WHOLE. YOU HAVE TO COME BACK FOR ME WITH THE *JOLLY ROGER!*
BUT WE'RE SO CLOSE TO FREEDOM.
THERE'S NO REASON WE HAVE TO LEAVE TONIGHT, KILLIAN!
LET'S STAY IN THE SHOALS A BIT LONGER! SEARCH OUT OTHER LOST SOULS WHO MAY BE HIDDEN IN THE MISTS.
WE CAN TRY FOR FREE WATERS ANOTHER DAY.
PLEASE, COME BACK FOR ME!

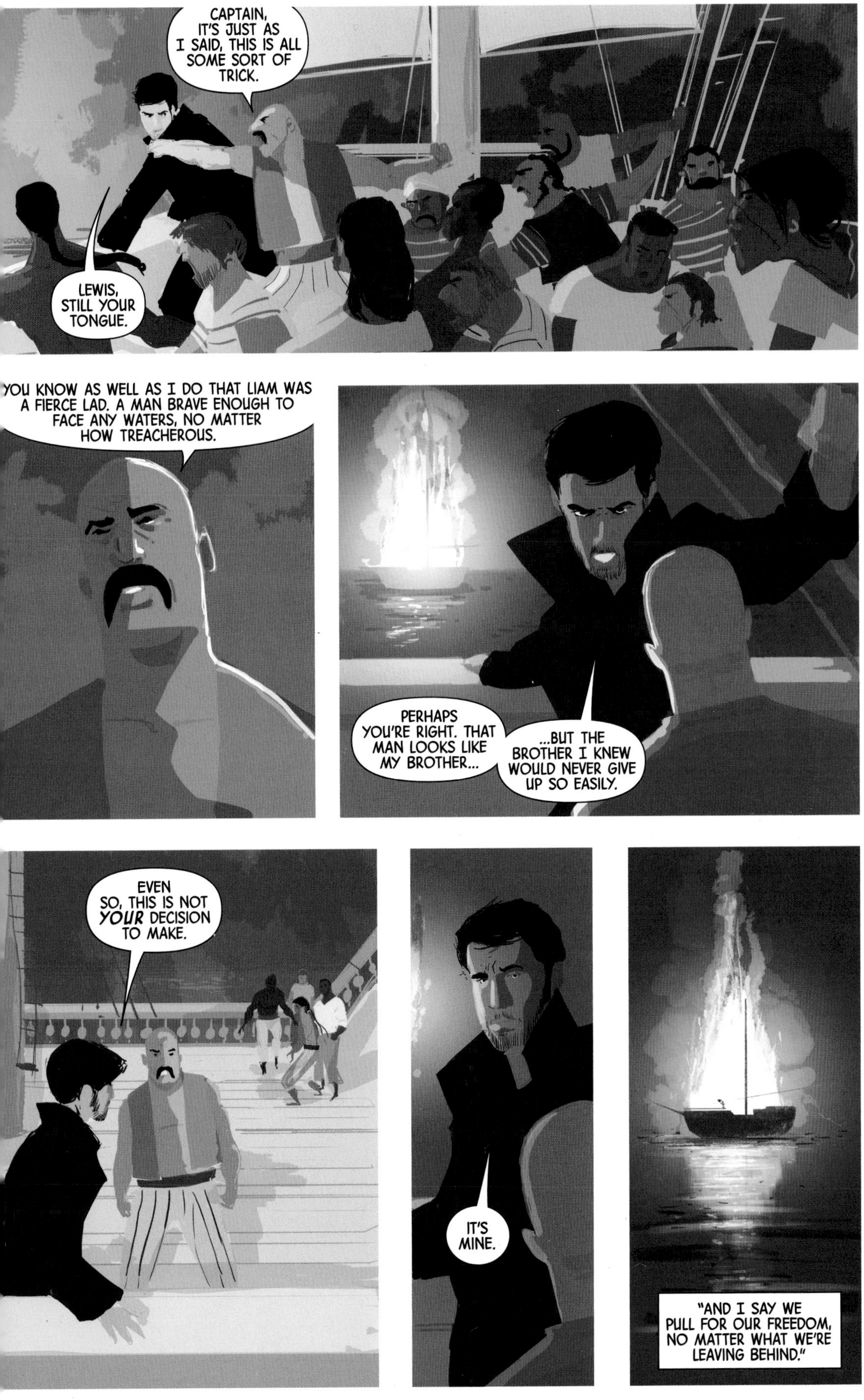
CAPTAIN, IT'S JUST AS I SAID, THIS IS ALL SOME SORT OF TRICK.
LEWIS, STILL YOUR TONGUE.
YOU KNOW AS WELL AS I DO THAT LIAM WAS A FIERCE LAD. A MAN BRAVE ENOUGH TO FACE ANY WATERS, NO MATTER HOW TREACHEROUS.
PERHAPS YOU'RE RIGHT. THAT MAN LOOKS LIKE MY BROTHER...
...BUT THE BROTHER I KNEW WOULD NEVER GIVE UP SO EASILY.
EVEN SO, THIS IS NOT *YOUR* DECISION TO MAKE.
IT'S MINE.
"AND I SAY WE PULL FOR OUR FREEDOM, NO MATTER WHAT WE'RE LEAVING BEHIND."

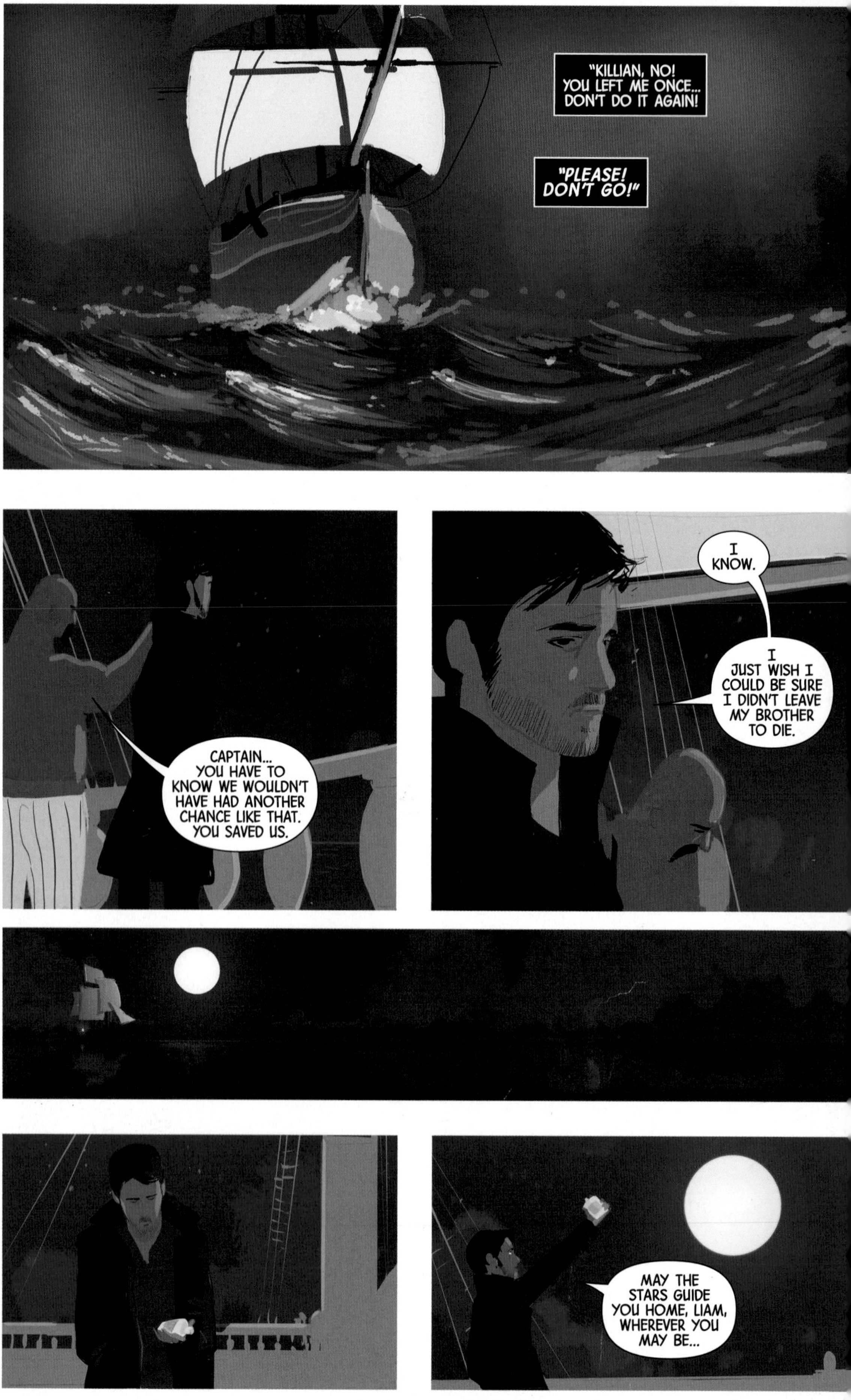
"KILLIAN, NO! YOU LEFT ME ONCE... DON'T DO IT AGAIN!
"PLEASE! DON'T GO!"
CAPTAIN... YOU HAVE TO KNOW WE WOULDN'T HAVE HAD ANOTHER CHANCE LIKE THAT. YOU SAVED US.
I KNOW.
I JUST WISH I COULD BE SURE I DIDN'T LEAVE MY BROTHER TO DIE.
MAY THE STARS GUIDE YOU HOME, LIAM, WHEREVER YOU MAY BE...

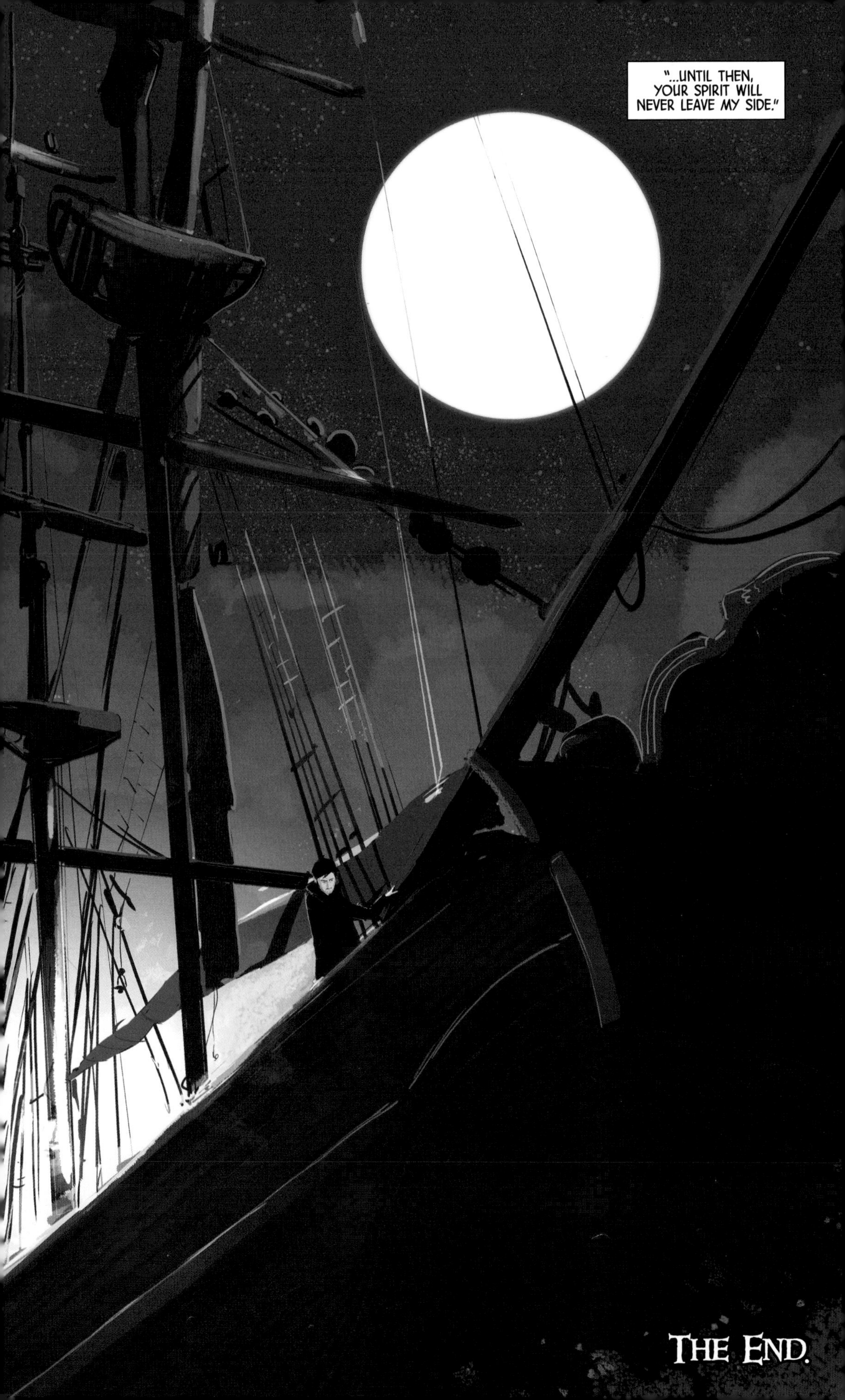
"...UNTIL THEN, YOUR SPIRIT WILL NEVER LEAVE MY SIDE."
THE END.

CHAPTER TWO

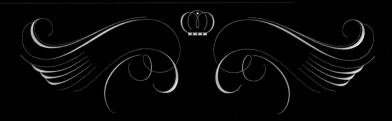

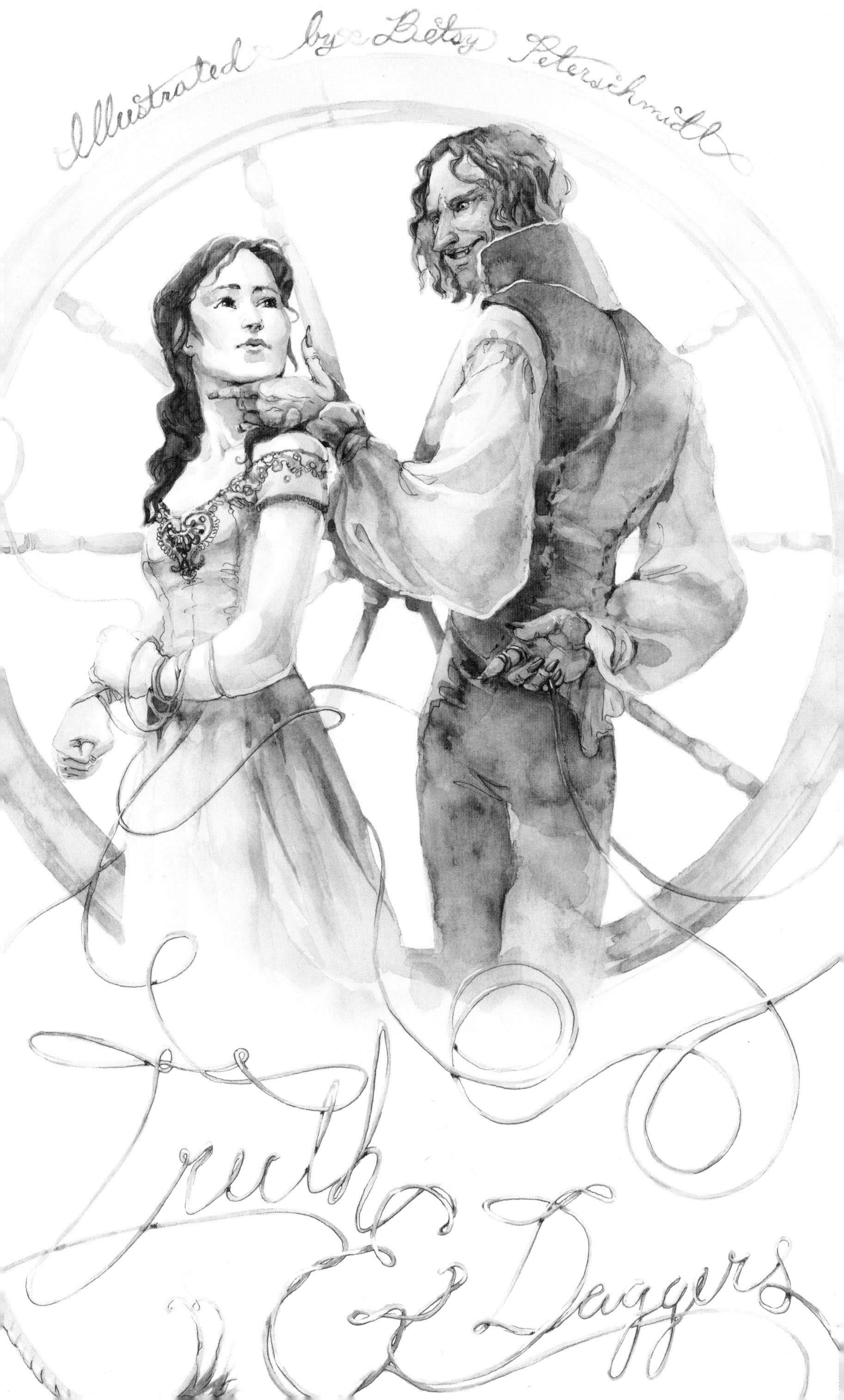
Illustrated by Betsy Peterschmidt
Truth & Daggers

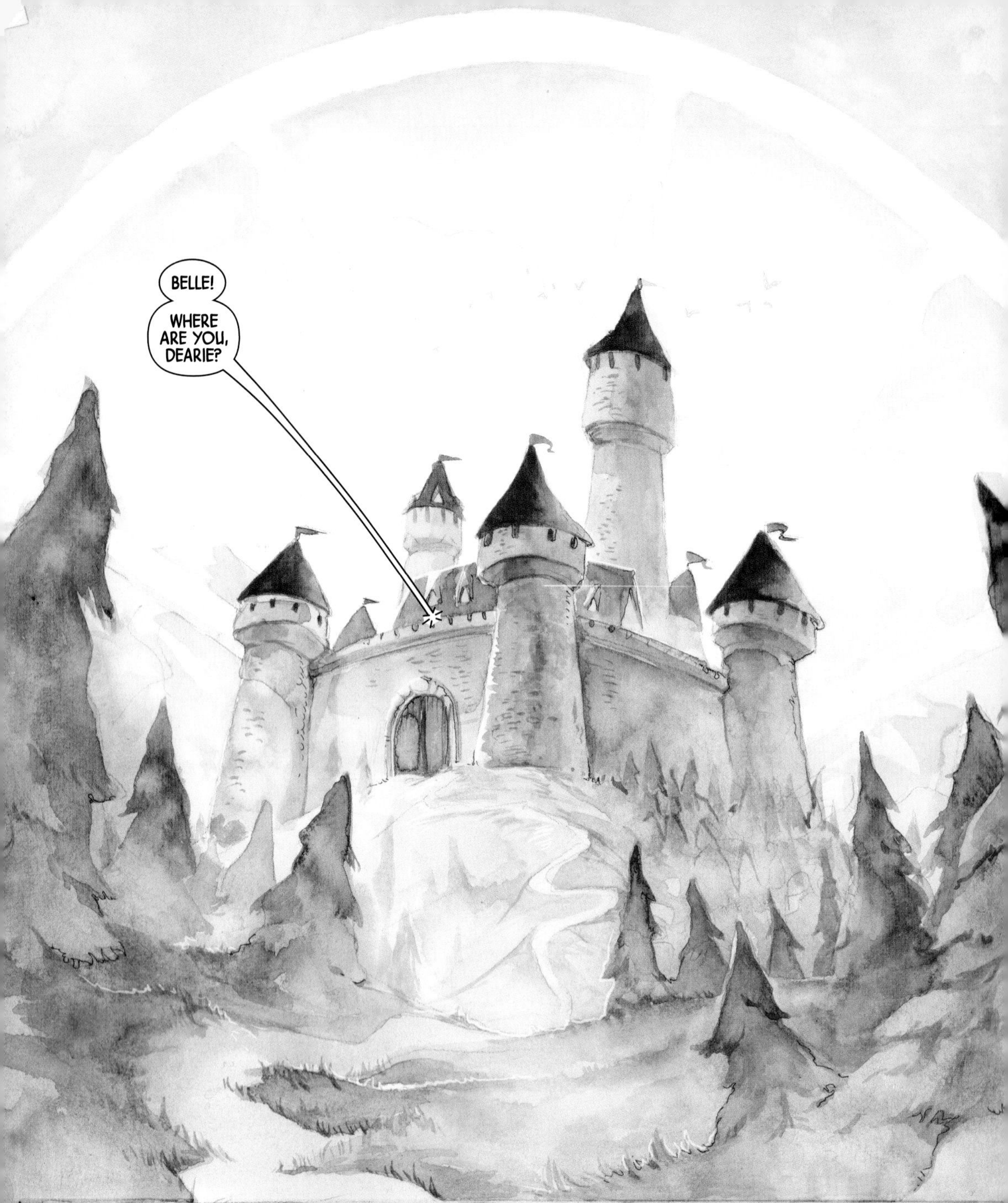
BELLE!
WHERE ARE YOU, DEARIE?

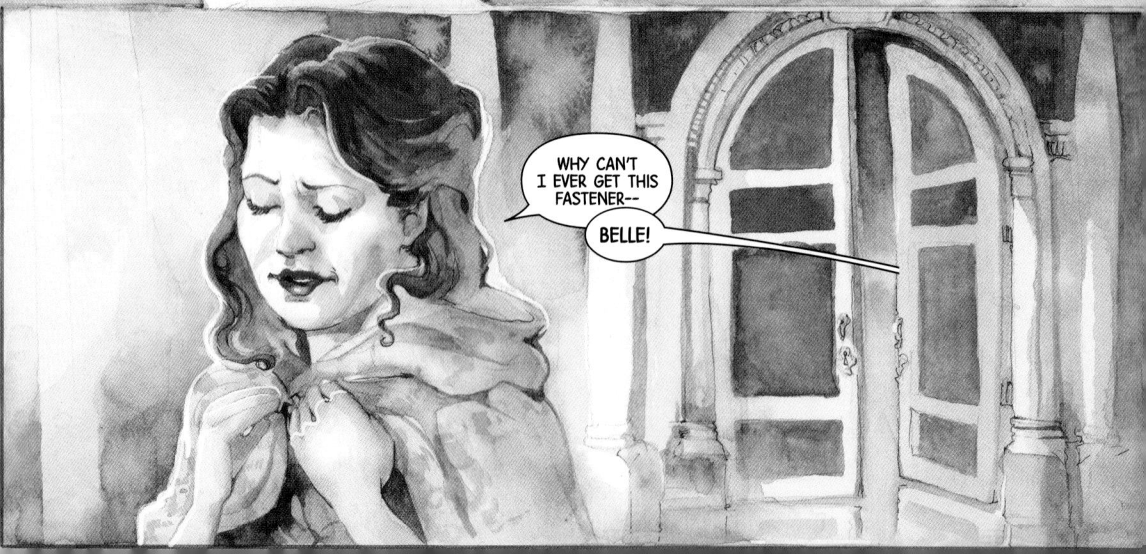
WHY CAN'T I EVER GET THIS FASTENER--
BELLE!

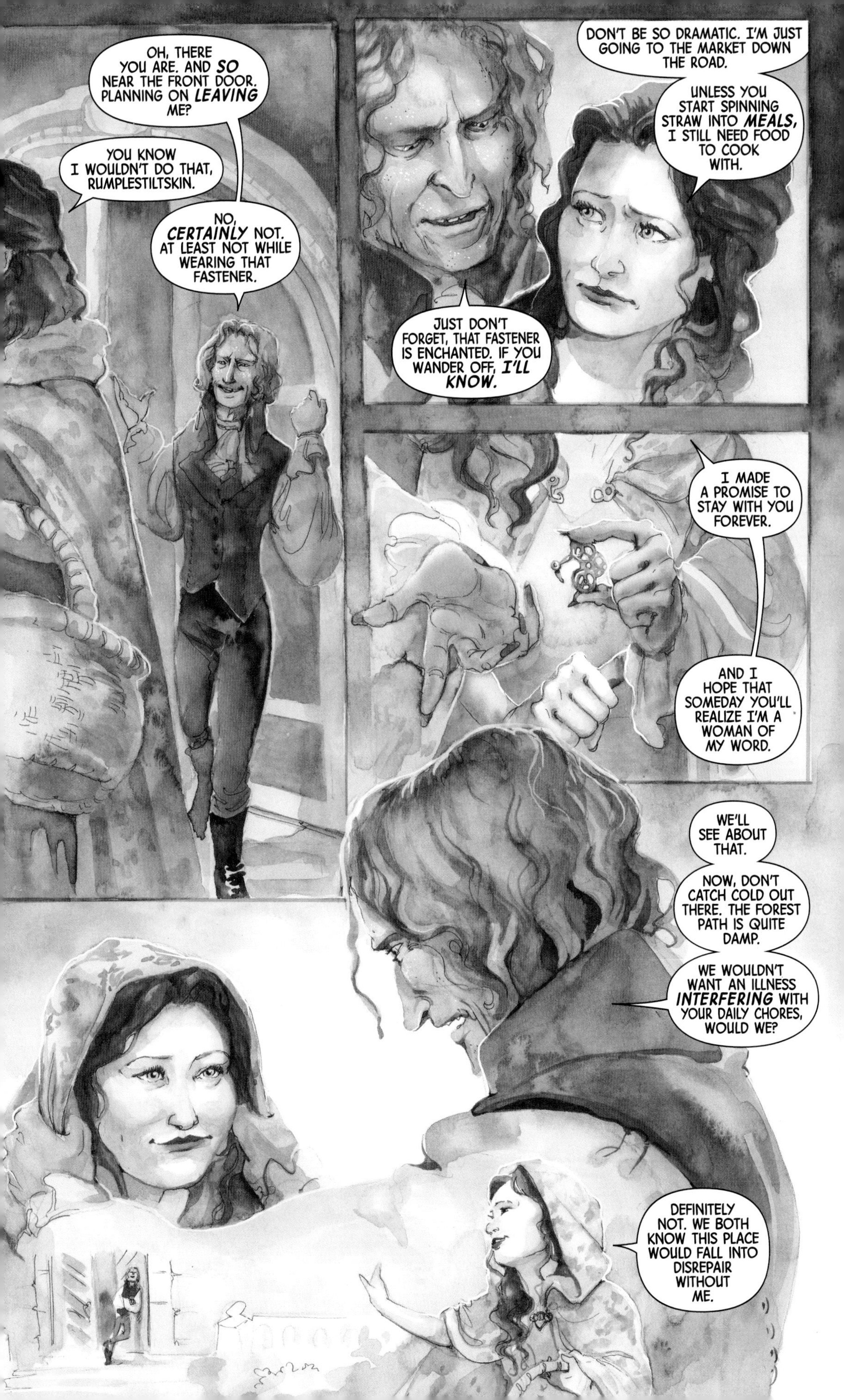

OH, THERE YOU ARE. AND SO NEAR THE FRONT DOOR. PLANNING ON LEAVING ME?
YOU KNOW I WOULDN'T DO THAT, RUMPLESTILTSKIN.
NO, CERTAINLY NOT. AT LEAST NOT WHILE WEARING THAT FASTENER.
DON'T BE SO DRAMATIC. I'M JUST GOING TO THE MARKET DOWN THE ROAD.
UNLESS YOU START SPINNING STRAW INTO MEALS, I STILL NEED FOOD TO COOK WITH.
JUST DON'T FORGET, THAT FASTENER IS ENCHANTED. IF YOU WANDER OFF, I'LL KNOW.
I MADE A PROMISE TO STAY WITH YOU FOREVER.
AND I HOPE THAT SOMEDAY YOU'LL REALIZE I'M A WOMAN OF MY WORD.
WE'LL SEE ABOUT THAT.
NOW, DON'T CATCH COLD OUT THERE. THE FOREST PATH IS QUITE DAMP.
WE WOULDN'T WANT AN ILLNESS INTERFERING WITH YOUR DAILY CHORES, WOULD WE?
DEFINITELY NOT. WE BOTH KNOW THIS PLACE WOULD FALL INTO DISREPAIR WITHOUT ME.

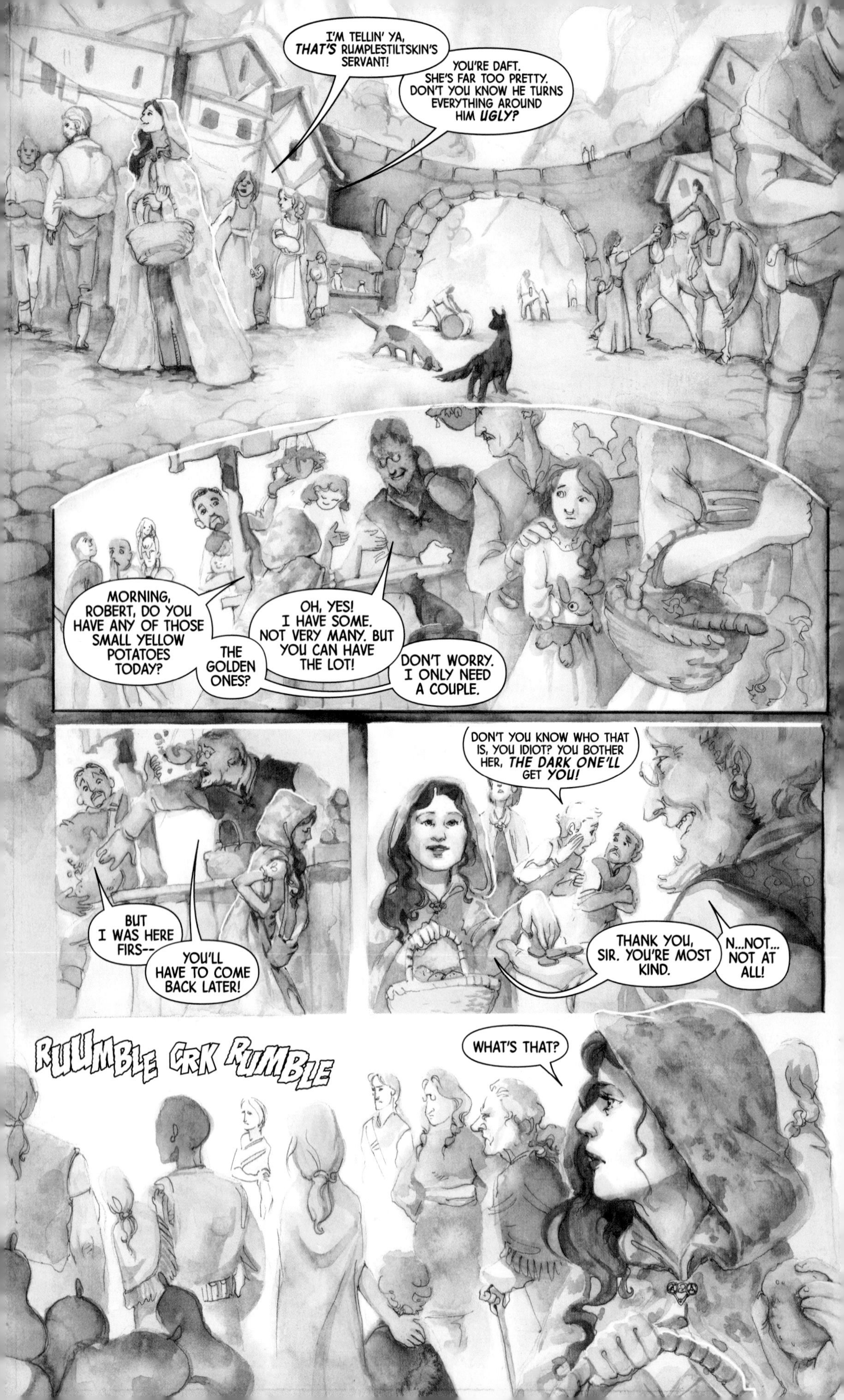
I'M TELLIN' YA, THAT'S RUMPLESTILTSKIN'S SERVANT!
YOU'RE DAFT. SHE'S FAR TOO PRETTY. DON'T YOU KNOW HE TURNS EVERYTHING AROUND HIM UGLY?
MORNING, ROBERT, DO YOU HAVE ANY OF THOSE SMALL YELLOW POTATOES TODAY?
THE GOLDEN ONES?
OH, YES! I HAVE SOME. NOT VERY MANY. BUT YOU CAN HAVE THE LOT!
DON'T WORRY. I ONLY NEED A COUPLE.
BUT I WAS HERE FIRS--
YOU'LL HAVE TO COME BACK LATER!
DON'T YOU KNOW WHO THAT IS, YOU IDIOT? YOU BOTHER HER, THE DARK ONE'LL GET YOU!
THANK YOU, SIR. YOU'RE MOST KIND.
N...NOT... NOT AT ALL!
RUUMBLE CRK RUMBLE
WHAT'S THAT?

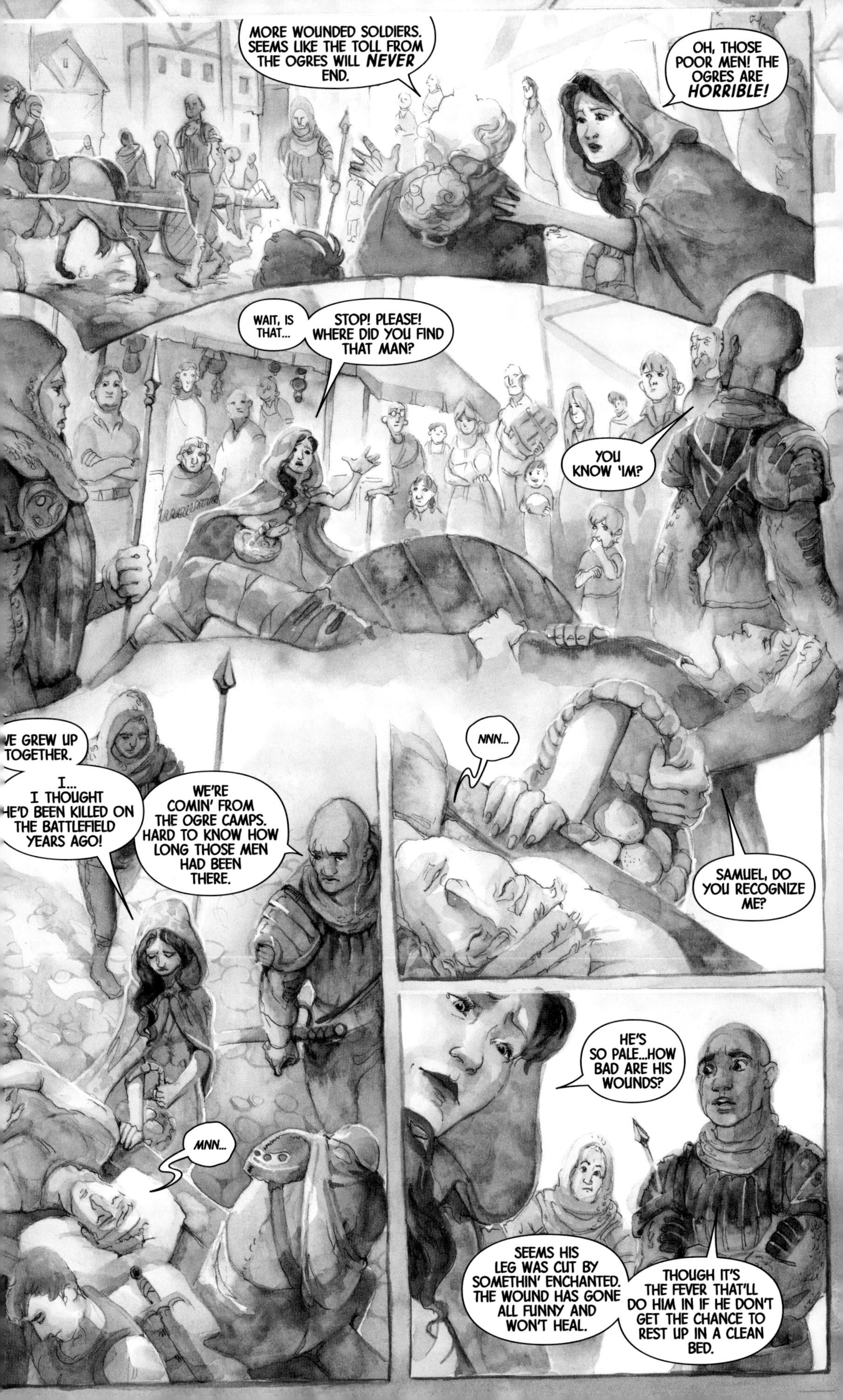

MORE WOUNDED SOLDIERS. SEEMS LIKE THE TOLL FROM THE OGRES WILL ***NEVER*** END.
OH, THOSE POOR MEN! THE OGRES ARE ***HORRIBLE!***
WAIT, IS THAT...
STOP! PLEASE! WHERE DID YOU FIND THAT MAN?
YOU KNOW 'IM?
WE GREW UP TOGETHER.
I... I THOUGHT HE'D BEEN KILLED ON THE BATTLEFIELD YEARS AGO!
WE'RE COMIN' FROM THE OGRE CAMPS. HARD TO KNOW HOW LONG THOSE MEN HAD BEEN THERE.
MNN...
NNN...
SAMUEL, DO YOU RECOGNIZE ME?
HE'S SO PALE...HOW BAD ARE HIS WOUNDS?
SEEMS HIS LEG WAS CUT BY SOMETHIN' ENCHANTED. THE WOUND HAS GONE ALL FUNNY AND WON'T HEAL.
THOUGH IT'S THE FEVER THAT'LL DO HIM IN IF HE DON'T GET THE CHANCE TO REST UP IN A CLEAN BED.

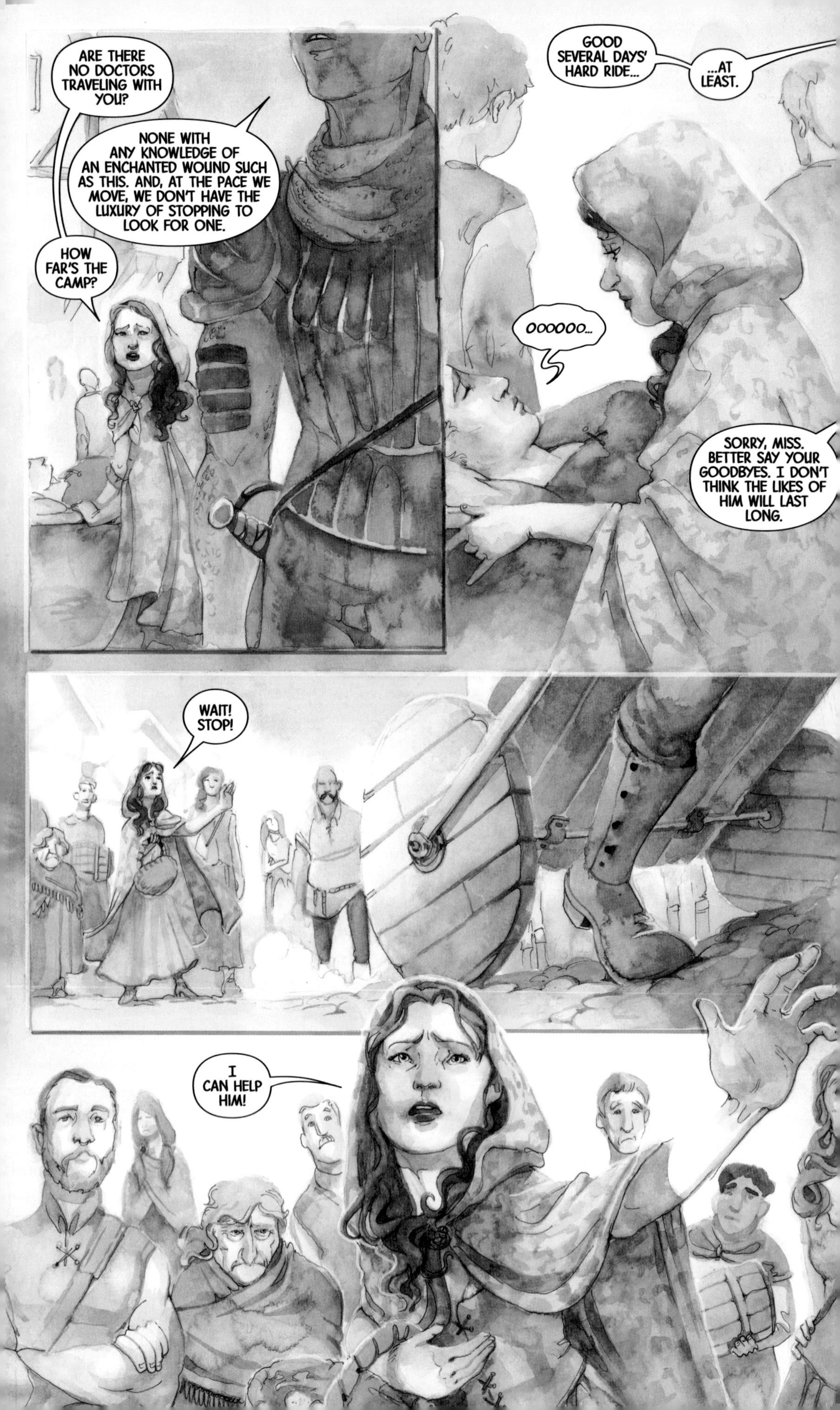

ARE THERE NO DOCTORS TRAVELING WITH YOU?
NONE WITH ANY KNOWLEDGE OF AN ENCHANTED WOUND SUCH AS THIS. AND, AT THE PACE WE MOVE, WE DON'T HAVE THE LUXURY OF STOPPING TO LOOK FOR ONE.
HOW FAR'S THE CAMP?
GOOD SEVERAL DAYS' HARD RIDE...
...AT LEAST.
OOOOOO...
SORRY, MISS. BETTER SAY YOUR GOODBYES. I DON'T THINK THE LIKES OF HIM WILL LAST LONG.
WAIT! STOP!
I CAN HELP HIM!

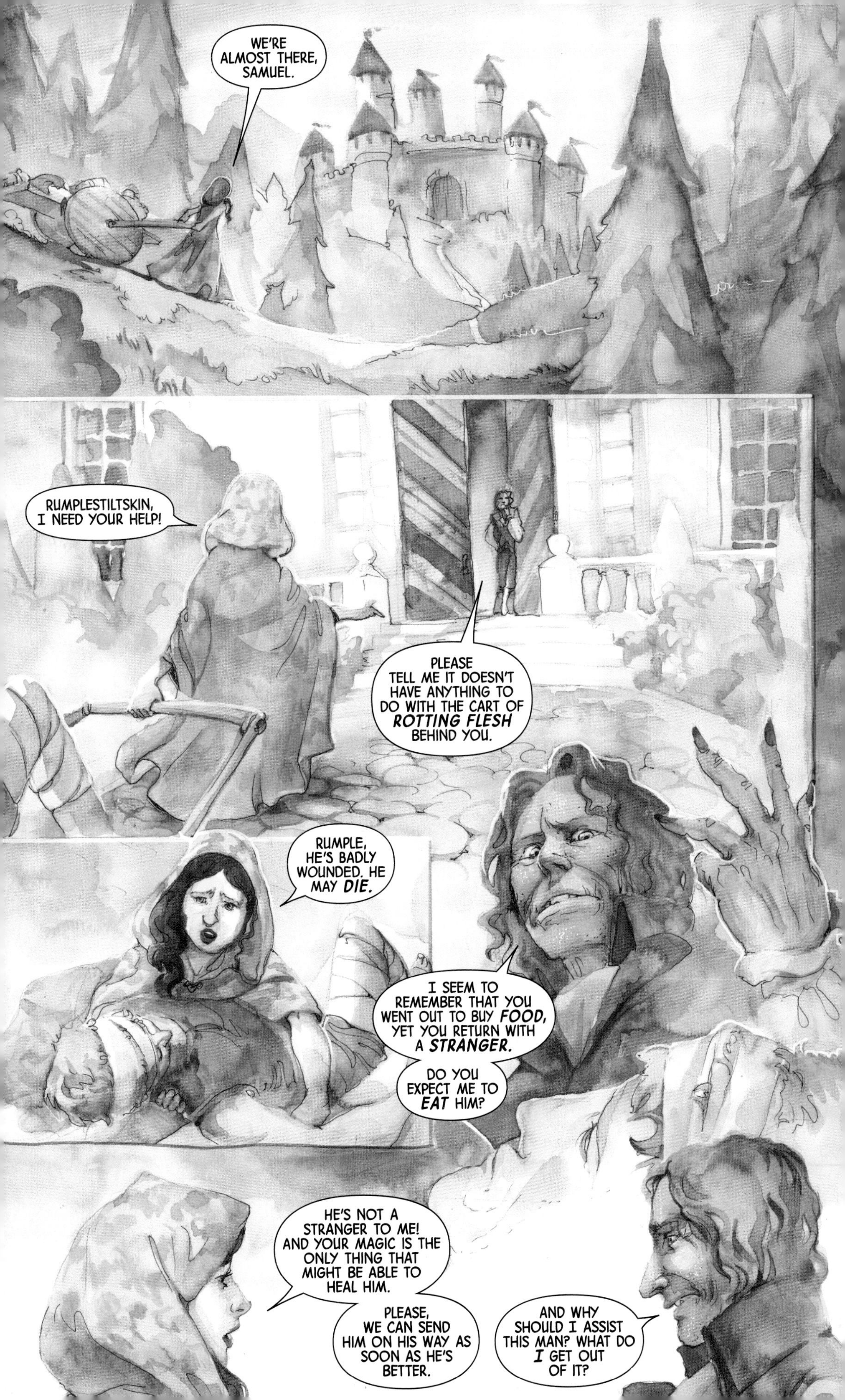
WE'RE ALMOST THERE, SAMUEL.
RUMPLESTILTSKIN, I NEED YOUR HELP!
PLEASE TELL ME IT DOESN'T HAVE ANYTHING TO DO WITH THE CART OF ROTTING FLESH BEHIND YOU.
RUMPLE, HE'S BADLY WOUNDED. HE MAY DIE.
I SEEM TO REMEMBER THAT YOU WENT OUT TO BUY FOOD, YET YOU RETURN WITH A STRANGER.
DO YOU EXPECT ME TO EAT HIM?
HE'S NOT A STRANGER TO ME! AND YOUR MAGIC IS THE ONLY THING THAT MIGHT BE ABLE TO HEAL HIM.
PLEASE, WE CAN SEND HIM ON HIS WAY AS SOON AS HE'S BETTER.
AND WHY SHOULD I ASSIST THIS MAN? WHAT DO I GET OUT OF IT?

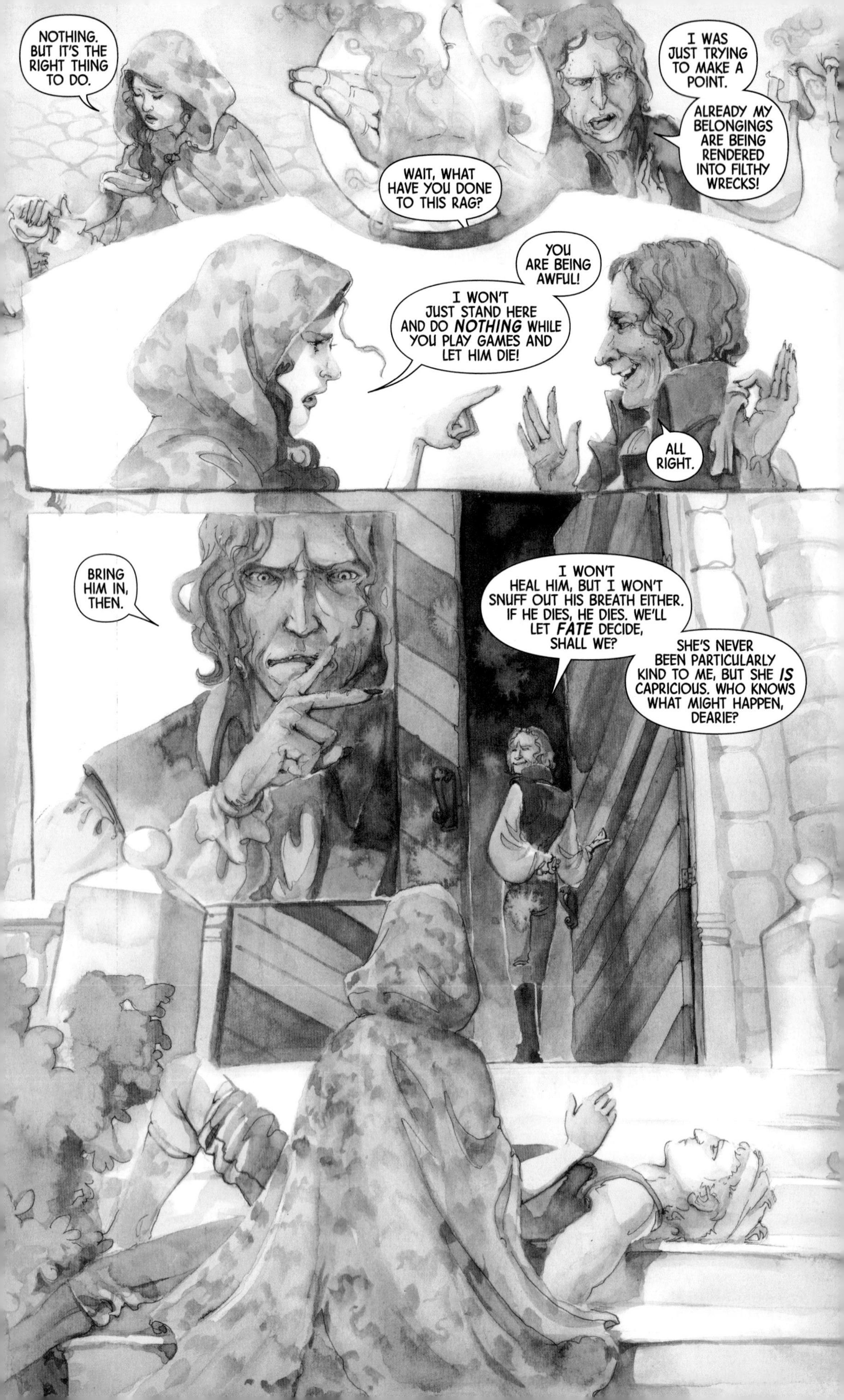
NOTHING. BUT IT'S THE RIGHT THING TO DO.
WAIT, WHAT HAVE YOU DONE TO THIS RAG?
I WAS JUST TRYING TO MAKE A POINT.
ALREADY MY BELONGINGS ARE BEING RENDERED INTO FILTHY WRECKS!
YOU ARE BEING AWFUL!
I WON'T JUST STAND HERE AND DO NOTHING WHILE YOU PLAY GAMES AND LET HIM DIE!
ALL RIGHT.
BRING HIM IN, THEN.
I WON'T HEAL HIM, BUT I WON'T SNUFF OUT HIS BREATH EITHER. IF HE DIES, HE DIES. WE'LL LET FATE DECIDE, SHALL WE?
SHE'S NEVER BEEN PARTICULARLY KIND TO ME, BUT SHE IS CAPRICIOUS. WHO KNOWS WHAT MIGHT HAPPEN, DEARIE?

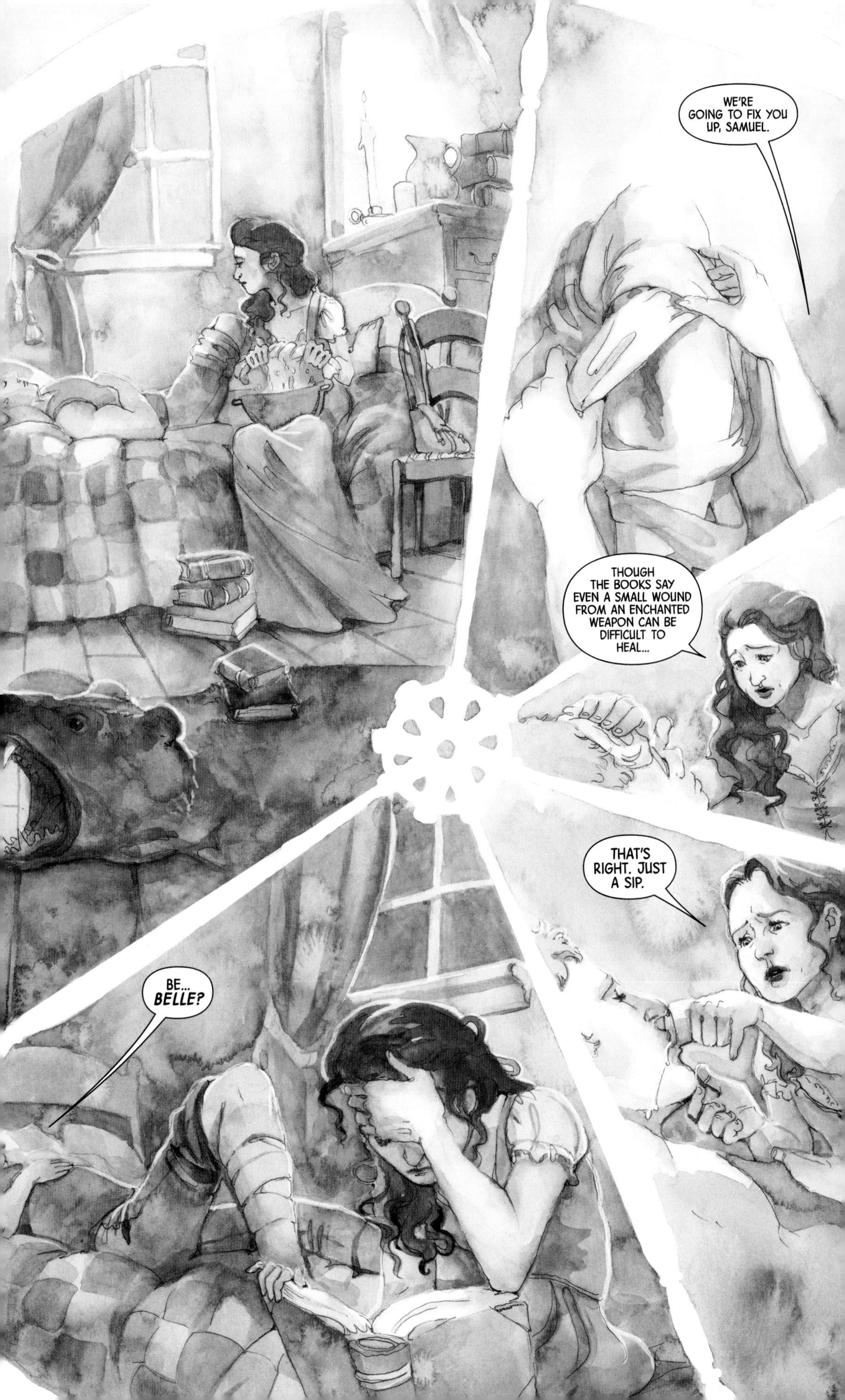
WE'RE GOING TO FIX YOU UP, SAMUEL.
THOUGH THE BOOKS SAY EVEN A SMALL WOUND FROM AN ENCHANTED WEAPON CAN BE DIFFICULT TO HEAL...
THAT'S RIGHT. JUST A SIP.
BE... BELLE?

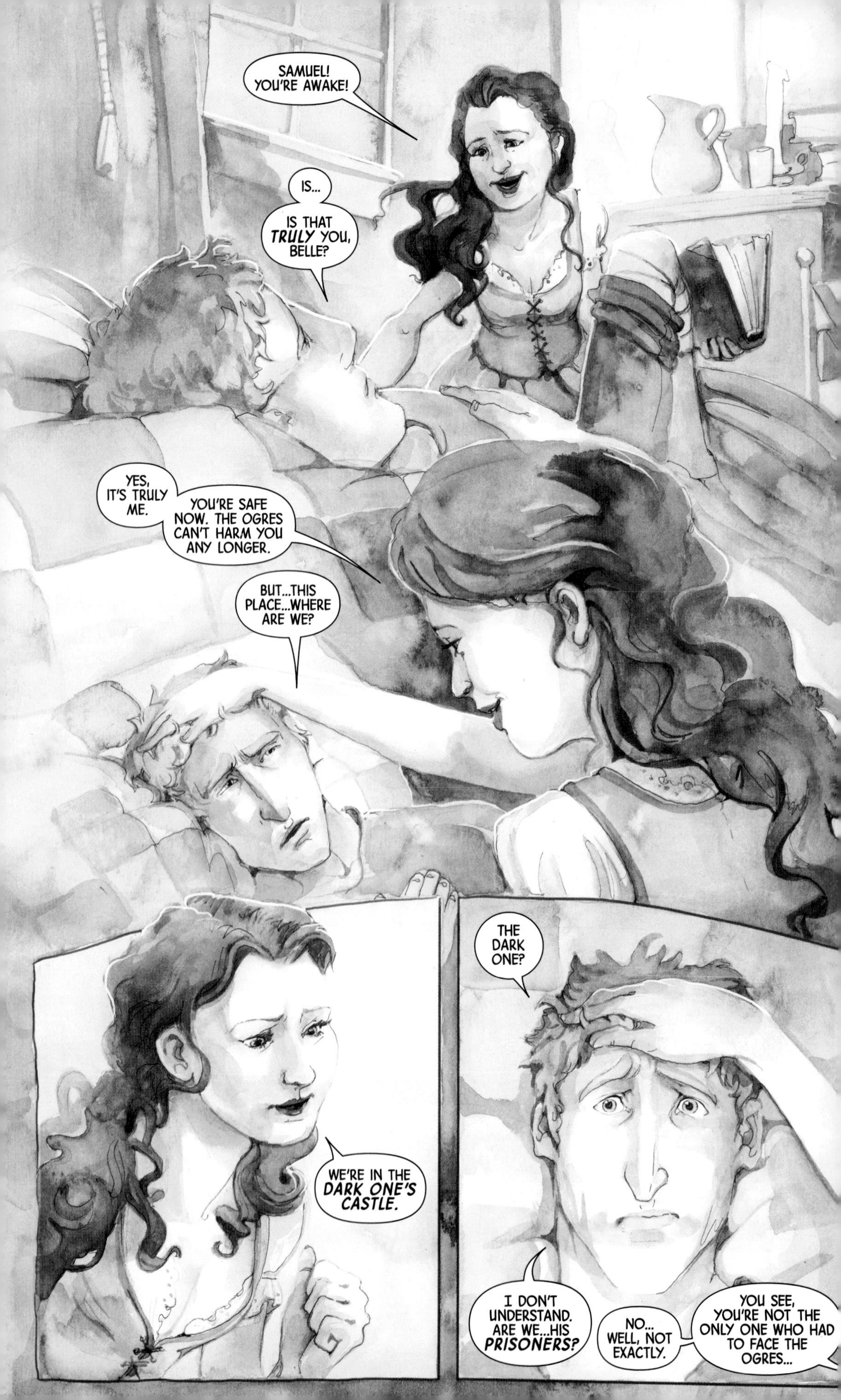
SAMUEL! YOU'RE AWAKE!
IS...
IS THAT *TRULY* YOU, BELLE?
YES, IT'S TRULY ME.
YOU'RE SAFE NOW. THE OGRES CAN'T HARM YOU ANY LONGER.
BUT...THIS PLACE...WHERE ARE WE?
WE'RE IN THE *DARK ONE'S CASTLE.*
THE DARK ONE?
I DON'T UNDERSTAND. ARE WE...HIS *PRISONERS?*
NO... WELL, NOT EXACTLY.
YOU SEE, YOU'RE NOT THE ONLY ONE WHO HAD TO FACE THE OGRES...

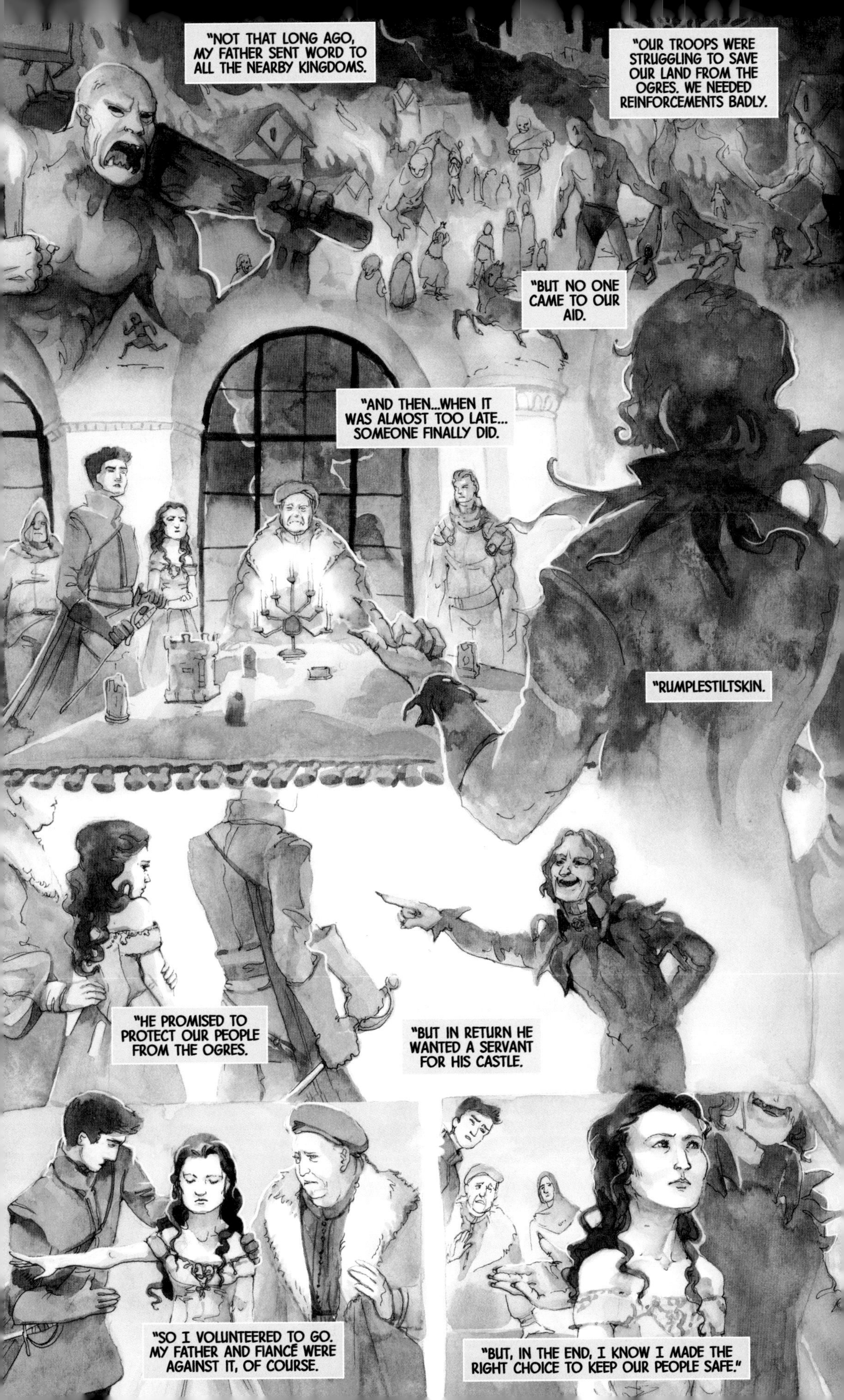
"NOT THAT LONG AGO, MY FATHER SENT WORD TO ALL THE NEARBY KINGDOMS.
"OUR TROOPS WERE STRUGGLING TO SAVE OUR LAND FROM THE OGRES. WE NEEDED REINFORCEMENTS BADLY.
"BUT NO ONE CAME TO OUR AID.
"AND THEN...WHEN IT WAS ALMOST TOO LATE... SOMEONE FINALLY DID.
"RUMPLESTILTSKIN.
"HE PROMISED TO PROTECT OUR PEOPLE FROM THE OGRES.
"BUT IN RETURN HE WANTED A SERVANT FOR HIS CASTLE.
"SO I VOLUNTEERED TO GO. MY FATHER AND FIANCÉ WERE AGAINST IT, OF COURSE.
"BUT, IN THE END, I KNOW I MADE THE RIGHT CHOICE TO KEEP OUR PEOPLE SAFE."

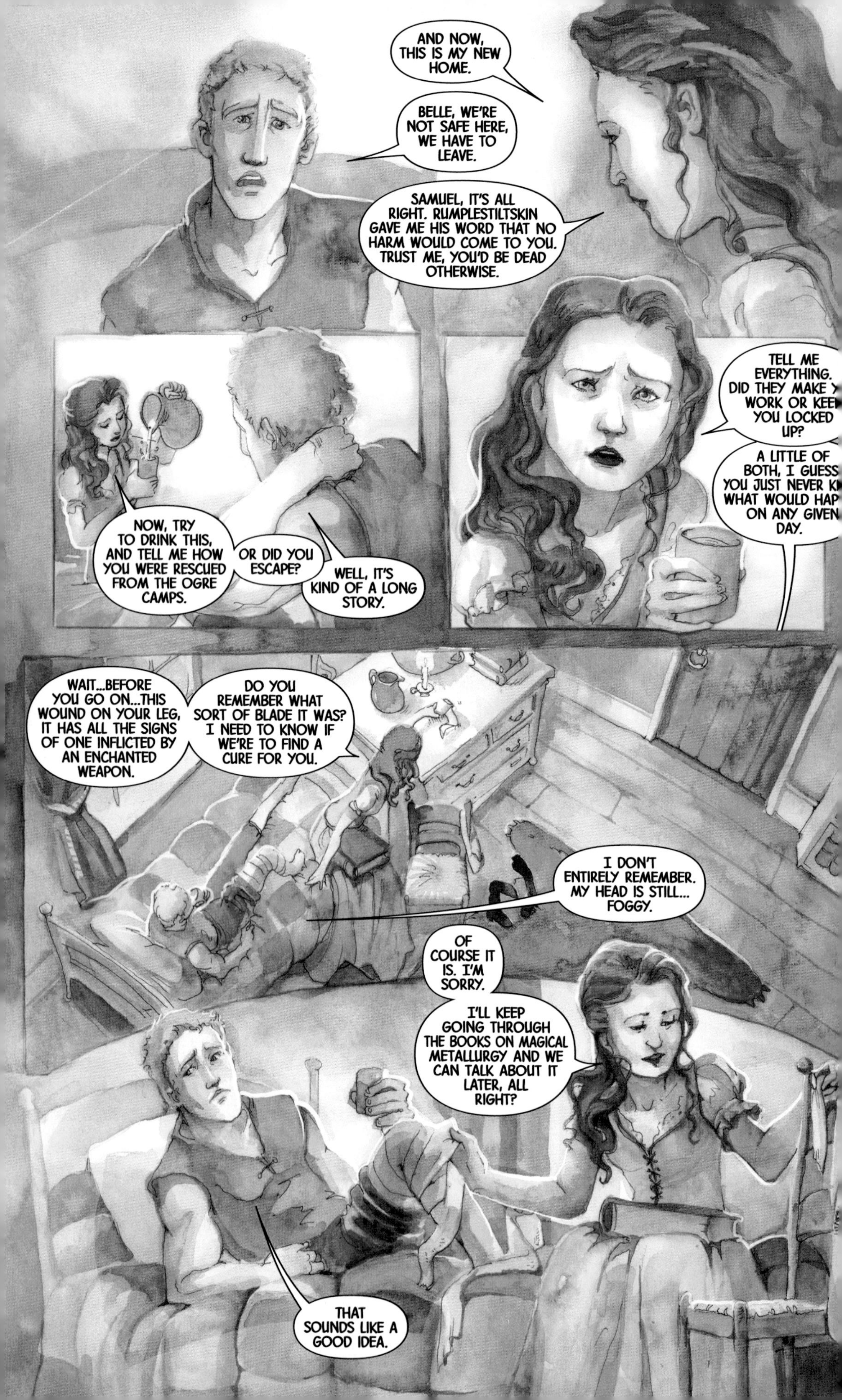

AND NOW, THIS IS MY NEW HOME.
BELLE, WE'RE NOT SAFE HERE, WE HAVE TO LEAVE.
SAMUEL, IT'S ALL RIGHT. RUMPLESTILTSKIN GAVE ME HIS WORD THAT NO HARM WOULD COME TO YOU. TRUST ME, YOU'D BE DEAD OTHERWISE.
NOW, TRY TO DRINK THIS, AND TELL ME HOW YOU WERE RESCUED FROM THE OGRE CAMPS.
OR DID YOU ESCAPE?
WELL, IT'S KIND OF A LONG STORY.
TELL ME EVERYTHING. DID THEY MAKE Y WORK OR KEE YOU LOCKED UP?
A LITTLE OF BOTH, I GUESS YOU JUST NEVER K WHAT WOULD HAP ON ANY GIVEN DAY.
WAIT...BEFORE YOU GO ON...THIS WOUND ON YOUR LEG, IT HAS ALL THE SIGNS OF ONE INFLICTED BY AN ENCHANTED WEAPON.
DO YOU REMEMBER WHAT SORT OF BLADE IT WAS? I NEED TO KNOW IF WE'RE TO FIND A CURE FOR YOU.
I DON'T ENTIRELY REMEMBER. MY HEAD IS STILL... FOGGY.
OF COURSE IT IS. I'M SORRY.
I'LL KEEP GOING THROUGH THE BOOKS ON MAGICAL METALLURGY AND WE CAN TALK ABOUT IT LATER, ALL RIGHT?
THAT SOUNDS LIKE A GOOD IDEA.

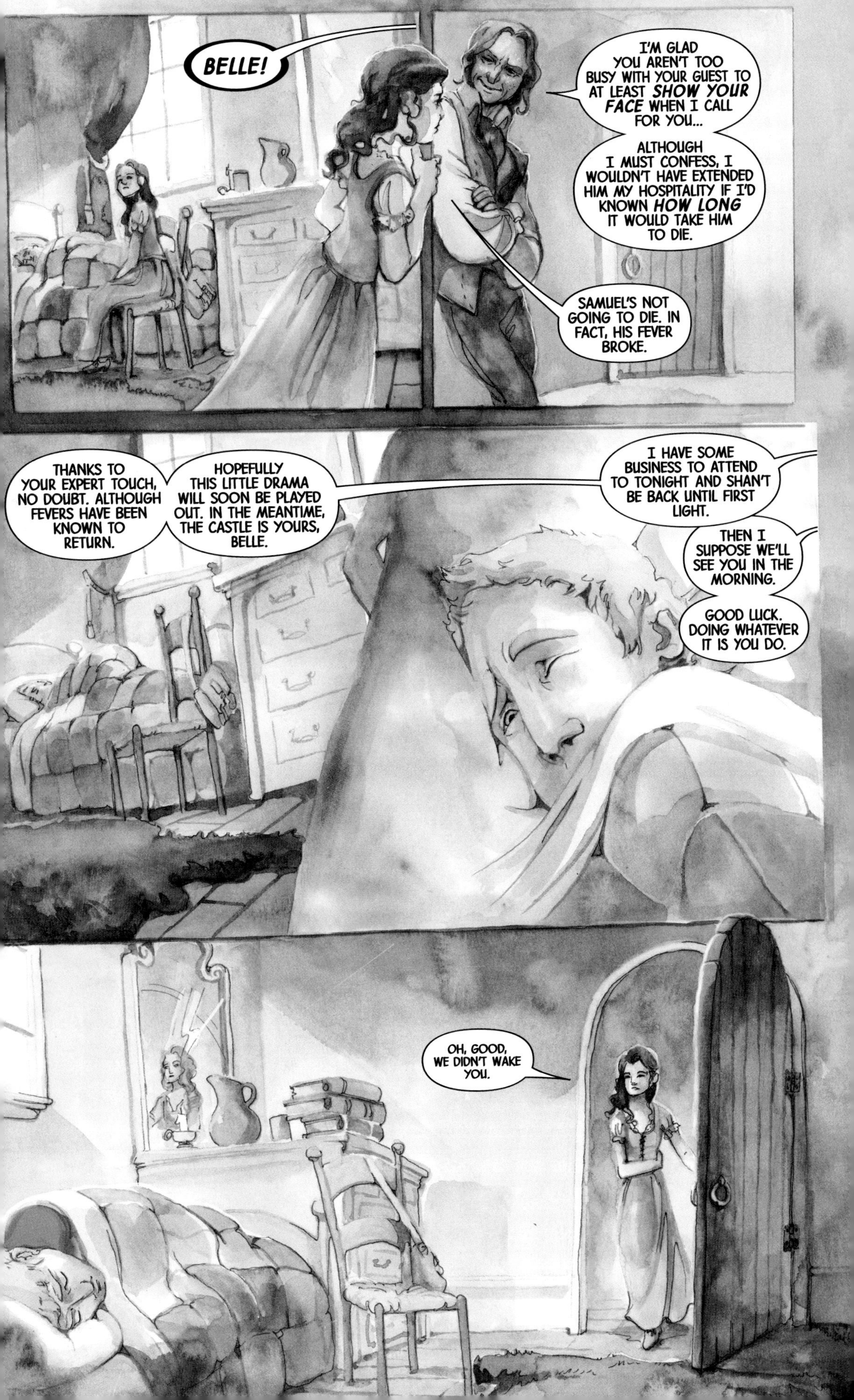
BELLE!
I'M GLAD YOU AREN'T TOO BUSY WITH YOUR GUEST TO AT LEAST *SHOW YOUR FACE* WHEN I CALL FOR YOU...
ALTHOUGH I MUST CONFESS, I WOULDN'T HAVE EXTENDED HIM MY HOSPITALITY IF I'D KNOWN *HOW LONG* IT WOULD TAKE HIM TO DIE.
SAMUEL'S NOT GOING TO DIE. IN FACT, HIS FEVER BROKE.
THANKS TO YOUR EXPERT TOUCH, NO DOUBT. ALTHOUGH FEVERS HAVE BEEN KNOWN TO RETURN.
HOPEFULLY THIS LITTLE DRAMA WILL SOON BE PLAYED OUT. IN THE MEANTIME, THE CASTLE IS YOURS, BELLE.
I HAVE SOME BUSINESS TO ATTEND TO TONIGHT AND SHAN'T BE BACK UNTIL FIRST LIGHT.
THEN I SUPPOSE WE'LL SEE YOU IN THE MORNING.
GOOD LUCK. DOING WHATEVER IT IS YOU DO.
OH, GOOD, WE DIDN'T WAKE YOU.

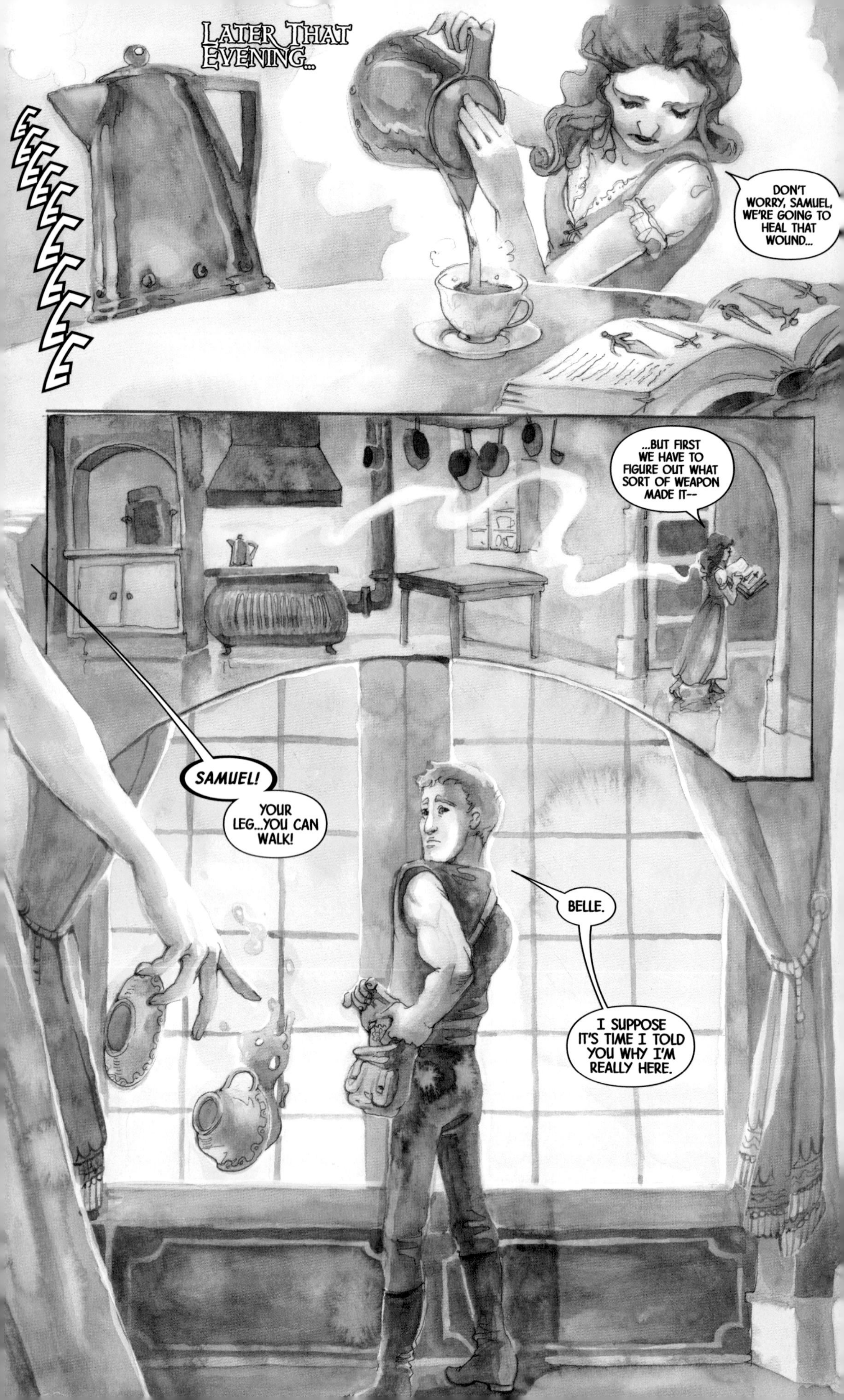
LATER THAT EVENING...
EEEEEEEEEE
DON'T WORRY, SAMUEL, WE'RE GOING TO HEAL THAT WOUND...
...BUT FIRST WE HAVE TO FIGURE OUT WHAT SORT OF WEAPON MADE IT--
SAMUEL!
YOUR LEG...YOU CAN WALK!
BELLE.
I SUPPOSE IT'S TIME I TOLD YOU WHY I'M REALLY HERE.

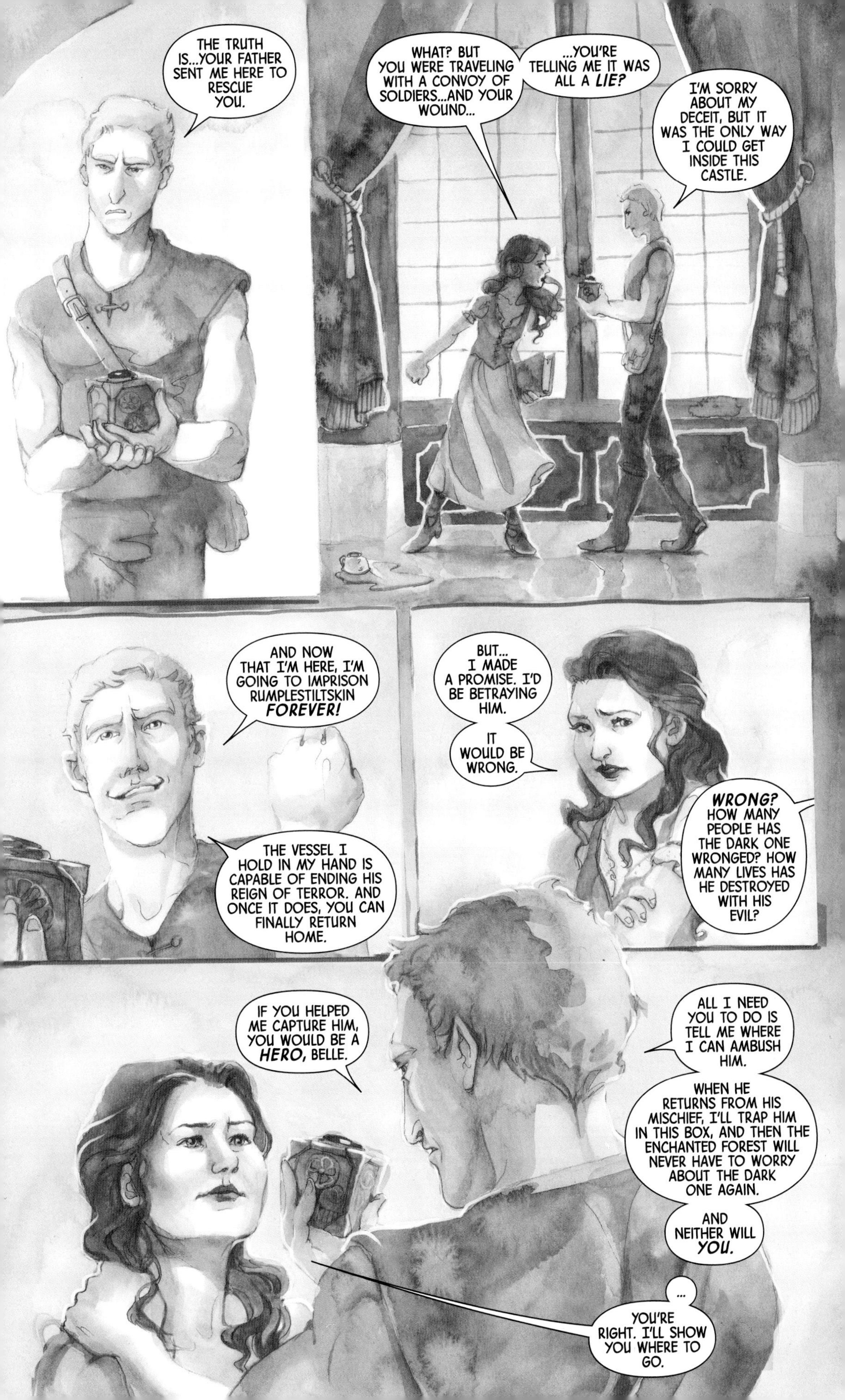
THE TRUTH IS...YOUR FATHER SENT ME HERE TO RESCUE YOU.
WHAT? BUT YOU WERE TRAVELING WITH A CONVOY OF SOLDIERS...AND YOUR WOUND...
...YOU'RE TELLING ME IT WAS ALL A LIE?
I'M SORRY ABOUT MY DECEIT, BUT IT WAS THE ONLY WAY I COULD GET INSIDE THIS CASTLE.
AND NOW THAT I'M HERE, I'M GOING TO IMPRISON RUMPLESTILTSKIN FOREVER!
THE VESSEL I HOLD IN MY HAND IS CAPABLE OF ENDING HIS REIGN OF TERROR. AND ONCE IT DOES, YOU CAN FINALLY RETURN HOME.
BUT... I MADE A PROMISE. I'D BE BETRAYING HIM.
IT WOULD BE WRONG.
WRONG? HOW MANY PEOPLE HAS THE DARK ONE WRONGED? HOW MANY LIVES HAS HE DESTROYED WITH HIS EVIL?
IF YOU HELPED ME CAPTURE HIM, YOU WOULD BE A HERO, BELLE.
ALL I NEED YOU TO DO IS TELL ME WHERE I CAN AMBUSH HIM.
WHEN HE RETURNS FROM HIS MISCHIEF, I'LL TRAP HIM IN THIS BOX, AND THEN THE ENCHANTED FOREST WILL NEVER HAVE TO WORRY ABOUT THE DARK ONE AGAIN.
AND NEITHER WILL YOU.
...
YOU'RE RIGHT. I'LL SHOW YOU WHERE TO GO.

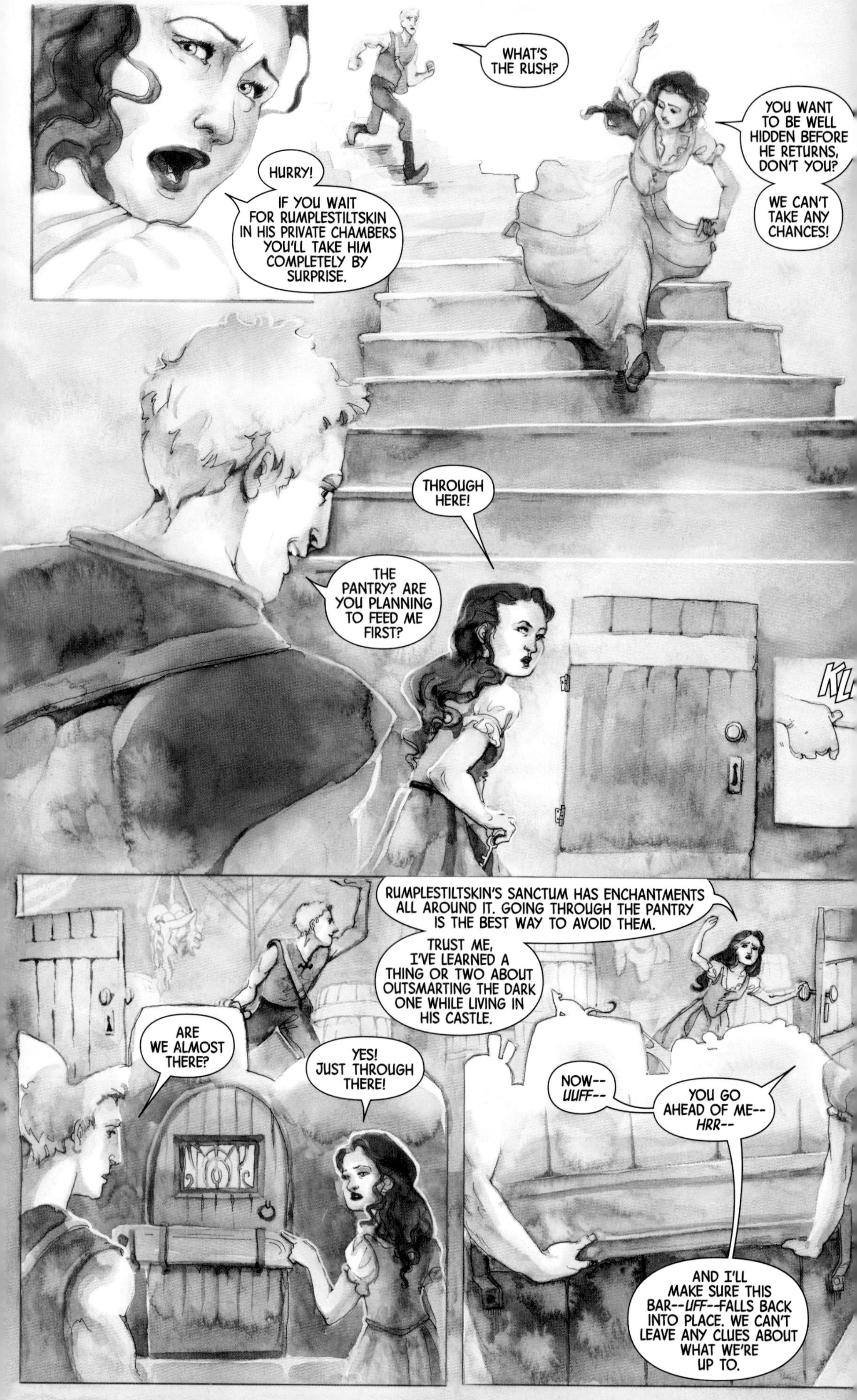
HURRY!
IF YOU WAIT FOR RUMPLESTILTSKIN IN HIS PRIVATE CHAMBERS YOU'LL TAKE HIM COMPLETELY BY SURPRISE.
WHAT'S THE RUSH?
YOU WANT TO BE WELL HIDDEN BEFORE HE RETURNS, DON'T YOU?
WE CAN'T TAKE ANY CHANCES!
THROUGH HERE!
THE PANTRY? ARE YOU PLANNING TO FEED ME FIRST?
KL
RUMPLESTILTSKIN'S SANCTUM HAS ENCHANTMENTS ALL AROUND IT. GOING THROUGH THE PANTRY IS THE BEST WAY TO AVOID THEM.
TRUST ME, I'VE LEARNED A THING OR TWO ABOUT OUTSMARTING THE DARK ONE WHILE LIVING IN HIS CASTLE.
ARE WE ALMOST THERE?
YES! JUST THROUGH THERE!
NOW-- *UUFF*--
YOU GO AHEAD OF ME-- *HRR*--
AND I'LL MAKE SURE THIS BAR--*UFF*--FALLS BACK INTO PLACE. WE CAN'T LEAVE ANY CLUES ABOUT WHAT WE'RE UP TO.

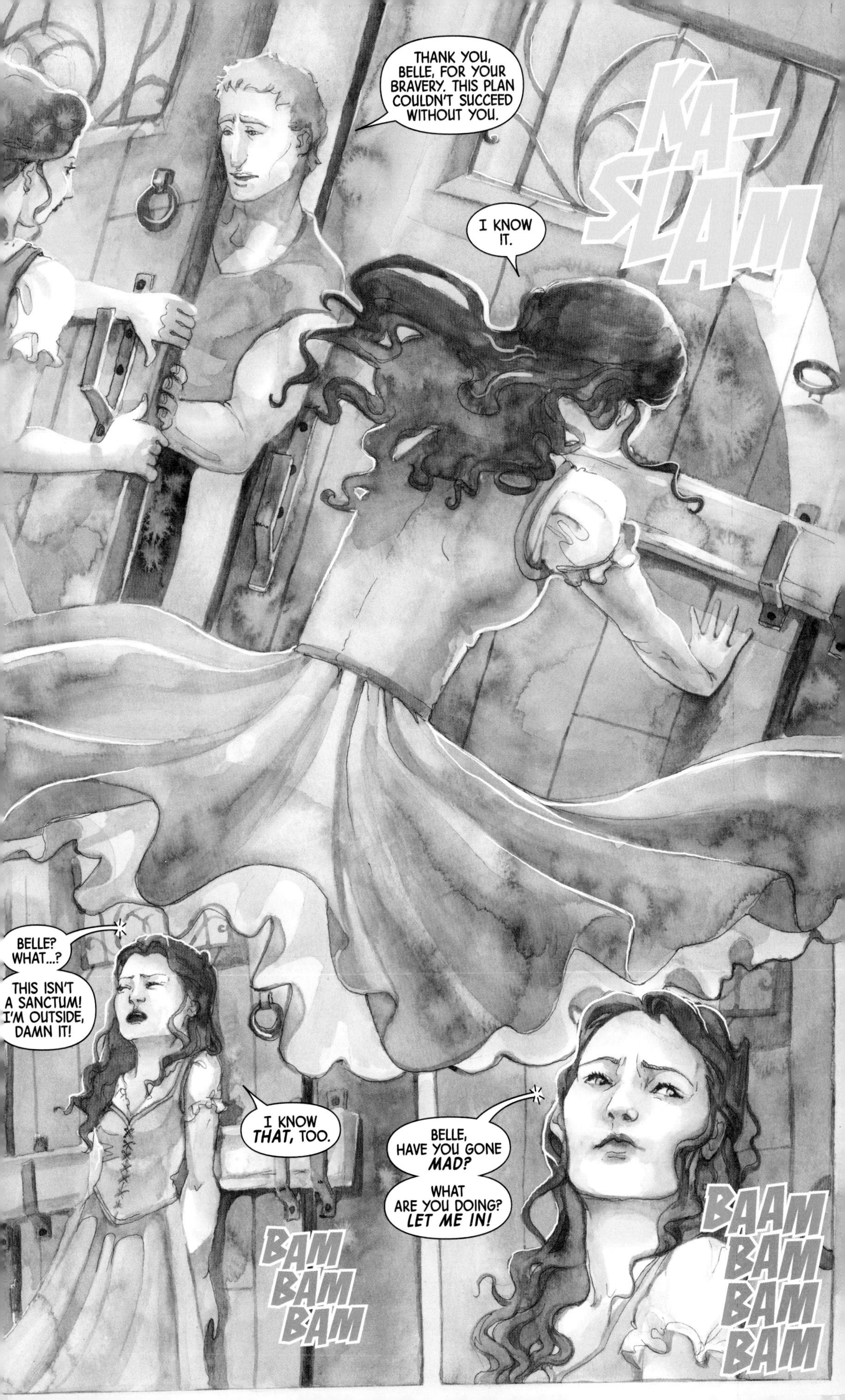
THANK YOU, BELLE, FOR YOUR BRAVERY. THIS PLAN COULDN'T SUCCEED WITHOUT YOU.
KA-SLAM
I KNOW IT.
BELLE? WHAT...?
THIS ISN'T A SANCTUM! I'M OUTSIDE, DAMN IT!
I KNOW THAT, TOO.
BELLE, HAVE YOU GONE MAD?
WHAT ARE YOU DOING? LET ME IN!
BAM BAM BAM
BAAM BAM BAM BAM

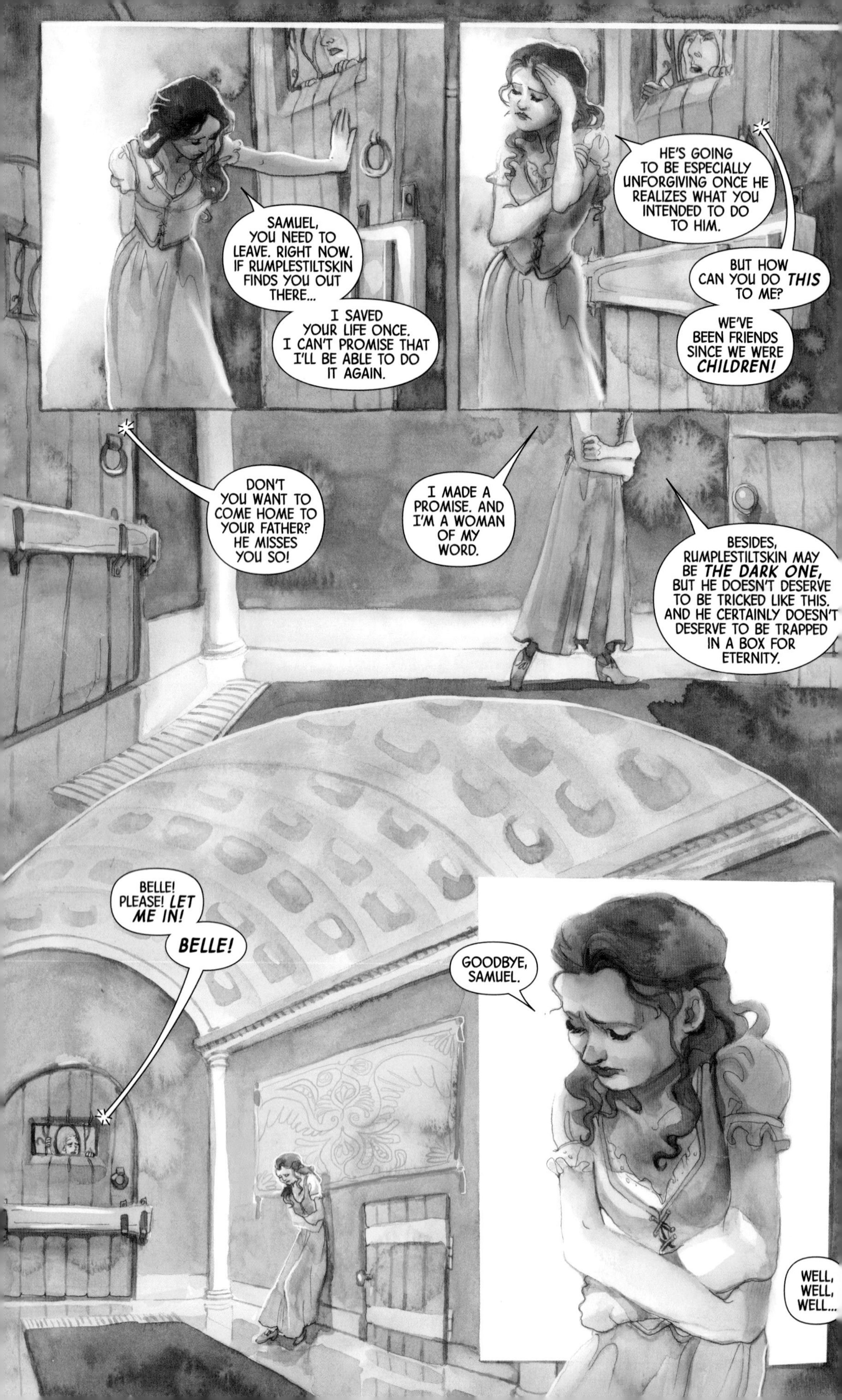
SAMUEL, YOU NEED TO LEAVE. RIGHT NOW. IF RUMPLESTILTSKIN FINDS YOU OUT THERE...
I SAVED YOUR LIFE ONCE. I CAN'T PROMISE THAT I'LL BE ABLE TO DO IT AGAIN.
HE'S GOING TO BE ESPECIALLY UNFORGIVING ONCE HE REALIZES WHAT YOU INTENDED TO DO TO HIM.
BUT HOW CAN YOU DO *THIS* TO ME?
WE'VE BEEN FRIENDS SINCE WE WERE *CHILDREN!*
DON'T YOU WANT TO COME HOME TO YOUR FATHER? HE MISSES YOU SO!
I MADE A PROMISE. AND I'M A WOMAN OF MY WORD.
BESIDES, RUMPLESTILTSKIN MAY BE *THE DARK ONE,* BUT HE DOESN'T DESERVE TO BE TRICKED LIKE THIS. AND HE CERTAINLY DOESN'T DESERVE TO BE TRAPPED IN A BOX FOR ETERNITY.
BELLE! PLEASE! *LET ME IN!*
BELLE!
GOODBYE, SAMUEL.
WELL, WELL, WELL...

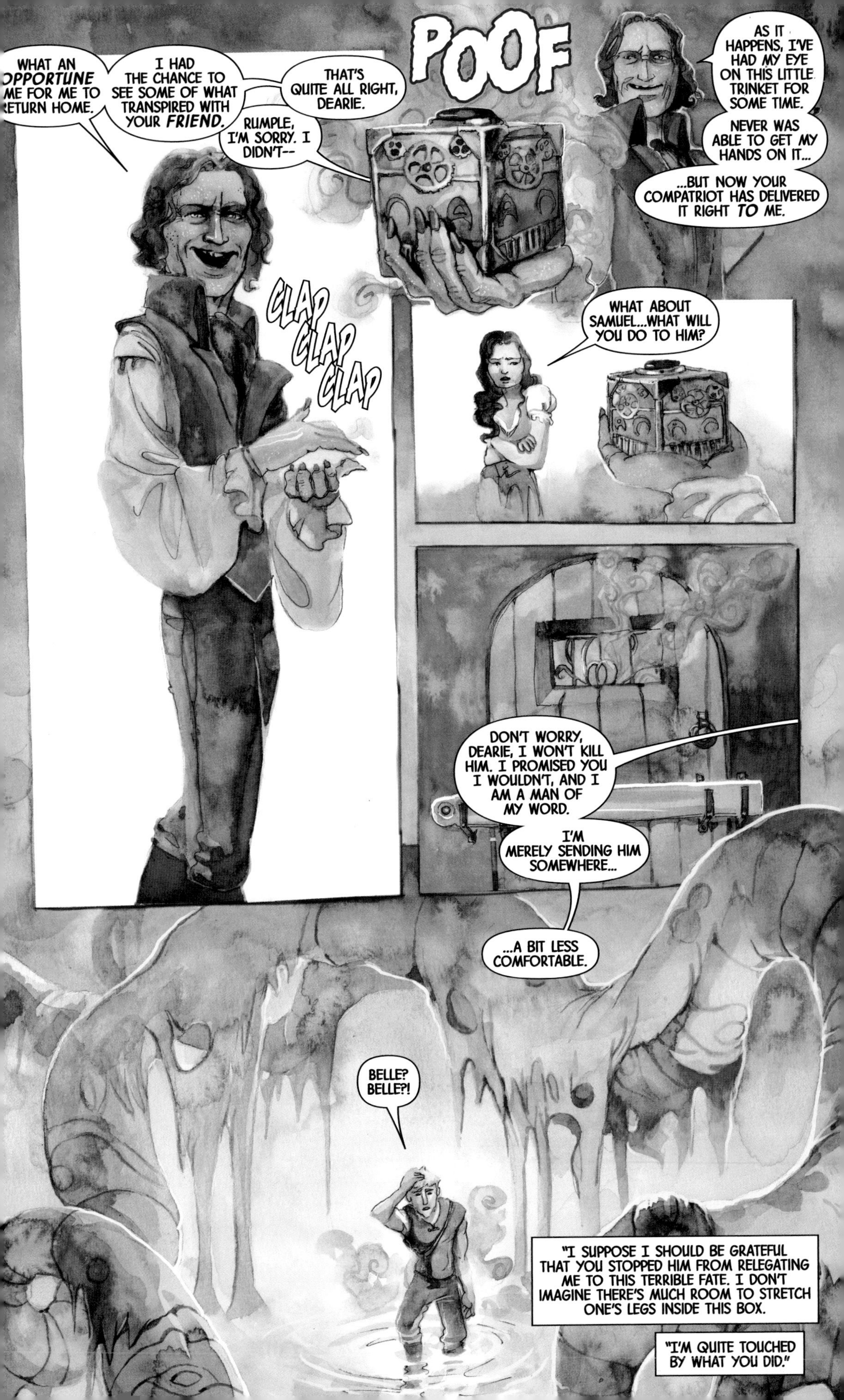
WHAT AN OPPORTUNE ME FOR ME TO ETURN HOME.
I HAD THE CHANCE TO SEE SOME OF WHAT TRANSPIRED WITH YOUR FRIEND.
RUMPLE, I'M SORRY. I DIDN'T--
THAT'S QUITE ALL RIGHT, DEARIE.
CLAP CLAP CLAP
POOF
AS IT HAPPENS, I'VE HAD MY EYE ON THIS LITTLE TRINKET FOR SOME TIME.
NEVER WAS ABLE TO GET MY HANDS ON IT...
...BUT NOW YOUR COMPATRIOT HAS DELIVERED IT RIGHT TO ME.
WHAT ABOUT SAMUEL...WHAT WILL YOU DO TO HIM?
DON'T WORRY, DEARIE, I WON'T KILL HIM. I PROMISED YOU I WOULDN'T, AND I AM A MAN OF MY WORD.
I'M MERELY SENDING HIM SOMEWHERE...
...A BIT LESS COMFORTABLE.
BELLE? BELLE?!
"I SUPPOSE I SHOULD BE GRATEFUL THAT YOU STOPPED HIM FROM RELEGATING ME TO THIS TERRIBLE FATE. I DON'T IMAGINE THERE'S MUCH ROOM TO STRETCH ONE'S LEGS INSIDE THIS BOX.
"I'M QUITE TOUCHED BY WHAT YOU DID."

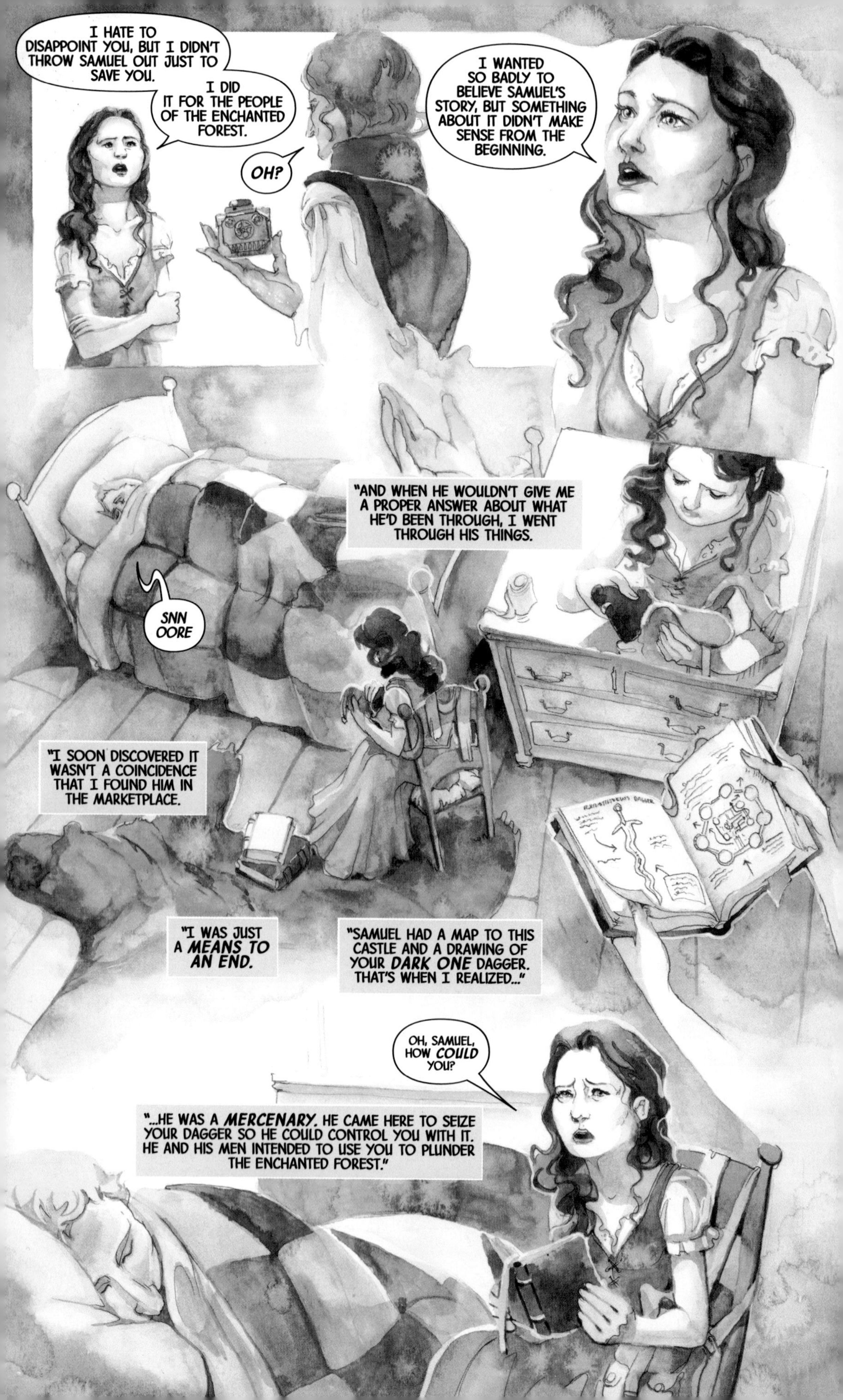

I HATE TO DISAPPOINT YOU, BUT I DIDN'T THROW SAMUEL OUT JUST TO SAVE YOU.
I DID IT FOR THE PEOPLE OF THE ENCHANTED FOREST.
OH?
I WANTED SO BADLY TO BELIEVE SAMUEL'S STORY, BUT SOMETHING ABOUT IT DIDN'T MAKE SENSE FROM THE BEGINNING.
"AND WHEN HE WOULDN'T GIVE ME A PROPER ANSWER ABOUT WHAT HE'D BEEN THROUGH, I WENT THROUGH HIS THINGS.
SNN OORE
"I SOON DISCOVERED IT WASN'T A COINCIDENCE THAT I FOUND HIM IN THE MARKETPLACE.
"I WAS JUST A ***MEANS TO AN END.***
"SAMUEL HAD A MAP TO THIS CASTLE AND A DRAWING OF YOUR ***DARK ONE*** DAGGER. THAT'S WHEN I REALIZED..."
OH, SAMUEL, HOW ***COULD*** YOU?
"...HE WAS A ***MERCENARY.*** HE CAME HERE TO SEIZE YOUR DAGGER SO HE COULD CONTROL YOU WITH IT. HE AND HIS MEN INTENDED TO USE YOU TO PLUNDER THE ENCHANTED FOREST."

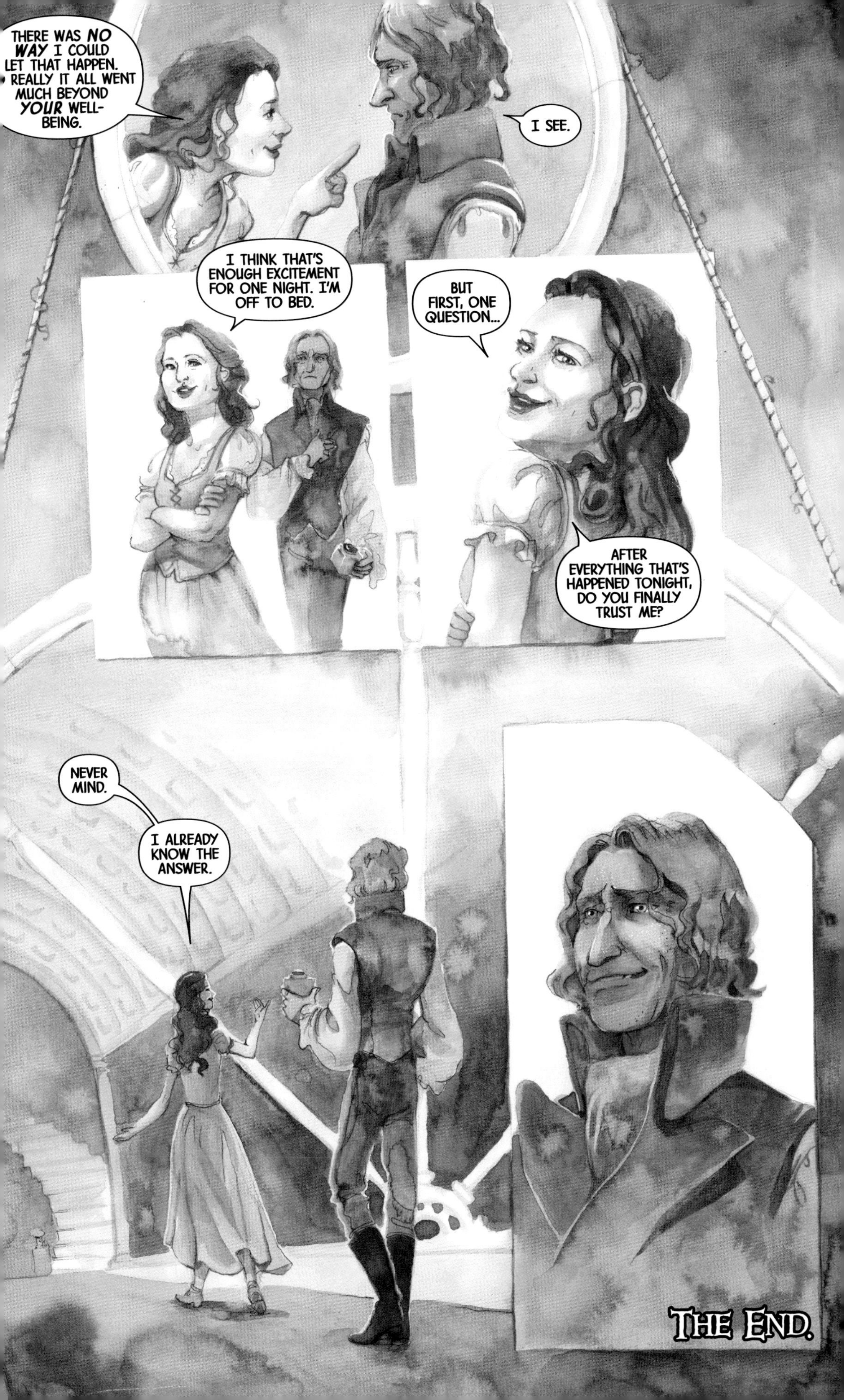
THERE WAS NO WAY I COULD LET THAT HAPPEN. REALLY IT ALL WENT MUCH BEYOND YOUR WELL-BEING.
I SEE.
I THINK THAT'S ENOUGH EXCITEMENT FOR ONE NIGHT. I'M OFF TO BED.
BUT FIRST, ONE QUESTION...
AFTER EVERYTHING THAT'S HAPPENED TONIGHT, DO YOU FINALLY TRUST ME?
NEVER MIND.
I ALREADY KNOW THE ANSWER.
THE END.

CHAPTER THREE

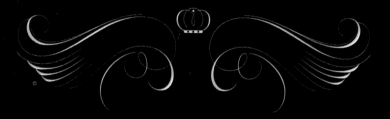

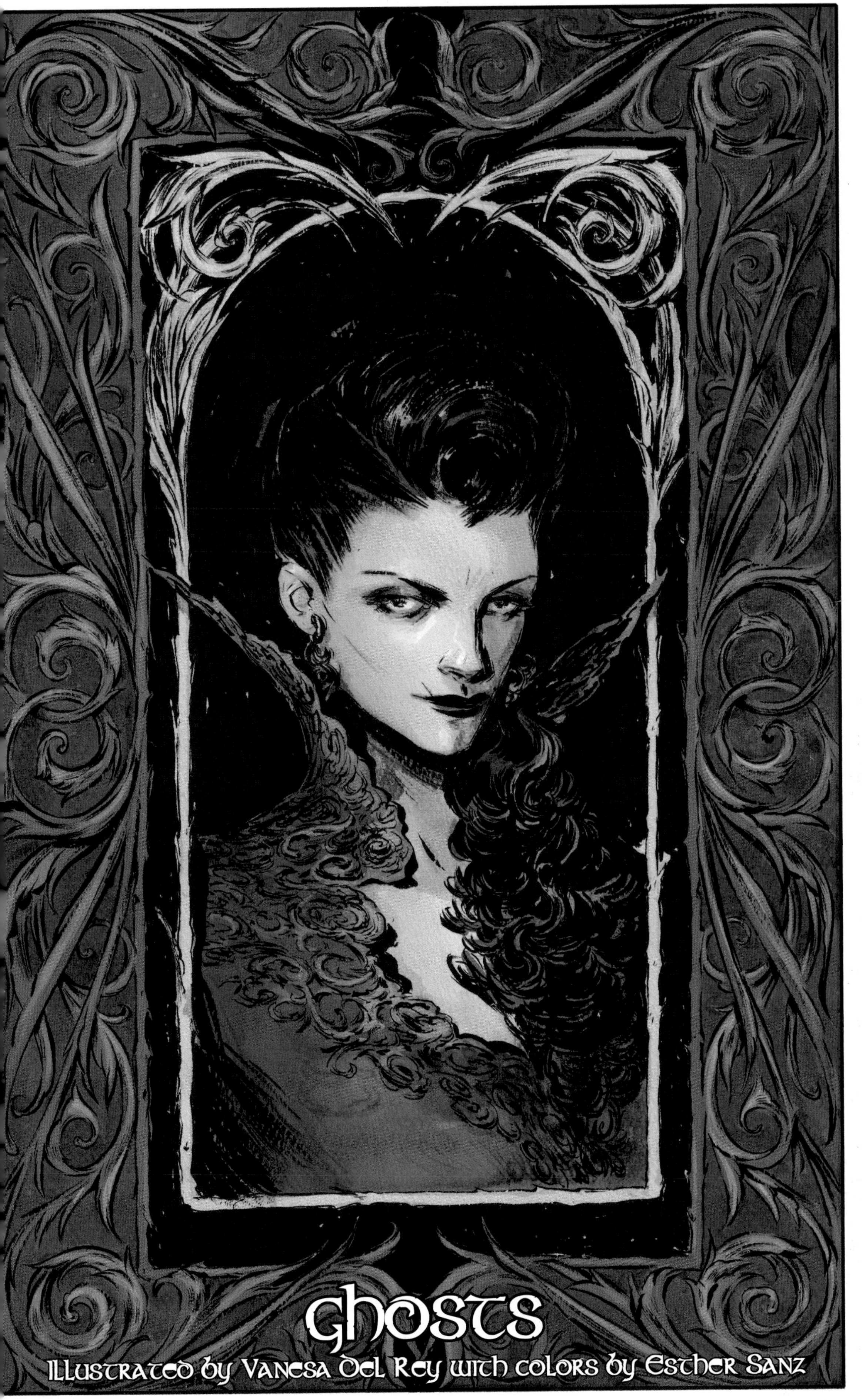

Ghosts

Illustrated by Vanesa Del Rey with colors by Esther Sanz

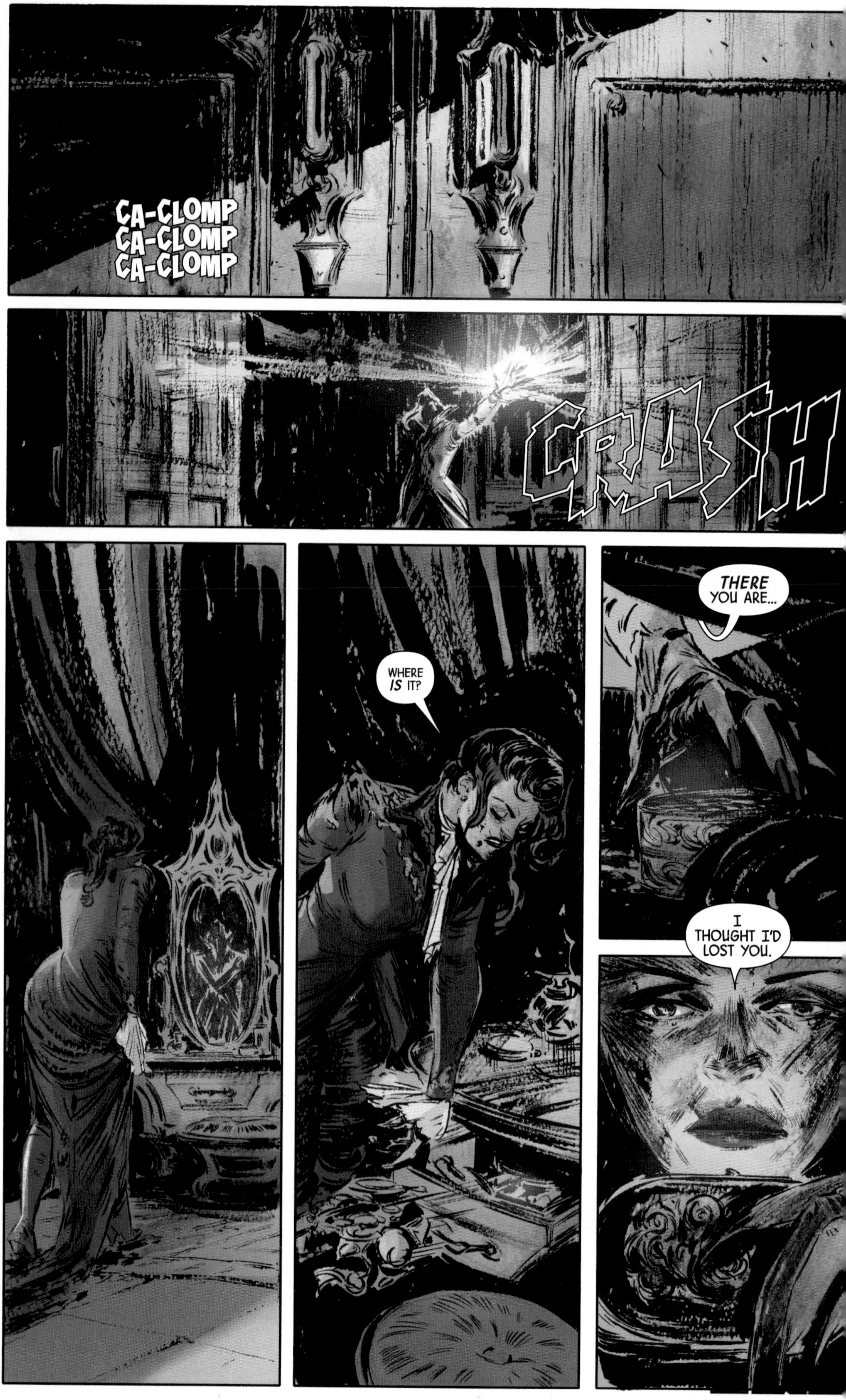
CA-CLOMP
CA-CLOMP
CA-CLOMP
CRASH
WHERE IS IT?
THERE YOU ARE...
I THOUGHT I'D LOST YOU.

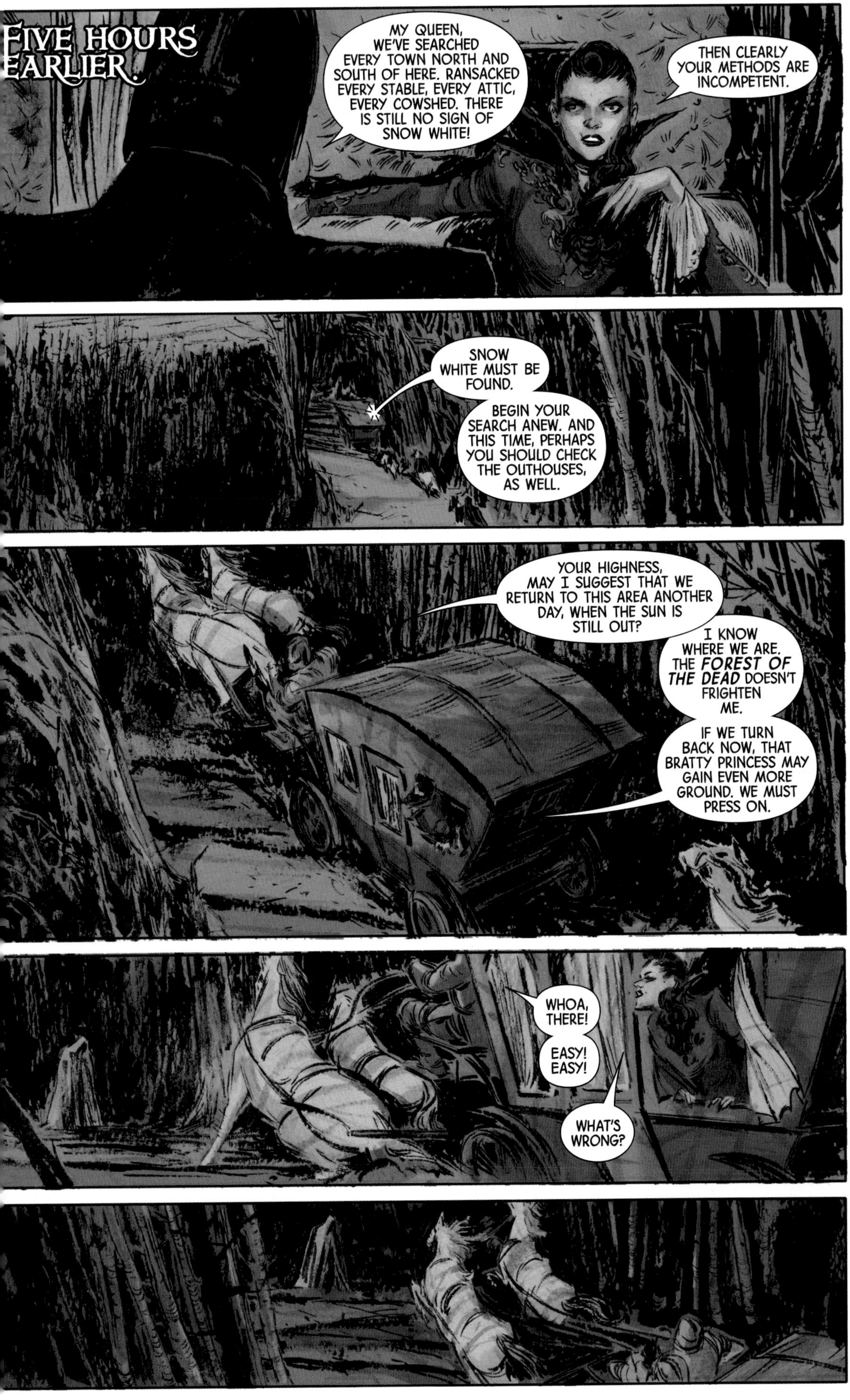

FIVE HOURS EARLIER.
MY QUEEN, WE'VE SEARCHED EVERY TOWN NORTH AND SOUTH OF HERE. RANSACKED EVERY STABLE, EVERY ATTIC, EVERY COWSHED. THERE IS STILL NO SIGN OF SNOW WHITE!
THEN CLEARLY YOUR METHODS ARE INCOMPETENT.
SNOW WHITE MUST BE FOUND.
BEGIN YOUR SEARCH ANEW. AND THIS TIME, PERHAPS YOU SHOULD CHECK THE OUTHOUSES, AS WELL.
YOUR HIGHNESS, MAY I SUGGEST THAT WE RETURN TO THIS AREA ANOTHER DAY, WHEN THE SUN IS STILL OUT?
I KNOW WHERE WE ARE. THE FOREST OF THE DEAD DOESN'T FRIGHTEN ME.
IF WE TURN BACK NOW, THAT BRATTY PRINCESS MAY GAIN EVEN MORE GROUND. WE MUST PRESS ON.
WHOA, THERE!
EASY! EASY!
WHAT'S WRONG?

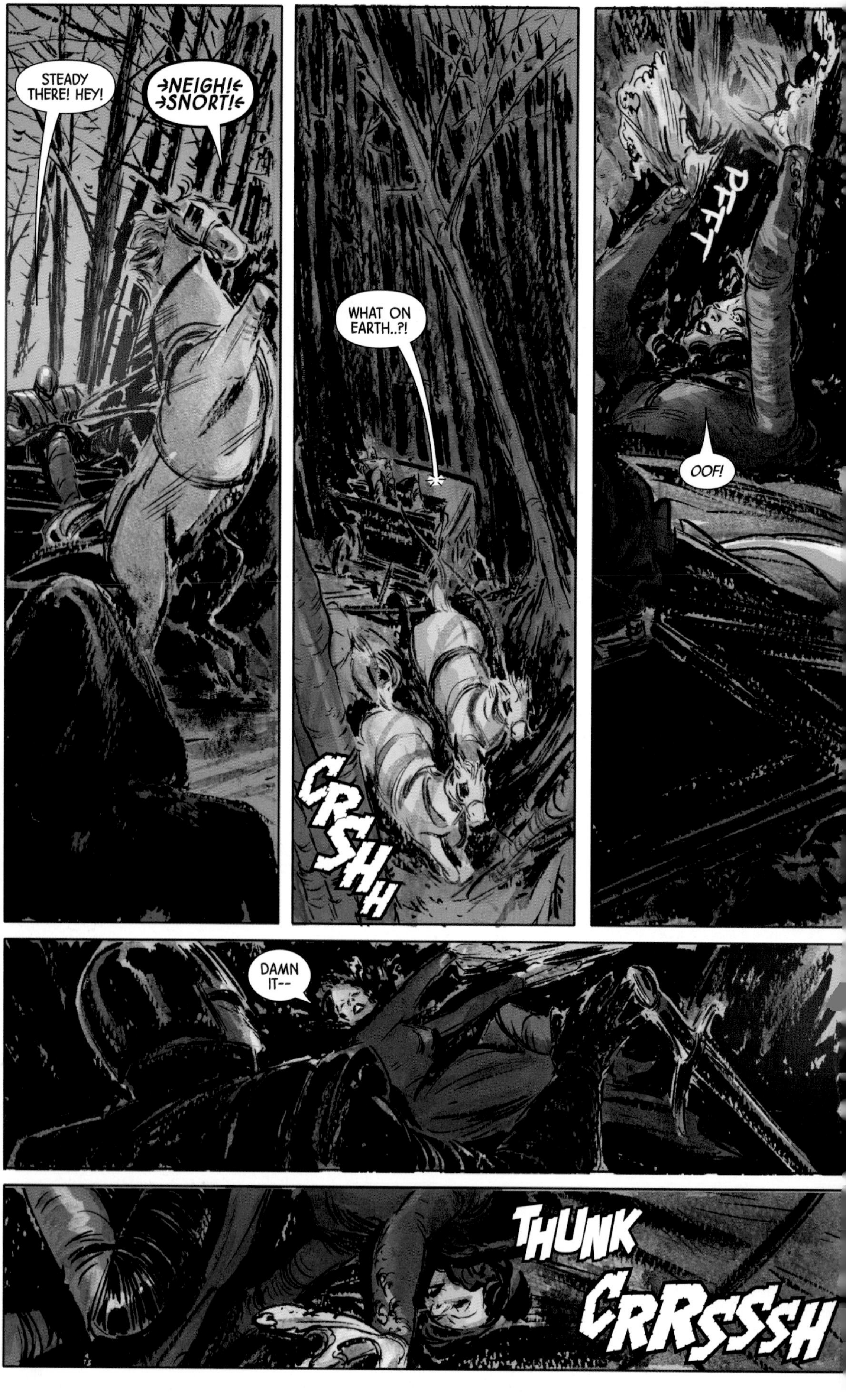
STEADY THERE! HEY!
→NEIGH!← →SNORT!←
WHAT ON EARTH..?!
CRSHH
PFFFT
OOF!
DAMN IT--
THUNK
CRRSSSH

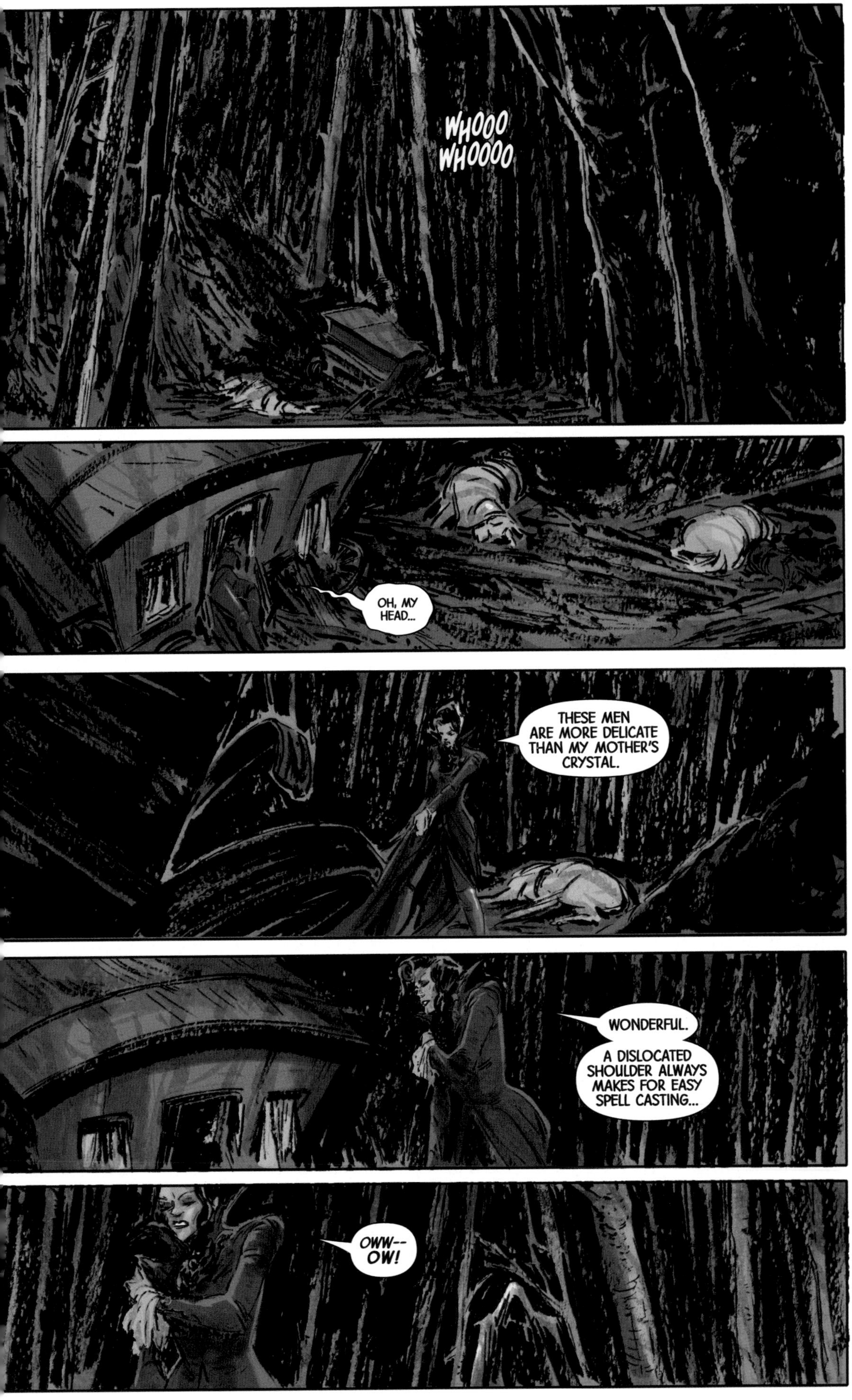
WHOOO WHOOOO
OH, MY HEAD...
THESE MEN ARE MORE DELICATE THAN MY MOTHER'S CRYSTAL.
WONDERFUL.
A DISLOCATED SHOULDER ALWAYS MAKES FOR EASY SPELL CASTING...
OWW-- OW!

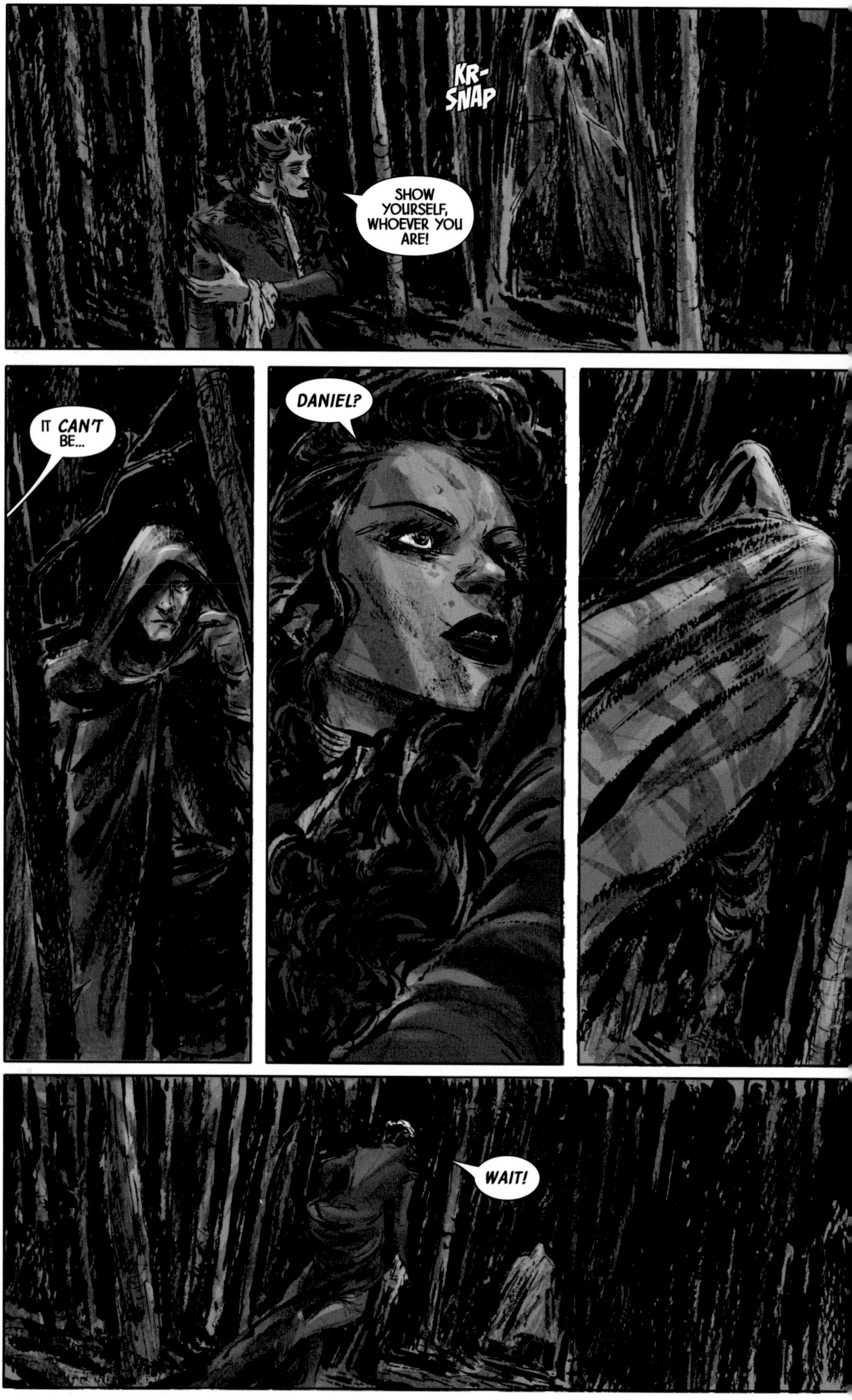
KR-SNAP
SHOW YOURSELF, WHOEVER YOU ARE!
IT CAN'T BE...
DANIEL?
WAIT!

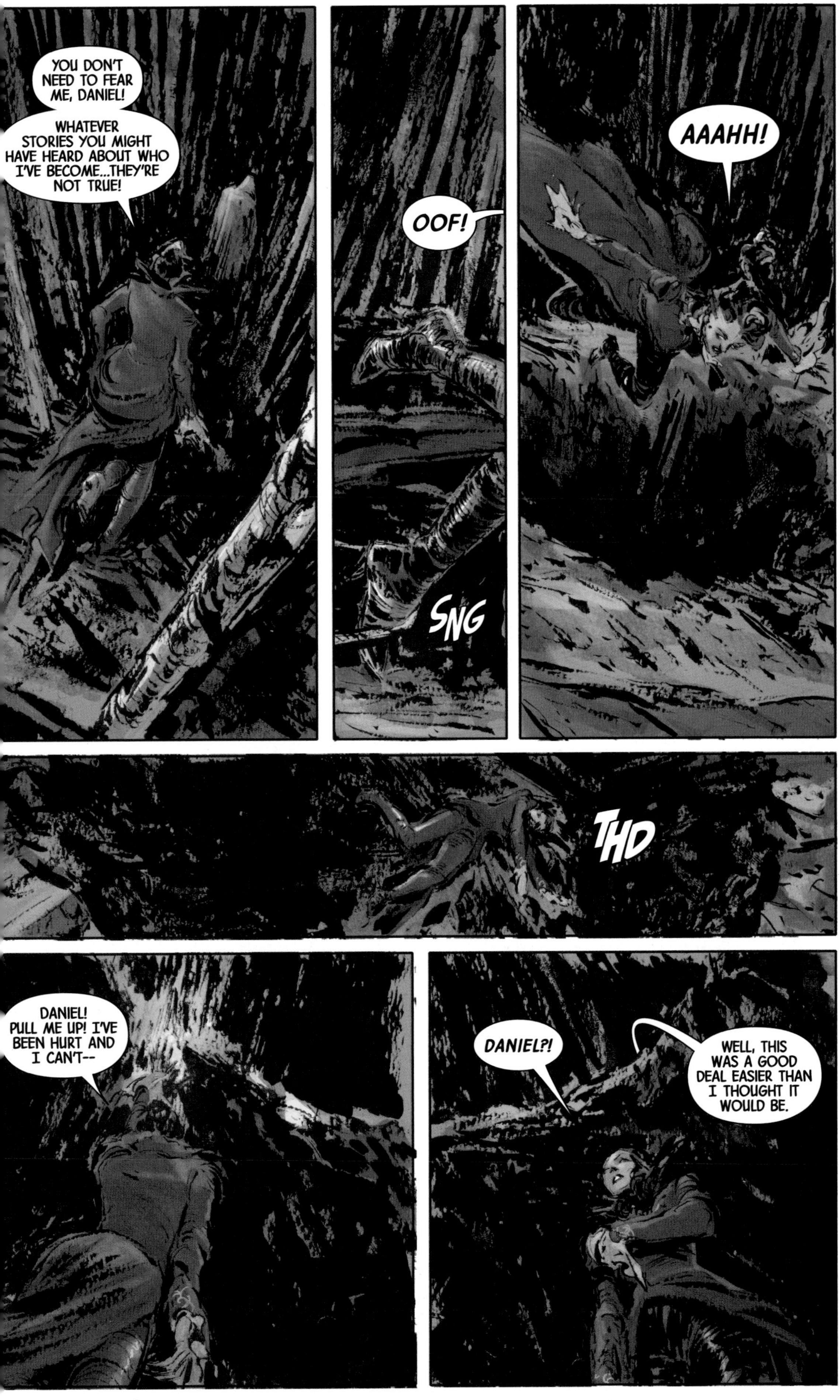
YOU DON'T NEED TO FEAR ME, DANIEL!
WHATEVER STORIES YOU MIGHT HAVE HEARD ABOUT WHO I'VE BECOME...THEY'RE NOT TRUE!
OOF!
SNG
AAAHH!
THD
DANIEL! PULL ME UP! I'VE BEEN HURT AND I CAN'T--
DANIEL?!
WELL, THIS WAS A GOOD DEAL EASIER THAN I THOUGHT IT WOULD BE.

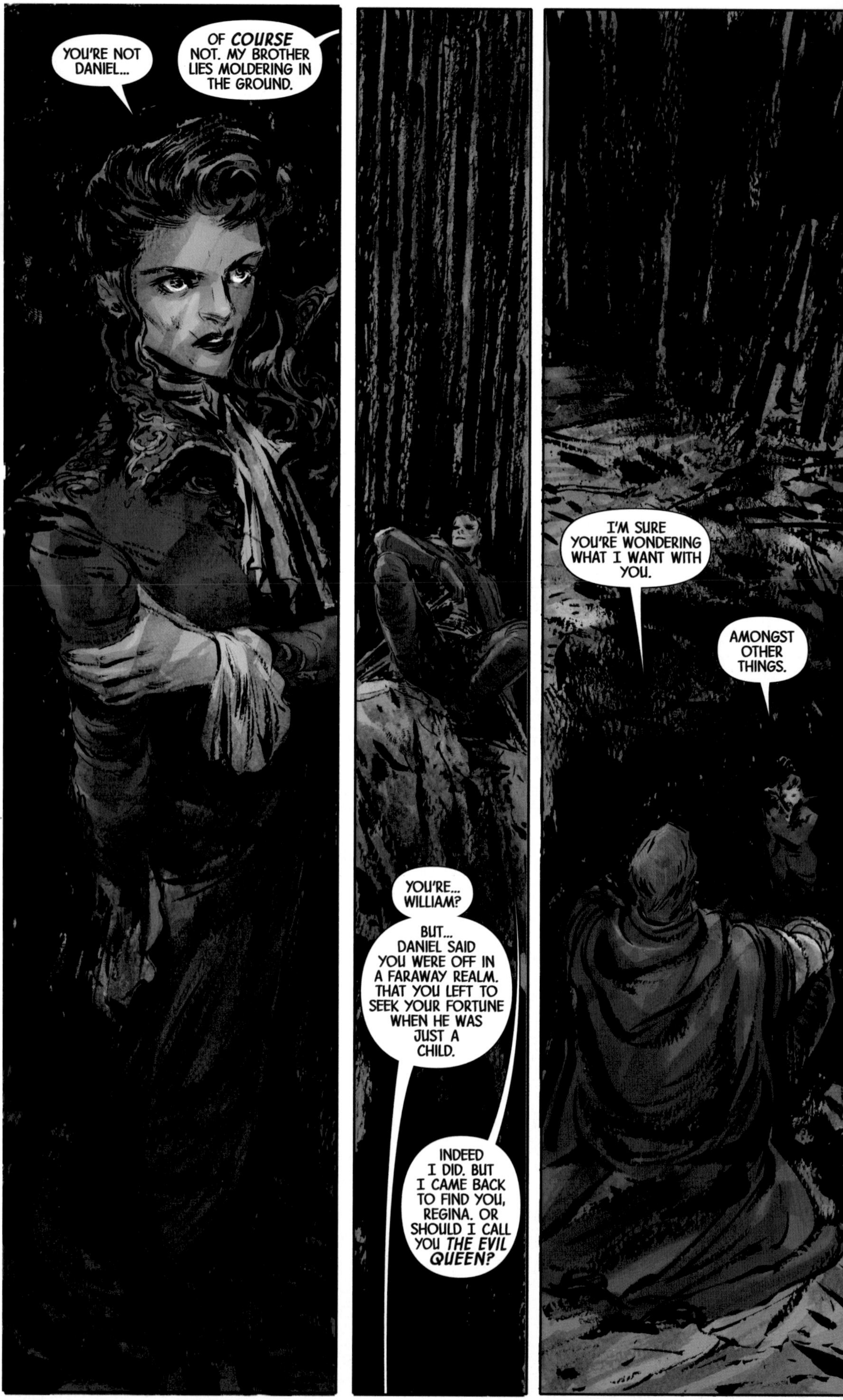
YOU'RE NOT DANIEL...
OF *COURSE* NOT. MY BROTHER LIES MOLDERING IN THE GROUND.
YOU'RE... WILLIAM?
BUT... DANIEL SAID YOU WERE OFF IN A FARAWAY REALM. THAT YOU LEFT TO SEEK YOUR FORTUNE WHEN HE WAS JUST A CHILD.
INDEED I DID. BUT I CAME BACK TO FIND YOU, REGINA. OR SHOULD I CALL YOU *THE EVIL QUEEN?*
I'M SURE YOU'RE WONDERING WHAT I WANT WITH YOU.
AMONGST OTHER THINGS.

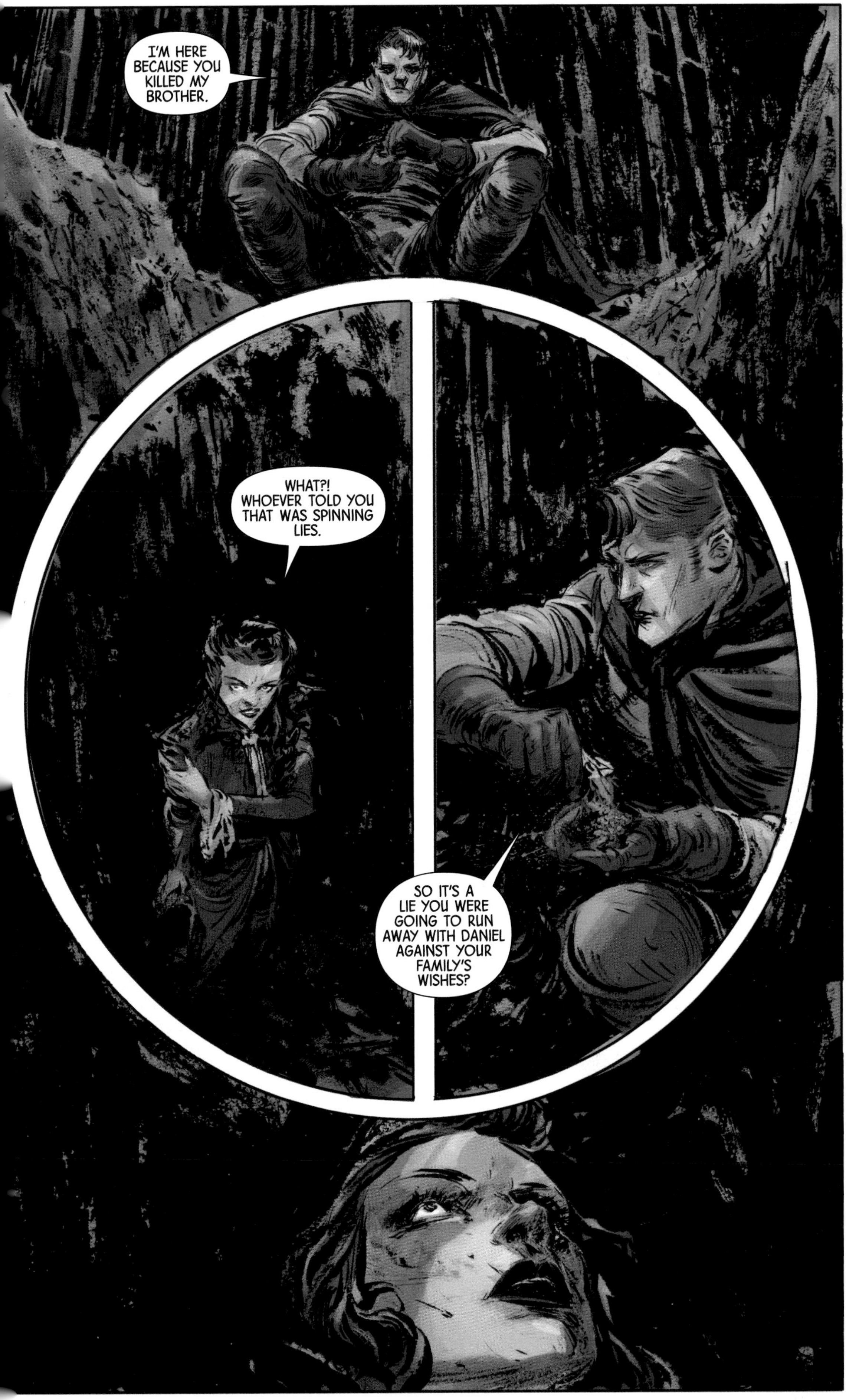
I'M HERE BECAUSE YOU KILLED MY BROTHER.
WHAT?! WHOEVER TOLD YOU THAT WAS SPINNING LIES.
SO IT'S A LIE YOU WERE GOING TO RUN AWAY WITH DANIEL AGAINST YOUR FAMILY'S WISHES?

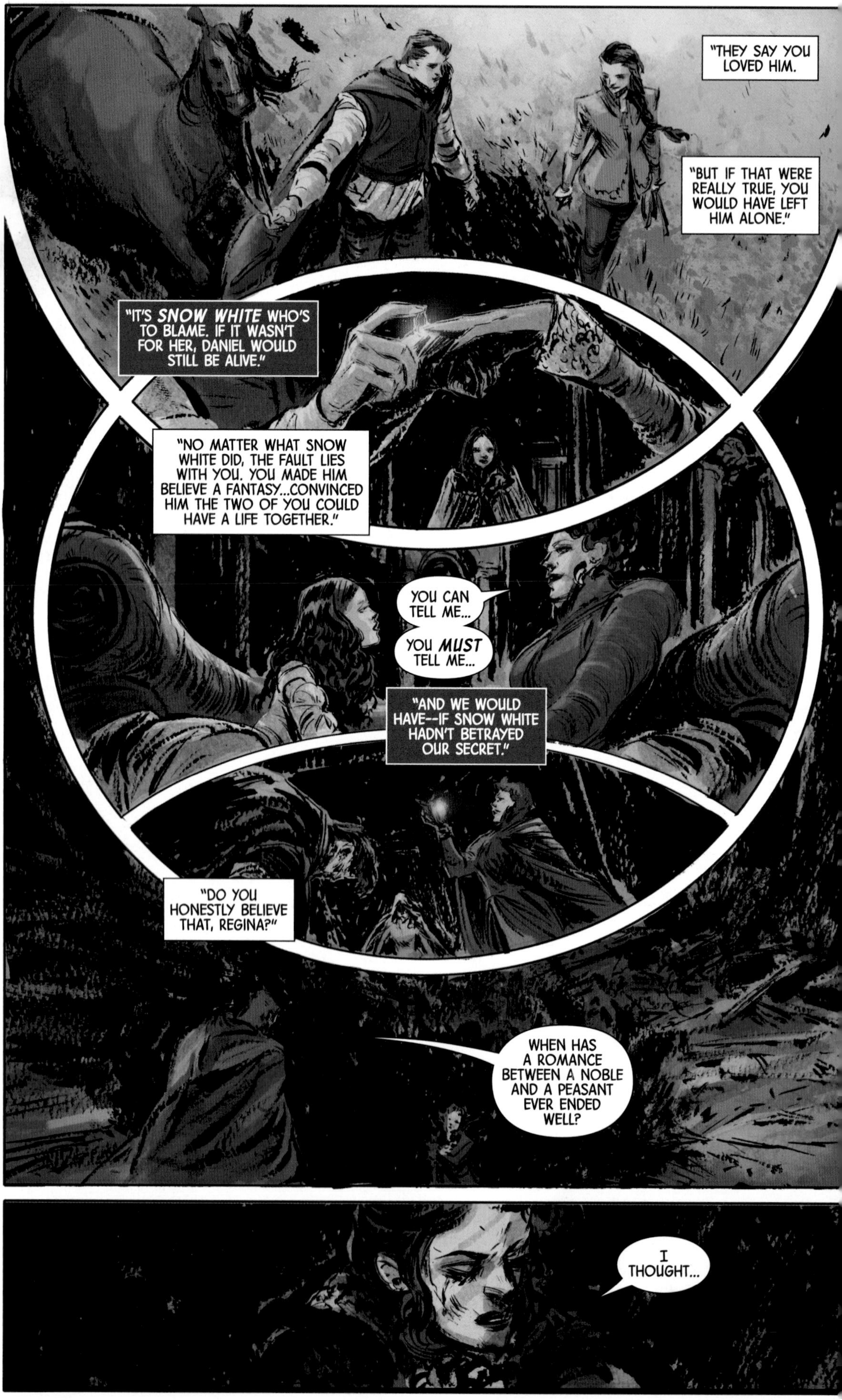
"THEY SAY YOU LOVED HIM.
"BUT IF THAT WERE REALLY TRUE, YOU WOULD HAVE LEFT HIM ALONE."
"IT'S SNOW WHITE WHO'S TO BLAME. IF IT WASN'T FOR HER, DANIEL WOULD STILL BE ALIVE."
"NO MATTER WHAT SNOW WHITE DID, THE FAULT LIES WITH YOU. YOU MADE HIM BELIEVE A FANTASY...CONVINCED HIM THE TWO OF YOU COULD HAVE A LIFE TOGETHER."
YOU CAN TELL ME...
YOU MUST TELL ME...
"AND WE WOULD HAVE--IF SNOW WHITE HADN'T BETRAYED OUR SECRET."
"DO YOU HONESTLY BELIEVE THAT, REGINA?"
WHEN HAS A ROMANCE BETWEEN A NOBLE AND A PEASANT EVER ENDED WELL?
I THOUGHT...

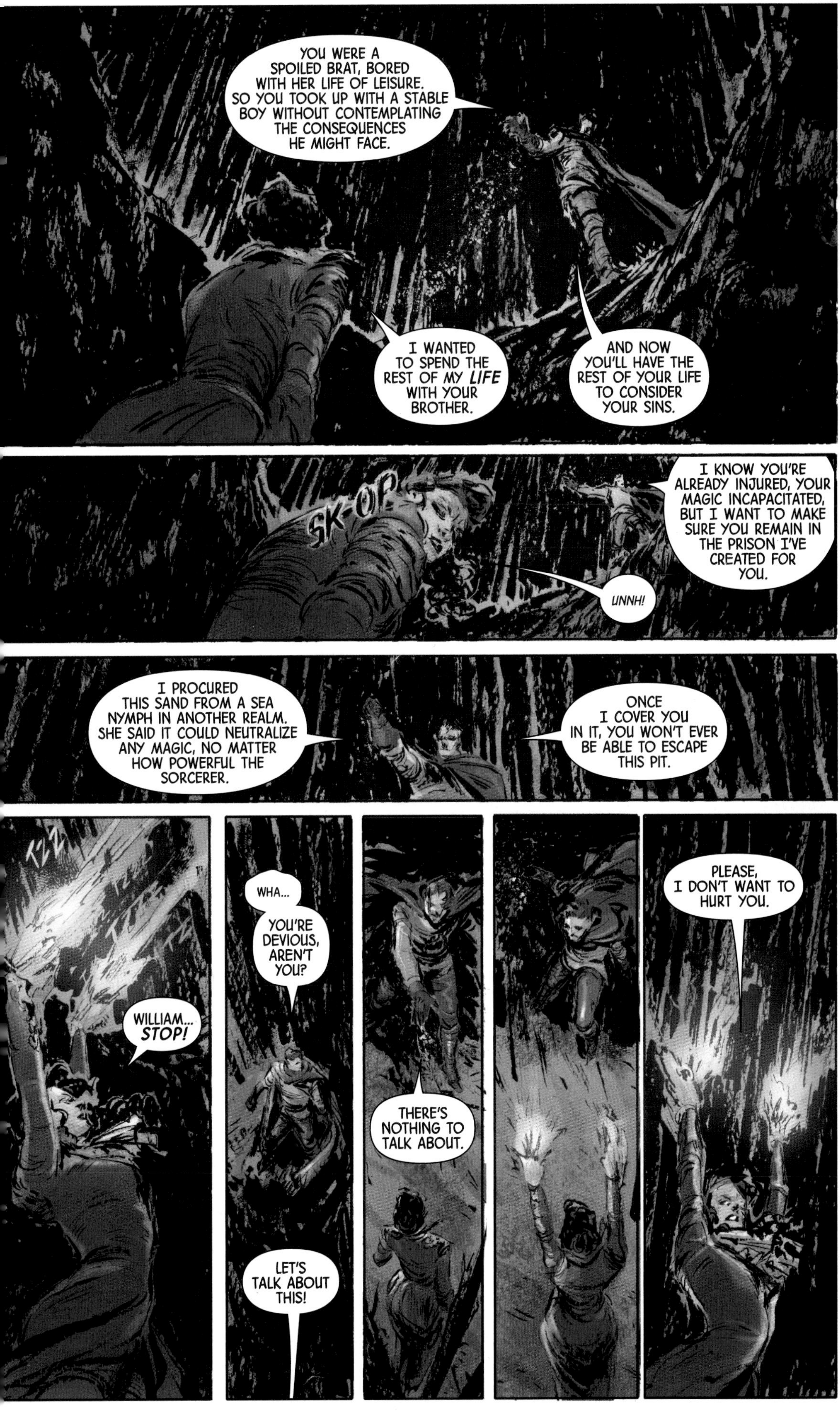

YOU WERE A SPOILED BRAT, BORED WITH HER LIFE OF LEISURE. SO YOU TOOK UP WITH A STABLE BOY WITHOUT CONTEMPLATING THE CONSEQUENCES HE MIGHT FACE.
I WANTED TO SPEND THE REST OF MY *LIFE* WITH YOUR BROTHER.
AND NOW YOU'LL HAVE THE REST OF YOUR LIFE TO CONSIDER YOUR SINS.
SK-OP
I KNOW YOU'RE ALREADY INJURED, YOUR MAGIC INCAPACITATED, BUT I WANT TO MAKE SURE YOU REMAIN IN THE PRISON I'VE CREATED FOR YOU.
UNNH!
I PROCURED THIS SAND FROM A SEA NYMPH IN ANOTHER REALM. SHE SAID IT COULD NEUTRALIZE ANY MAGIC, NO MATTER HOW POWERFUL THE SORCERER.
ONCE I COVER YOU IN IT, YOU WON'T EVER BE ABLE TO ESCAPE THIS PIT.
WILLIAM... **STOP!**
WHA...
YOU'RE DEVIOUS, AREN'T YOU?
LET'S TALK ABOUT THIS!
THERE'S NOTHING TO TALK ABOUT.
PLEASE, I DON'T WANT TO HURT YOU.

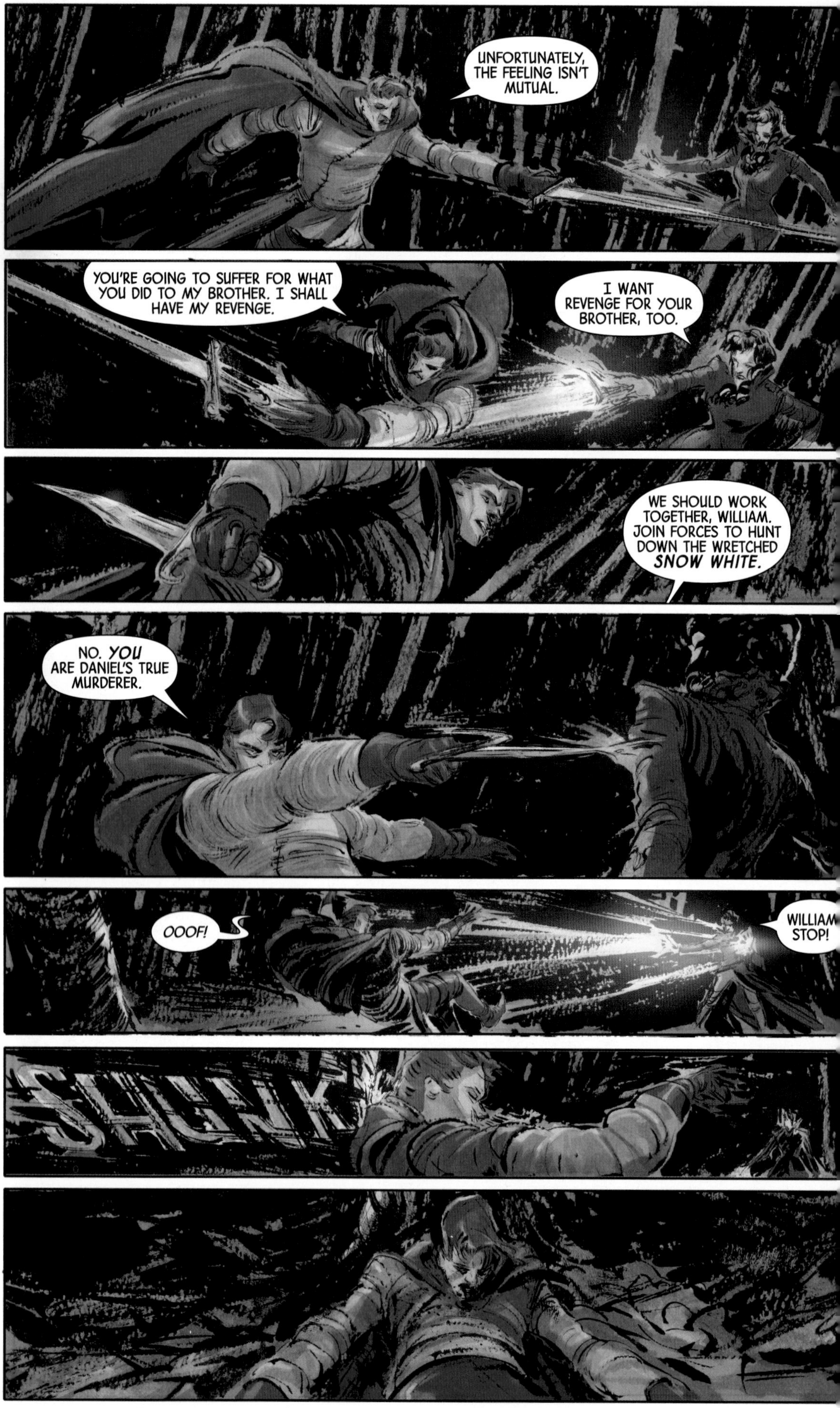
UNFORTUNATELY, THE FEELING ISN'T MUTUAL.
YOU'RE GOING TO SUFFER FOR WHAT YOU DID TO MY BROTHER. I SHALL HAVE MY REVENGE.
I WANT REVENGE FOR YOUR BROTHER, TOO.
WE SHOULD WORK TOGETHER, WILLIAM. JOIN FORCES TO HUNT DOWN THE WRETCHED SNOW WHITE.
NO. YOU ARE DANIEL'S TRUE MURDERER.
OOOF!
WILLIAM STOP!
SHUNK

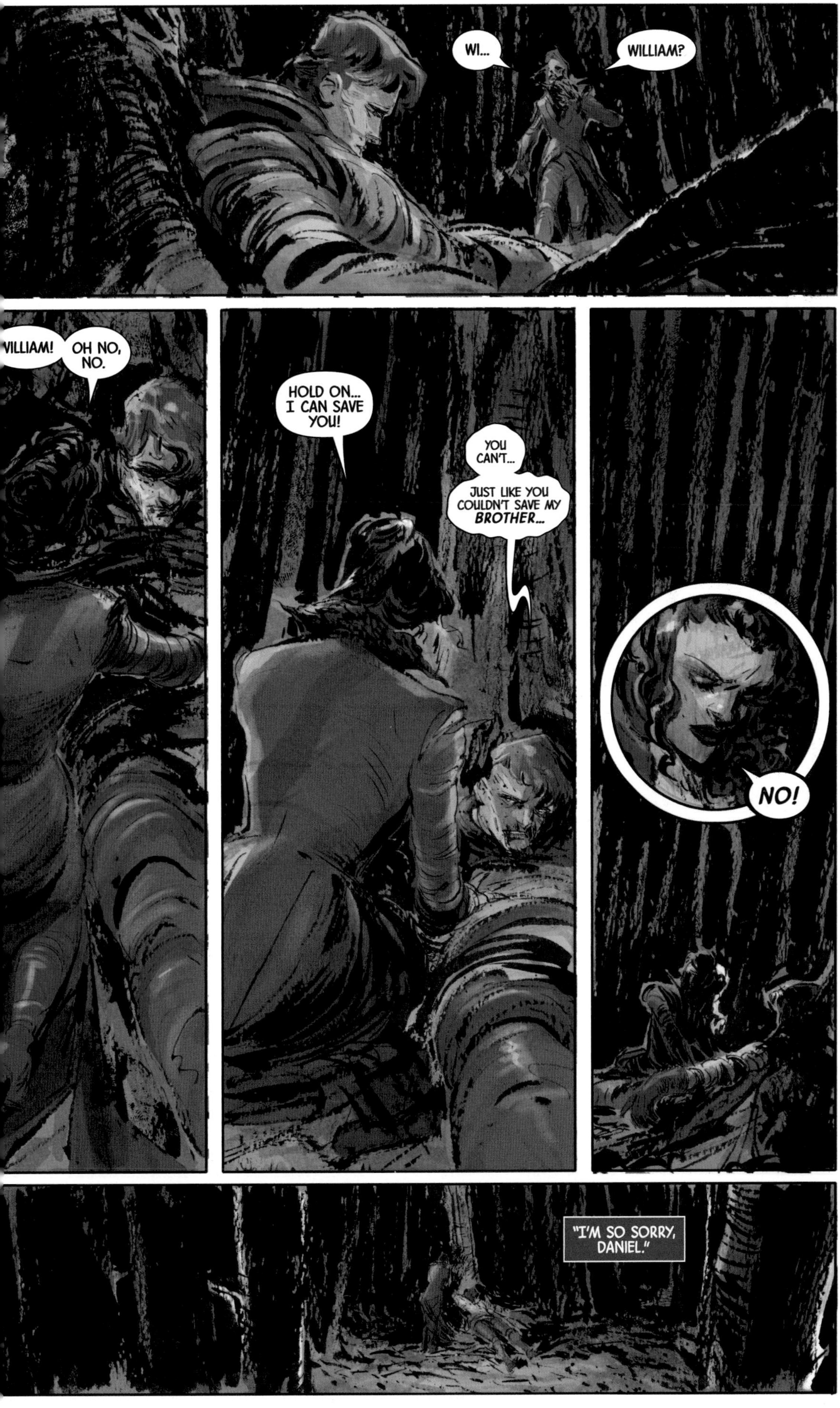
WI...
WILLIAM?
VILLIAM!
OH NO, NO.
HOLD ON... I CAN SAVE YOU!
YOU CAN'T...
JUST LIKE YOU COULDN'T SAVE MY *BROTHER*...
NO!
"I'M SO SORRY, DANIEL."

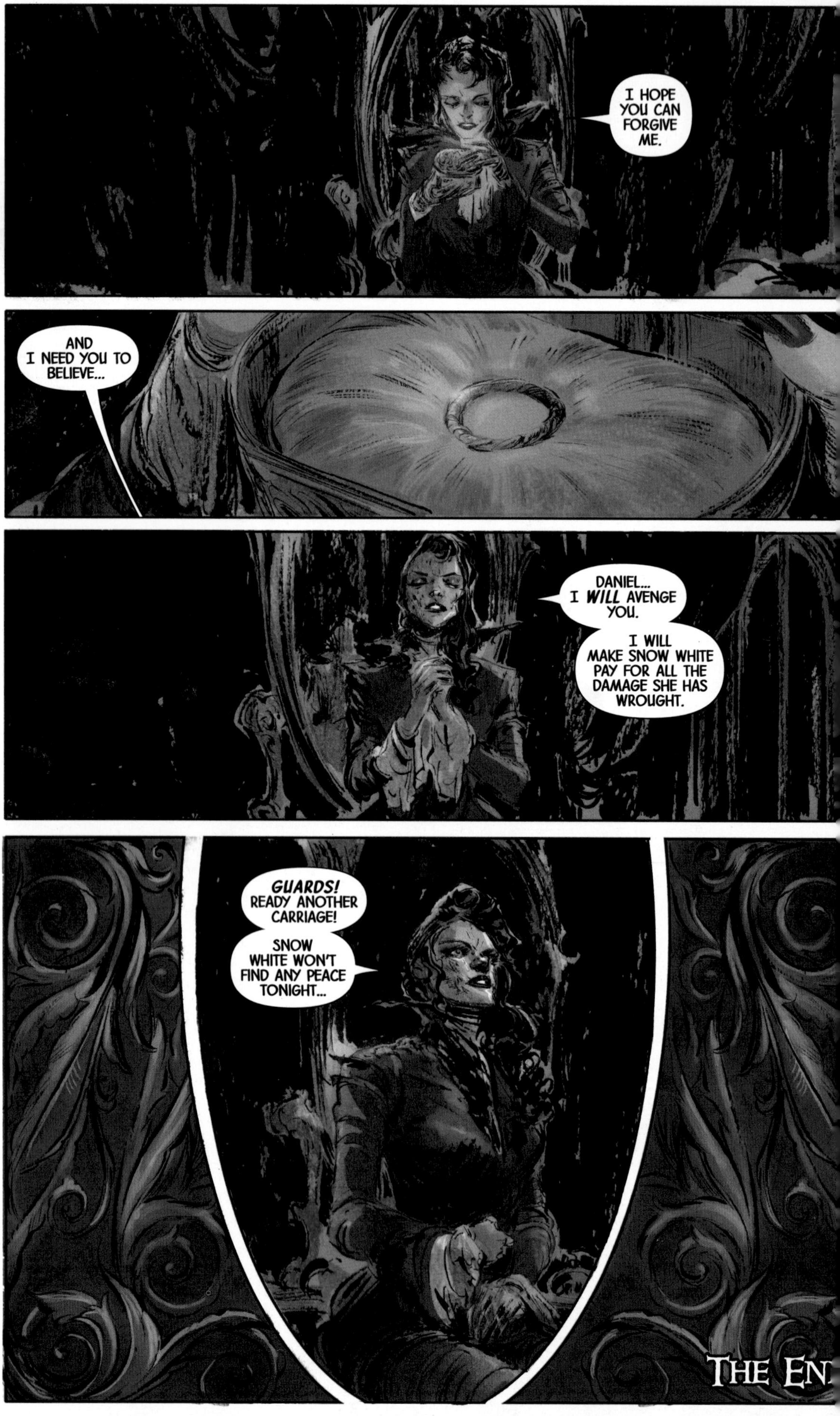
I HOPE YOU CAN FORGIVE ME.
AND I NEED YOU TO BELIEVE...
DANIEL... I WILL AVENGE YOU.
I WILL MAKE SNOW WHITE PAY FOR ALL THE DAMAGE SHE HAS WROUGHT.
GUARDS! READY ANOTHER CARRIAGE!
SNOW WHITE WON'T FIND ANY PEACE TONIGHT...

CHAPTER FOUR

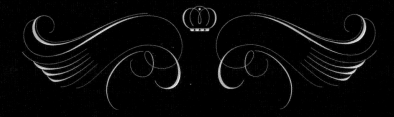

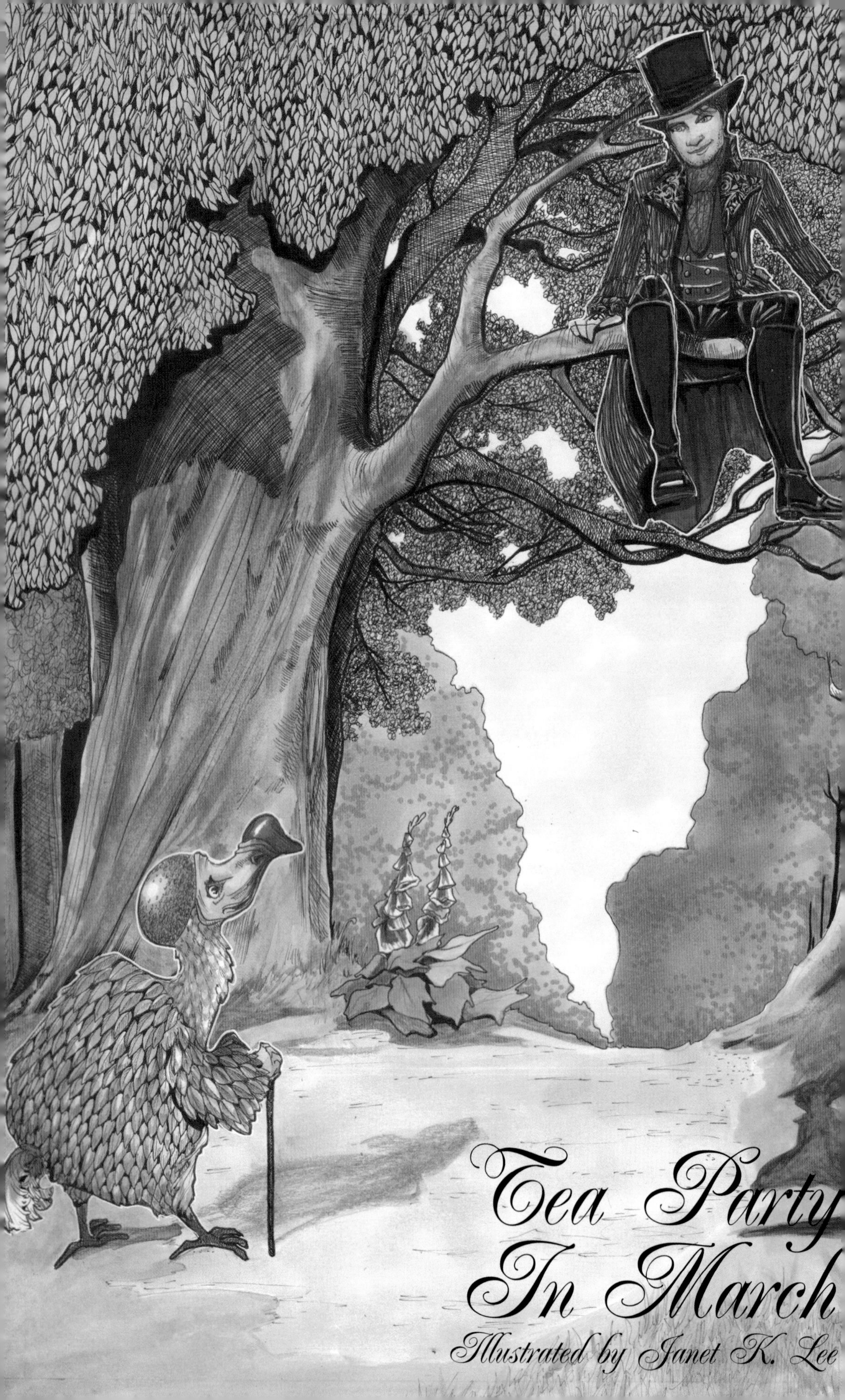
Tea Party
In March
Illustrated by Janet K. Lee

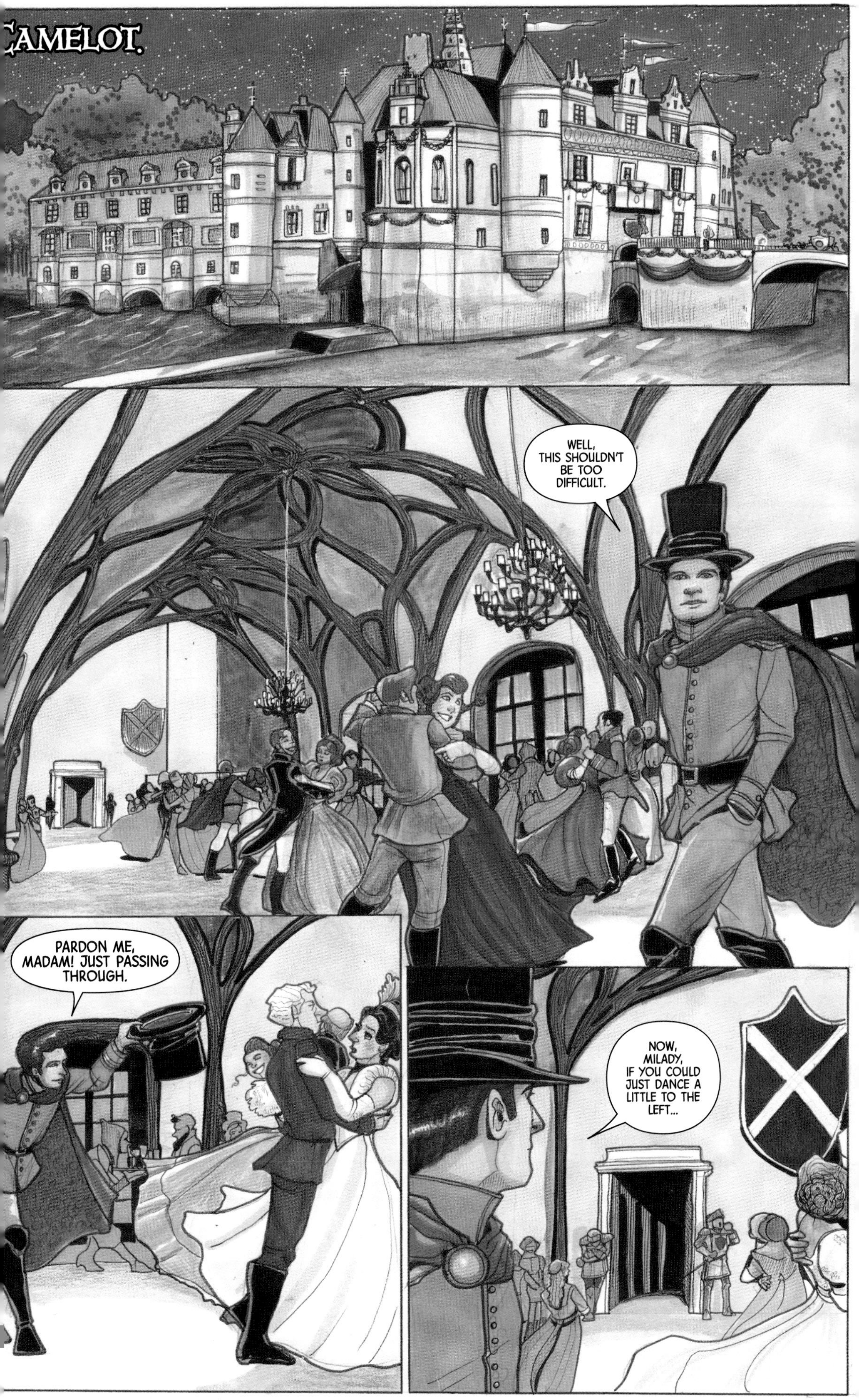
CAMELOT.
WELL, THIS SHOULDN'T BE TOO DIFFICULT.
PARDON ME, MADAM! JUST PASSING THROUGH.
NOW, MILADY, IF YOU COULD JUST DANCE A LITTLE TO THE LEFT...

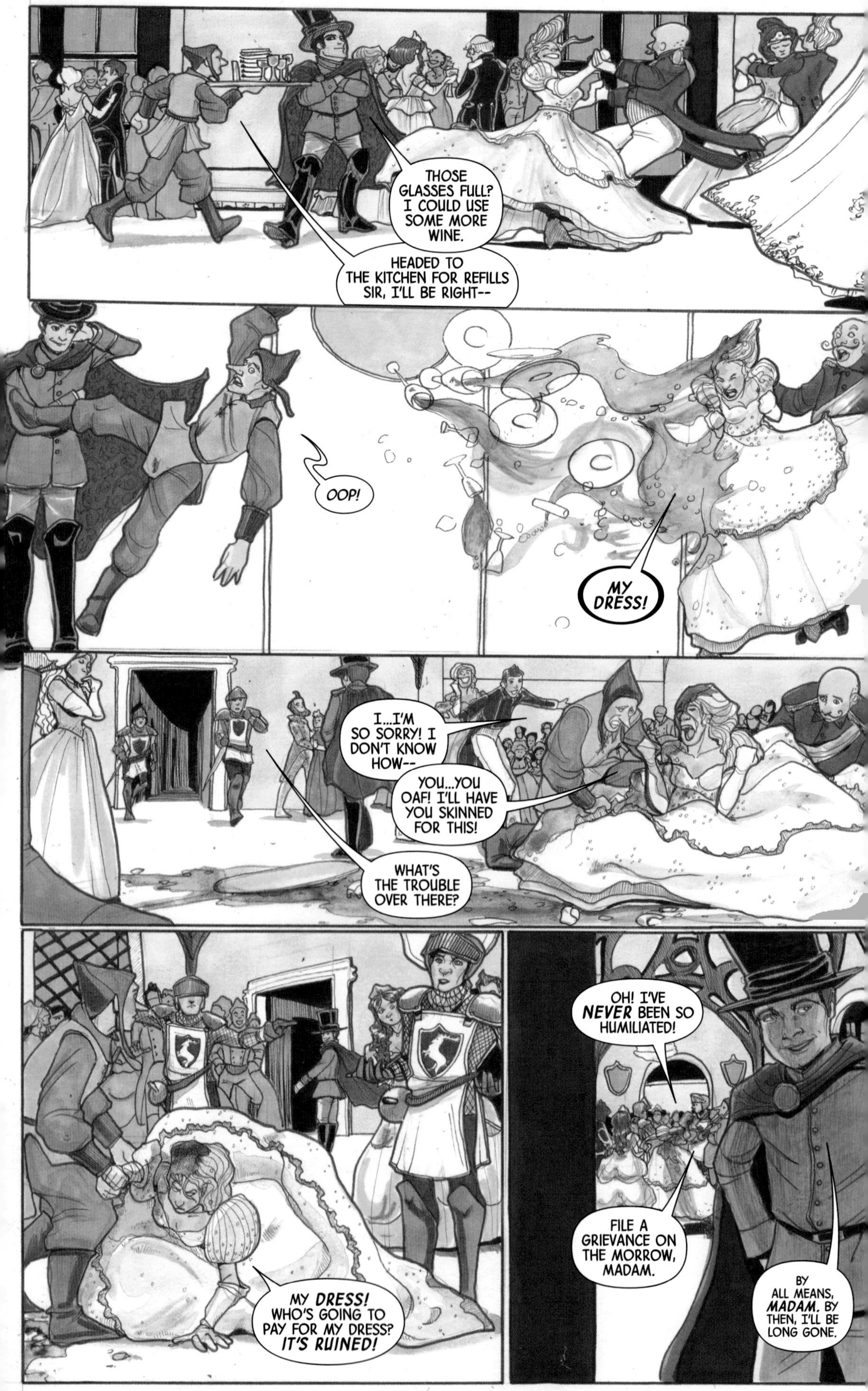
THOSE GLASSES FULL? I COULD USE SOME MORE WINE.
HEADED TO THE KITCHEN FOR REFILLS SIR, I'LL BE RIGHT--
OOP!
MY DRESS!
I...I'M SO SORRY! I DON'T KNOW HOW--
YOU...YOU OAF! I'LL HAVE YOU SKINNED FOR THIS!
WHAT'S THE TROUBLE OVER THERE?
MY DRESS! WHO'S GOING TO PAY FOR MY DRESS? IT'S RUINED!
OH! I'VE NEVER BEEN SO HUMILIATED!
FILE A GRIEVANCE ON THE MORROW, MADAM.
BY ALL MEANS, MADAM. BY THEN, I'LL BE LONG GONE.

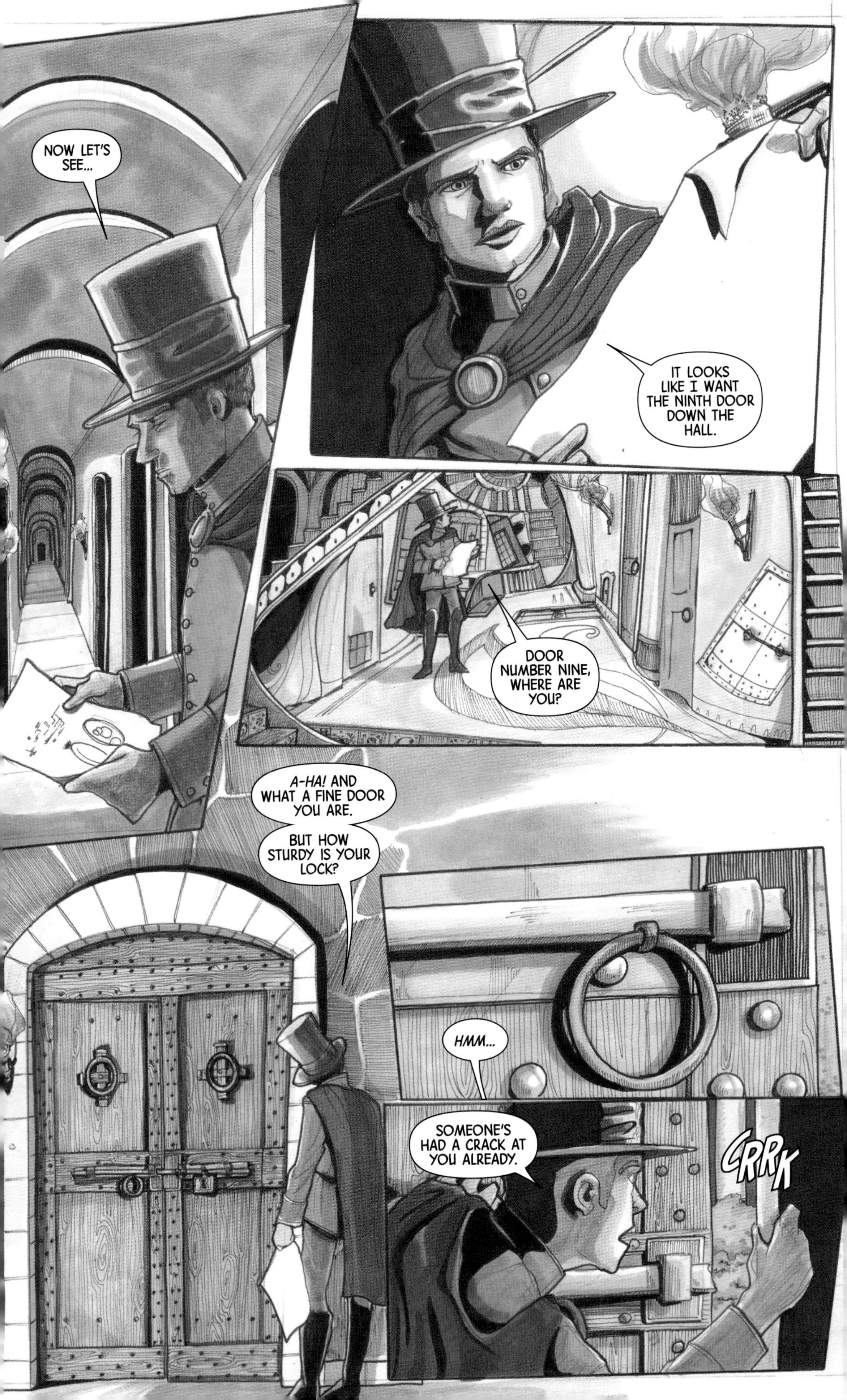
NOW LET'S SEE...
IT LOOKS LIKE I WANT THE NINTH DOOR DOWN THE HALL.
DOOR NUMBER NINE, WHERE ARE YOU?
A-HA! AND WHAT A FINE DOOR YOU ARE.
BUT HOW STURDY IS YOUR LOCK?
HMM...
SOMEONE'S HAD A CRACK AT YOU ALREADY.
CRRK

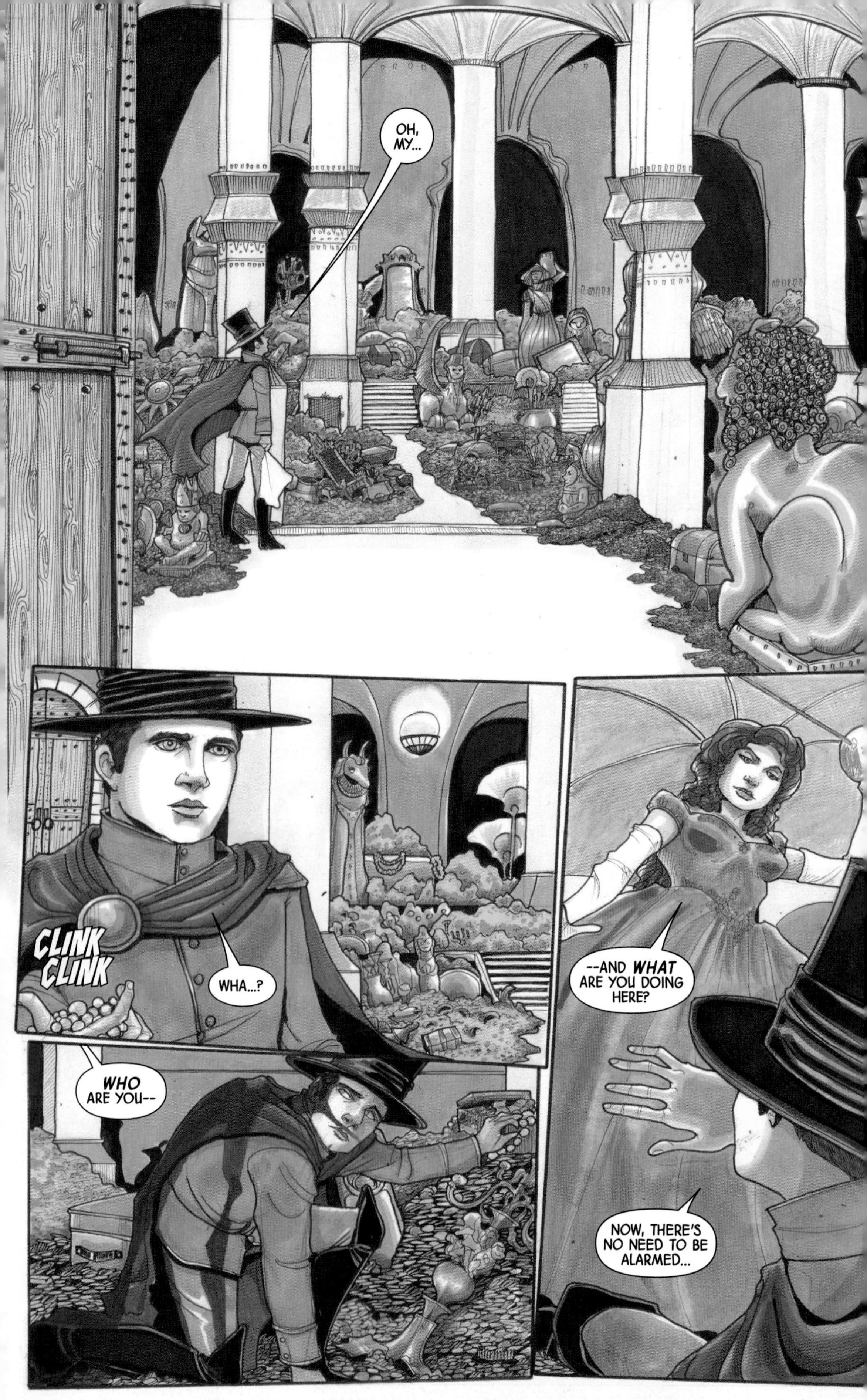
OH, MY...
CLINK CLINK
WHA...?
WHO ARE YOU--
--AND WHAT ARE YOU DOING HERE?
NOW, THERE'S NO NEED TO BE ALARMED...

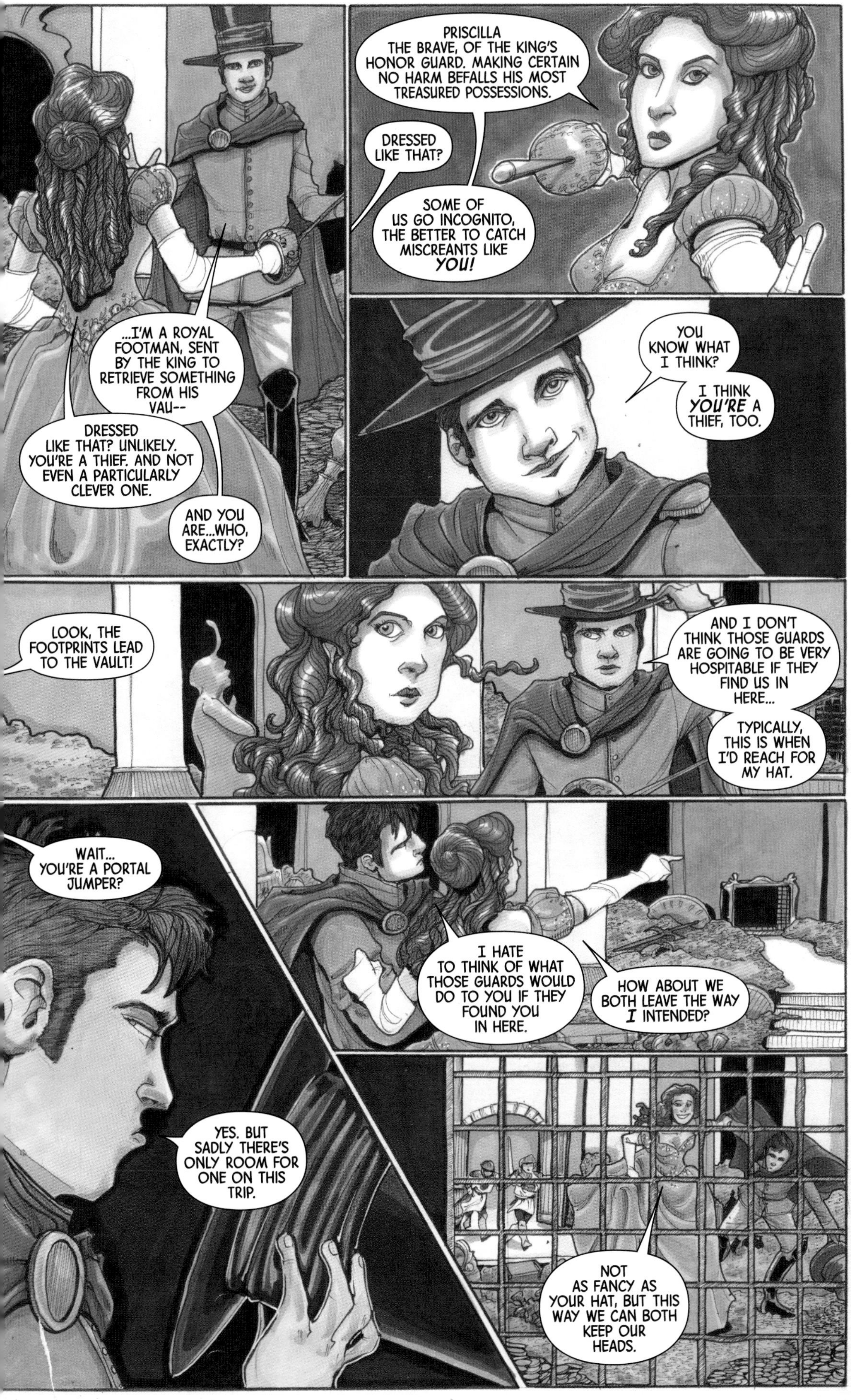
PRISCILLA THE BRAVE, OF THE KING'S HONOR GUARD. MAKING CERTAIN NO HARM BEFALLS HIS MOST TREASURED POSSESSIONS.
DRESSED LIKE THAT?
SOME OF US GO INCOGNITO, THE BETTER TO CATCH MISCREANTS LIKE YOU!
...I'M A ROYAL FOOTMAN, SENT BY THE KING TO RETRIEVE SOMETHING FROM HIS VAU--
DRESSED LIKE THAT? UNLIKELY. YOU'RE A THIEF. AND NOT EVEN A PARTICULARLY CLEVER ONE.
AND YOU ARE...WHO, EXACTLY?
YOU KNOW WHAT I THINK?
I THINK YOU'RE A THIEF, TOO.
LOOK, THE FOOTPRINTS LEAD TO THE VAULT!
AND I DON'T THINK THOSE GUARDS ARE GOING TO BE VERY HOSPITABLE IF THEY FIND US IN HERE...
TYPICALLY, THIS IS WHEN I'D REACH FOR MY HAT.
WAIT... YOU'RE A PORTAL JUMPER?
YES. BUT SADLY THERE'S ONLY ROOM FOR ONE ON THIS TRIP.
I HATE TO THINK OF WHAT THOSE GUARDS WOULD DO TO YOU IF THEY FOUND YOU IN HERE.
HOW ABOUT WE BOTH LEAVE THE WAY I INTENDED?
NOT AS FANCY AS YOUR HAT, BUT THIS WAY WE CAN BOTH KEEP OUR HEADS.

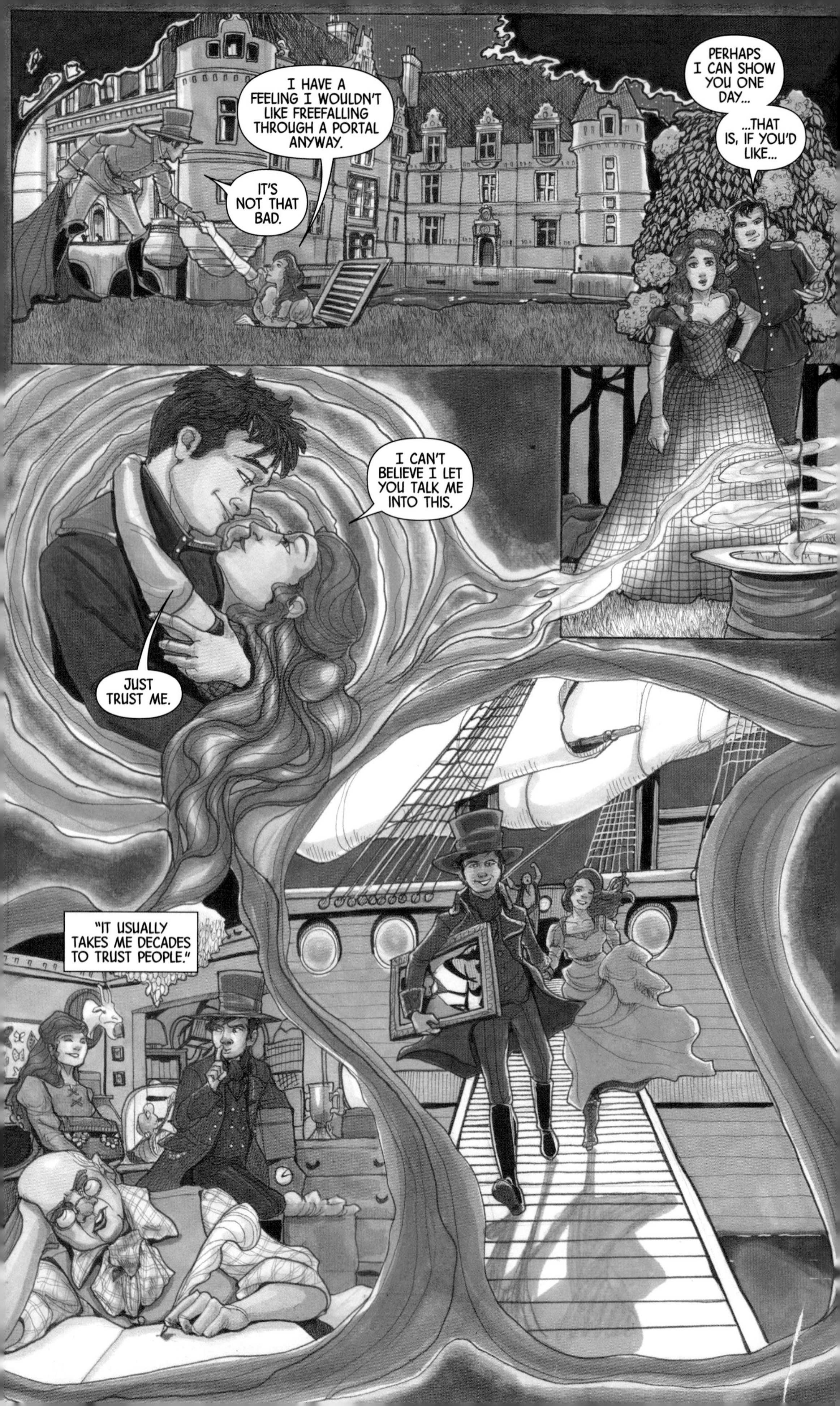
I HAVE A FEELING I WOULDN'T LIKE FREEFALLING THROUGH A PORTAL ANYWAY.
IT'S NOT THAT BAD.
PERHAPS I CAN SHOW YOU ONE DAY...
...THAT IS, IF YOU'D LIKE...
I CAN'T BELIEVE I LET YOU TALK ME INTO THIS.
JUST TRUST ME.
"IT USUALLY TAKES ME DECADES TO TRUST PEOPLE."

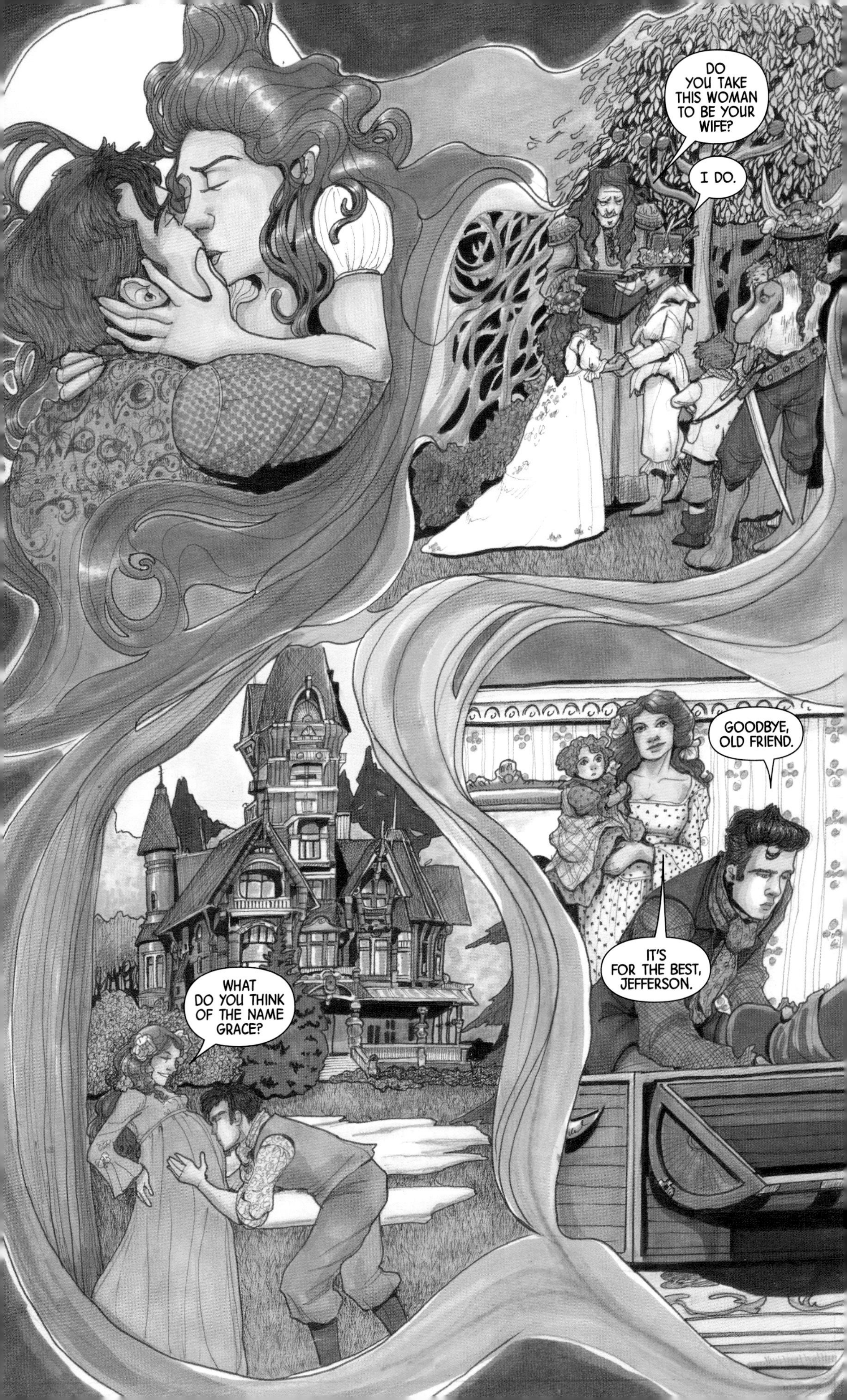
DO YOU TAKE THIS WOMAN TO BE YOUR WIFE?
I DO.
GOODBYE, OLD FRIEND.
IT'S FOR THE BEST, JEFFERSON.
WHAT DO YOU THINK OF THE NAME GRACE?

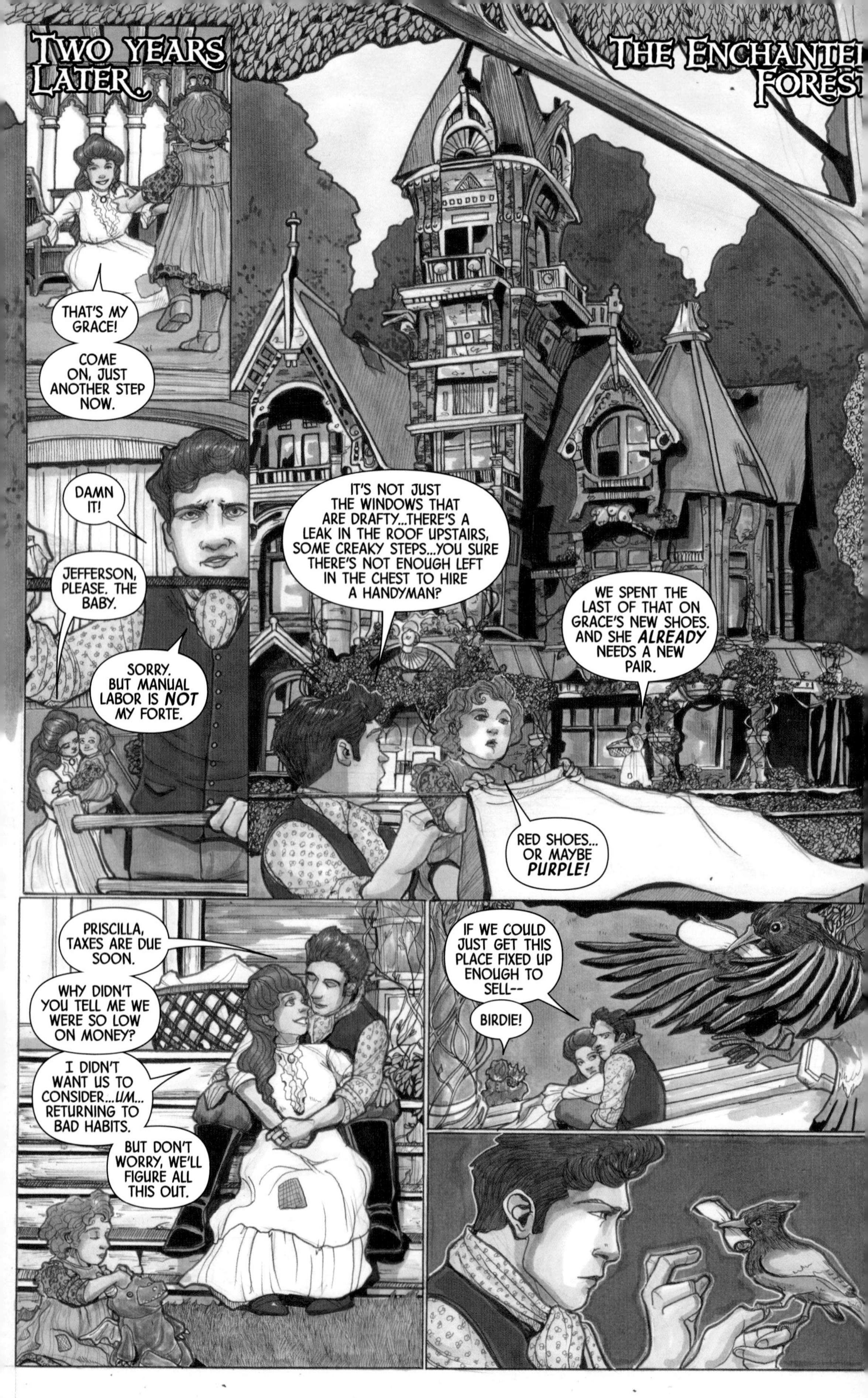
TWO YEARS LATER
THE ENCHANTED FOREST
THAT'S MY GRACE!
COME ON, JUST ANOTHER STEP NOW.
DAMN IT!
JEFFERSON, PLEASE. THE BABY.
SORRY. BUT MANUAL LABOR IS NOT MY FORTE.
IT'S NOT JUST THE WINDOWS THAT ARE DRAFTY...THERE'S A LEAK IN THE ROOF UPSTAIRS, SOME CREAKY STEPS...YOU SURE THERE'S NOT ENOUGH LEFT IN THE CHEST TO HIRE A HANDYMAN?
WE SPENT THE LAST OF THAT ON GRACE'S NEW SHOES. AND SHE ALREADY NEEDS A NEW PAIR.
RED SHOES... OR MAYBE PURPLE!
PRISCILLA, TAXES ARE DUE SOON.
WHY DIDN'T YOU TELL ME WE WERE SO LOW ON MONEY?
I DIDN'T WANT US TO CONSIDER...UM... RETURNING TO BAD HABITS.
BUT DON'T WORRY, WE'LL FIGURE ALL THIS OUT.
IF WE COULD JUST GET THIS PLACE FIXED UP ENOUGH TO SELL--
BIRDIE!

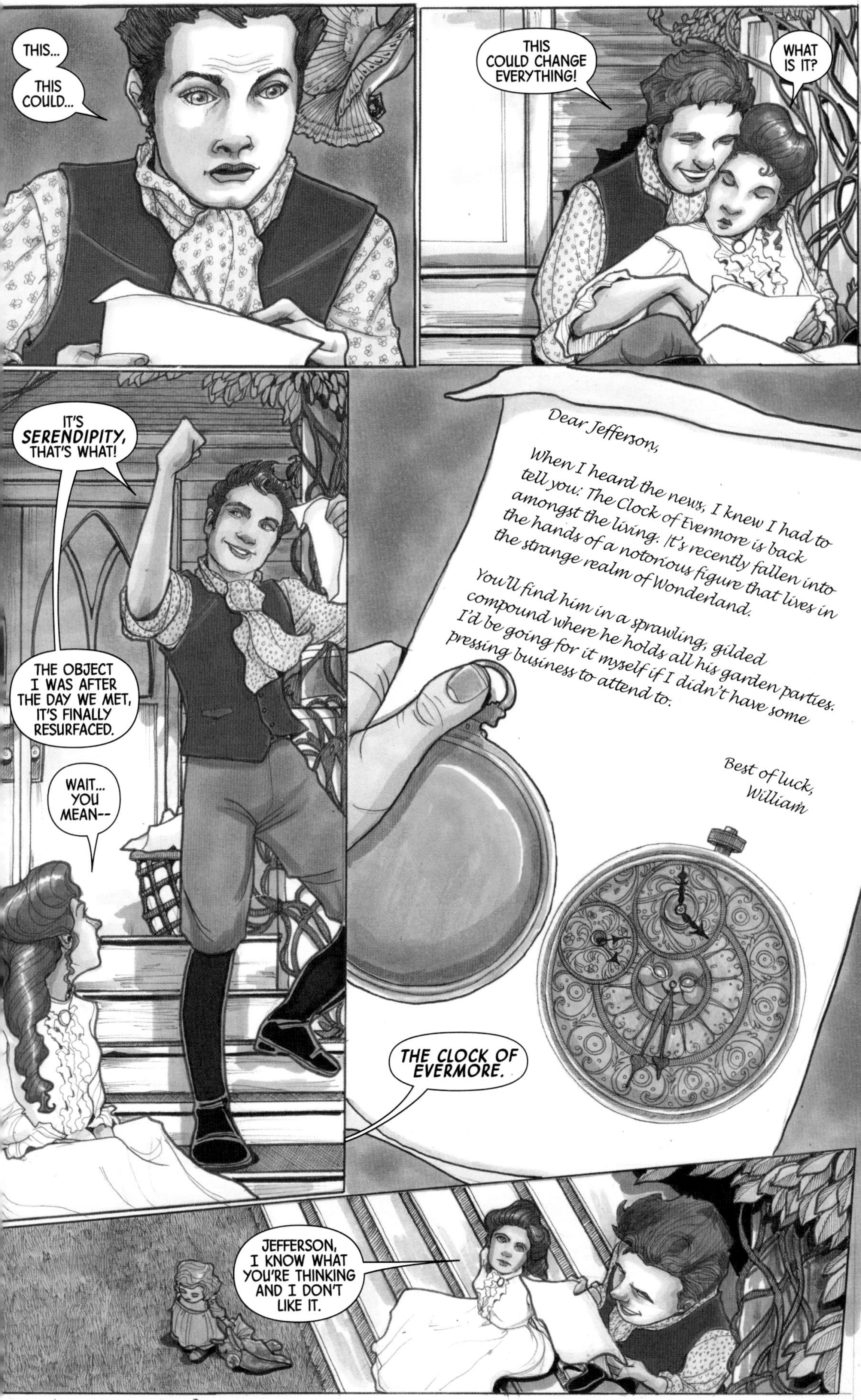
THIS...
THIS COULD...
THIS COULD CHANGE EVERYTHING!
WHAT IS IT?
IT'S *SERENDIPITY,* THAT'S WHAT!
THE OBJECT I WAS AFTER THE DAY WE MET, IT'S FINALLY RESURFACED.
WAIT... YOU MEAN--
Dear Jefferson,
When I heard the news, I knew I had to tell you: The Clock of Evermore is back amongst the living. It's recently fallen into the hands of a notorious figure that lives in the strange realm of Wonderland.
You'll find him in a sprawling, gilded compound where he holds all his garden parties. I'd be going for it myself if I didn't have some pressing business to attend to.
Best of luck,
William
THE CLOCK OF EVERMORE.
JEFFERSON, I KNOW WHAT YOU'RE THINKING AND I DON'T LIKE IT.

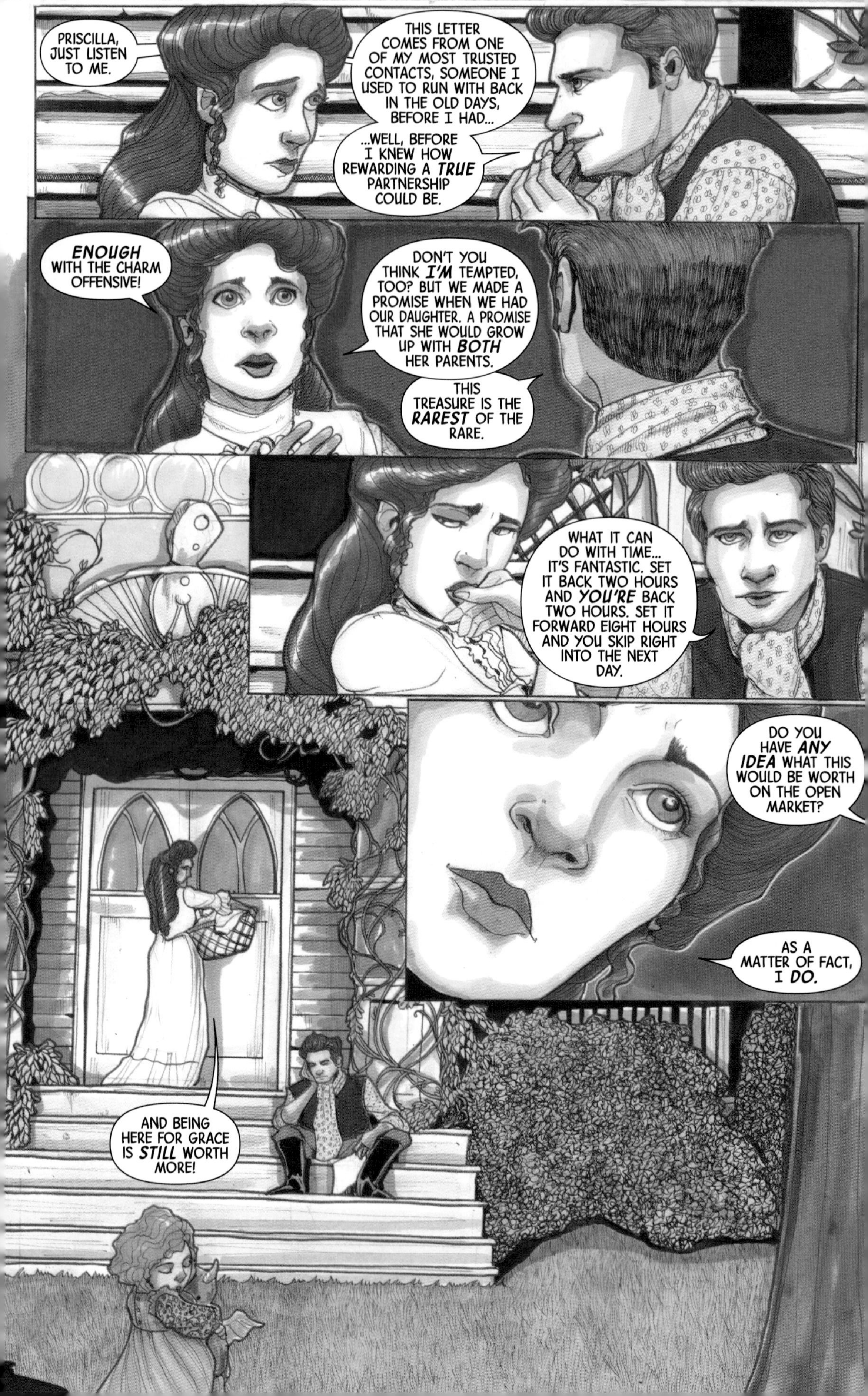
PRISCILLA, JUST LISTEN TO ME.
THIS LETTER COMES FROM ONE OF MY MOST TRUSTED CONTACTS, SOMEONE I USED TO RUN WITH BACK IN THE OLD DAYS, BEFORE I HAD...
...WELL, BEFORE I KNEW HOW REWARDING A *TRUE* PARTNERSHIP COULD BE.
ENOUGH WITH THE CHARM OFFENSIVE!
DON'T YOU THINK *I'M* TEMPTED, TOO? BUT WE MADE A PROMISE WHEN WE HAD OUR DAUGHTER. A PROMISE THAT SHE WOULD GROW UP WITH *BOTH* HER PARENTS.
THIS TREASURE IS THE *RAREST* OF THE RARE.
WHAT IT CAN DO WITH TIME... IT'S FANTASTIC. SET IT BACK TWO HOURS AND *YOU'RE* BACK TWO HOURS. SET IT FORWARD EIGHT HOURS AND YOU SKIP RIGHT INTO THE NEXT DAY.
DO YOU HAVE *ANY IDEA* WHAT THIS WOULD BE WORTH ON THE OPEN MARKET?
AS A MATTER OF FACT, I *DO.*
AND BEING HERE FOR GRACE IS *STILL* WORTH MORE!

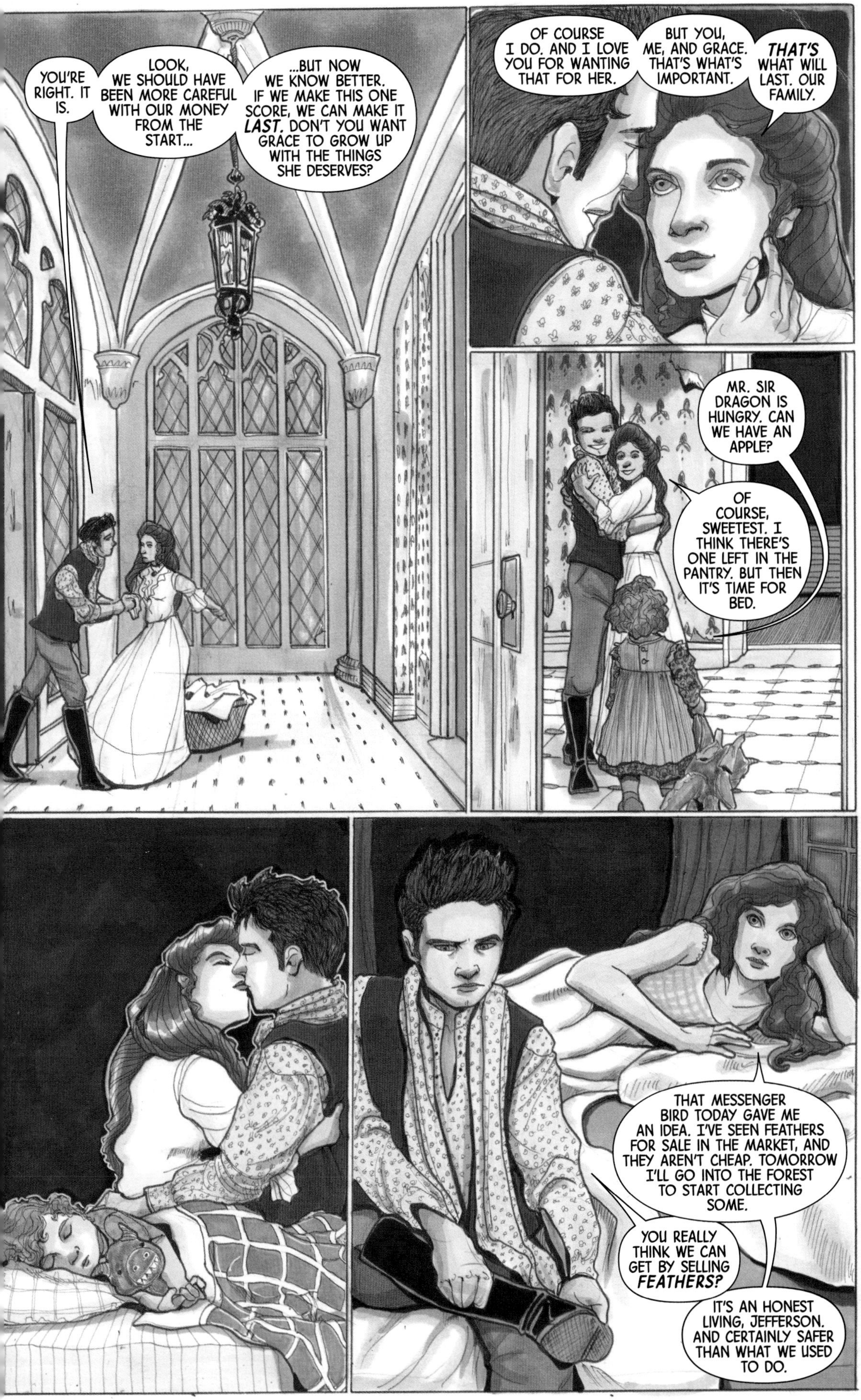
YOU'RE RIGHT. IT IS.
LOOK, WE SHOULD HAVE BEEN MORE CAREFUL WITH OUR MONEY FROM THE START...
...BUT NOW WE KNOW BETTER. IF WE MAKE THIS ONE SCORE, WE CAN MAKE IT LAST. DON'T YOU WANT GRACE TO GROW UP WITH THE THINGS SHE DESERVES?
OF COURSE I DO. AND I LOVE YOU FOR WANTING THAT FOR HER.
BUT YOU, ME, AND GRACE. THAT'S WHAT'S IMPORTANT.
THAT'S WHAT WILL LAST. OUR FAMILY.
MR. SIR DRAGON IS HUNGRY. CAN WE HAVE AN APPLE?
OF COURSE, SWEETEST. I THINK THERE'S ONE LEFT IN THE PANTRY. BUT THEN IT'S TIME FOR BED.
THAT MESSENGER BIRD TODAY GAVE ME AN IDEA. I'VE SEEN FEATHERS FOR SALE IN THE MARKET, AND THEY AREN'T CHEAP. TOMORROW I'LL GO INTO THE FOREST TO START COLLECTING SOME.
YOU REALLY THINK WE CAN GET BY SELLING FEATHERS?
IT'S AN HONEST LIVING, JEFFERSON. AND CERTAINLY SAFER THAN WHAT WE USED TO DO.

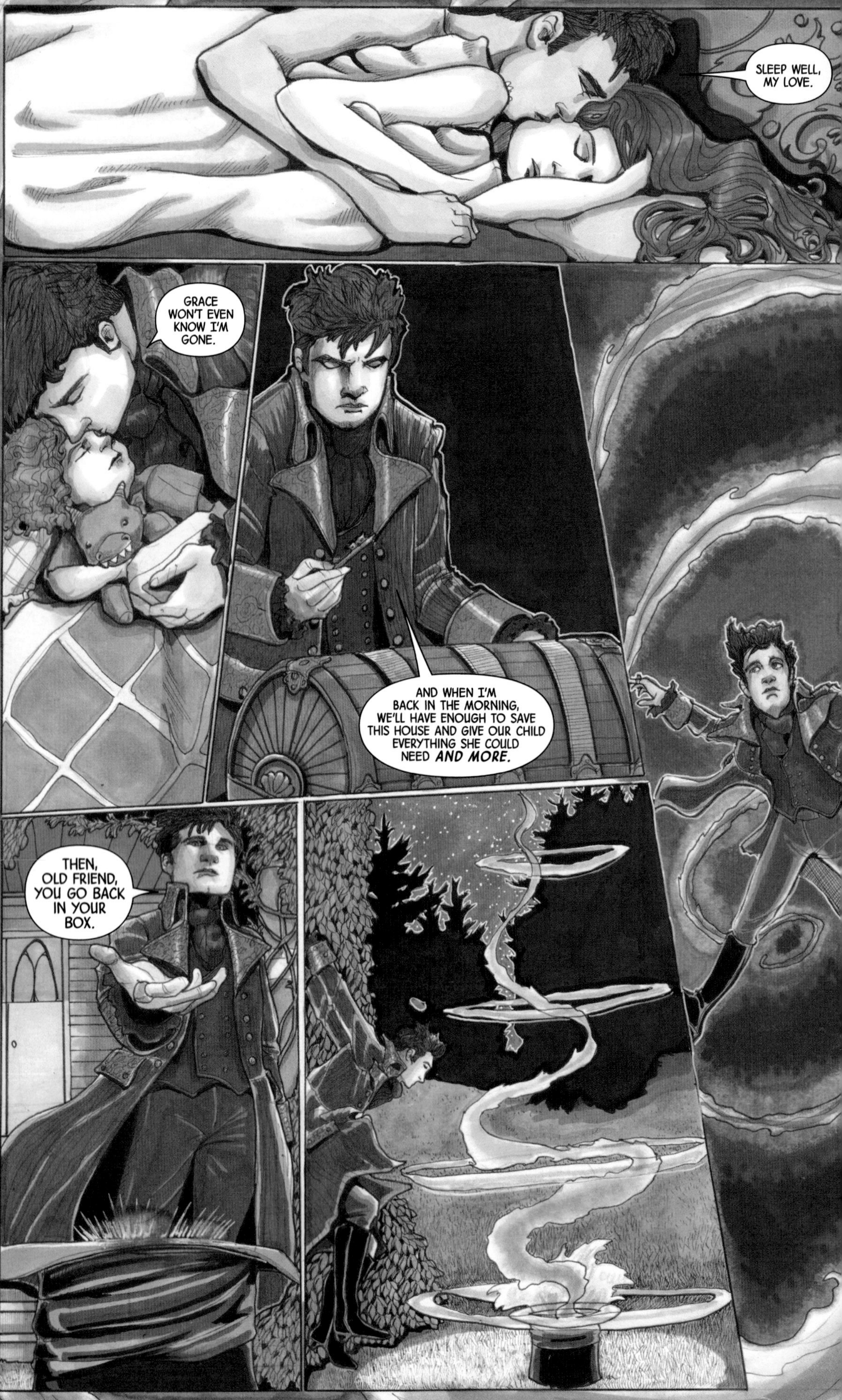
SLEEP WELL, MY LOVE.
GRACE WON'T EVEN KNOW I'M GONE.
AND WHEN I'M BACK IN THE MORNING, WE'LL HAVE ENOUGH TO SAVE THIS HOUSE AND GIVE OUR CHILD EVERYTHING SHE COULD NEED AND MORE.
THEN, OLD FRIEND, YOU GO BACK IN YOUR BOX.

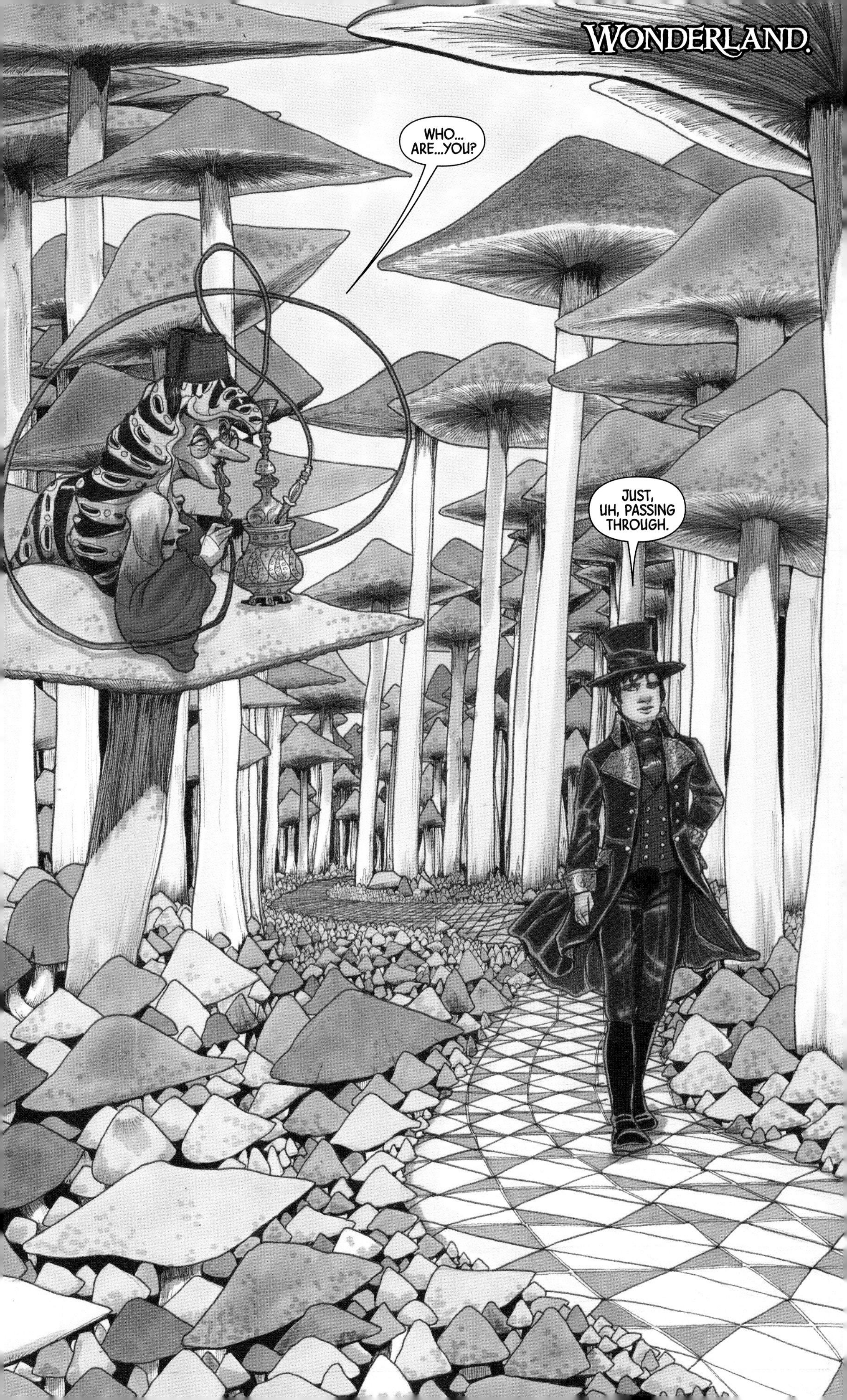
WONDERLAND.
WHO... ARE...YOU?
JUST, UH, PASSING THROUGH.

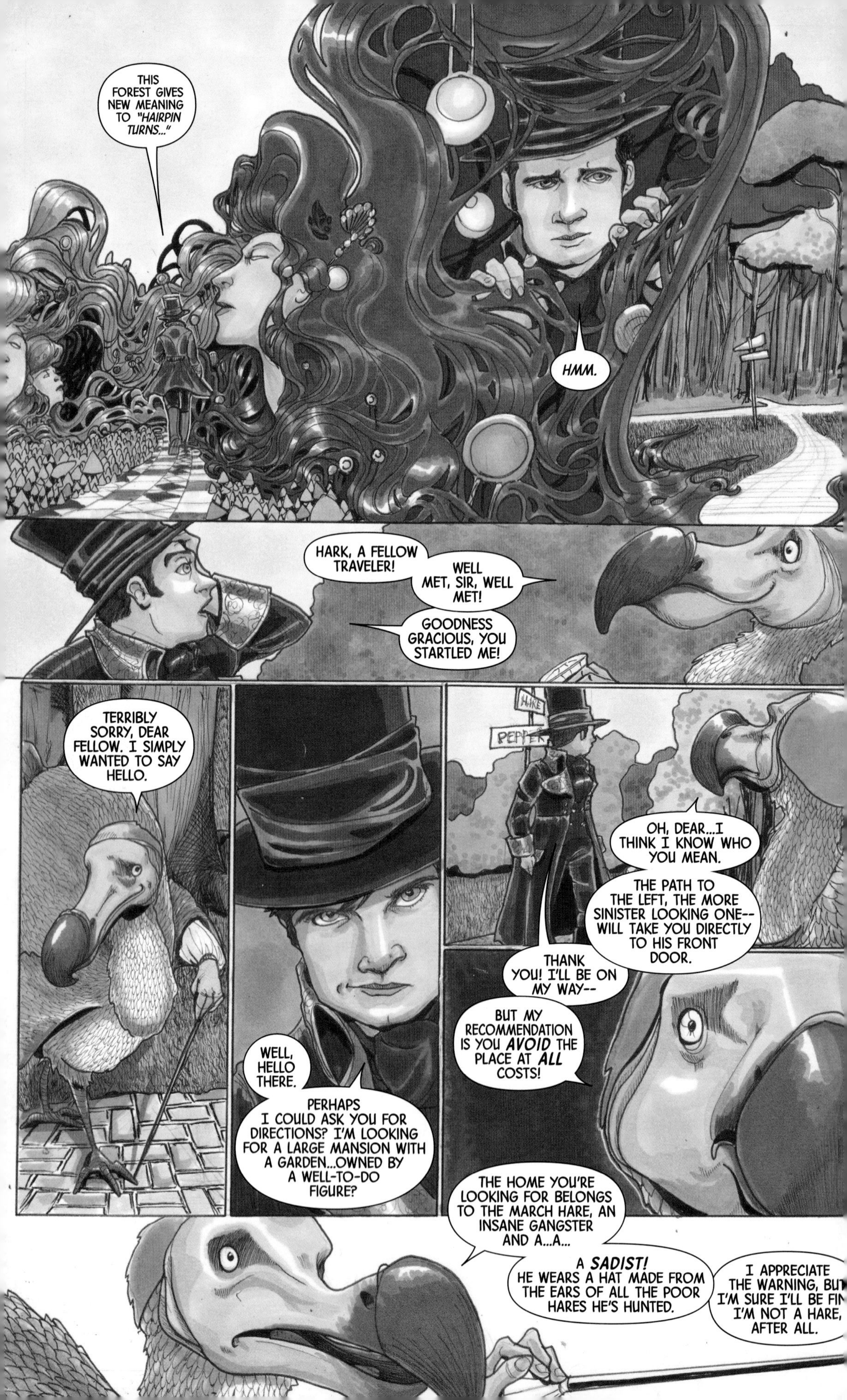
THIS FOREST GIVES NEW MEANING TO "HAIRPIN TURNS..."
HMM.
HARK, A FELLOW TRAVELER!
WELL MET, SIR, WELL MET!
GOODNESS GRACIOUS, YOU STARTLED ME!
TERRIBLY SORRY, DEAR FELLOW. I SIMPLY WANTED TO SAY HELLO.
WELL, HELLO THERE.
PERHAPS I COULD ASK YOU FOR DIRECTIONS? I'M LOOKING FOR A LARGE MANSION WITH A GARDEN...OWNED BY A WELL-TO-DO FIGURE?
HARE
PEPPER
OH, DEAR...I THINK I KNOW WHO YOU MEAN.
THE PATH TO THE LEFT, THE MORE SINISTER LOOKING ONE--WILL TAKE YOU DIRECTLY TO HIS FRONT DOOR.
THANK YOU! I'LL BE ON MY WAY--
BUT MY RECOMMENDATION IS YOU AVOID THE PLACE AT ALL COSTS!
THE HOME YOU'RE LOOKING FOR BELONGS TO THE MARCH HARE, AN INSANE GANGSTER AND A...A...
A SADIST! HE WEARS A HAT MADE FROM THE EARS OF ALL THE POOR HARES HE'S HUNTED.
I APPRECIATE THE WARNING, BUT I'M SURE I'LL BE FIN I'M NOT A HARE, AFTER ALL.

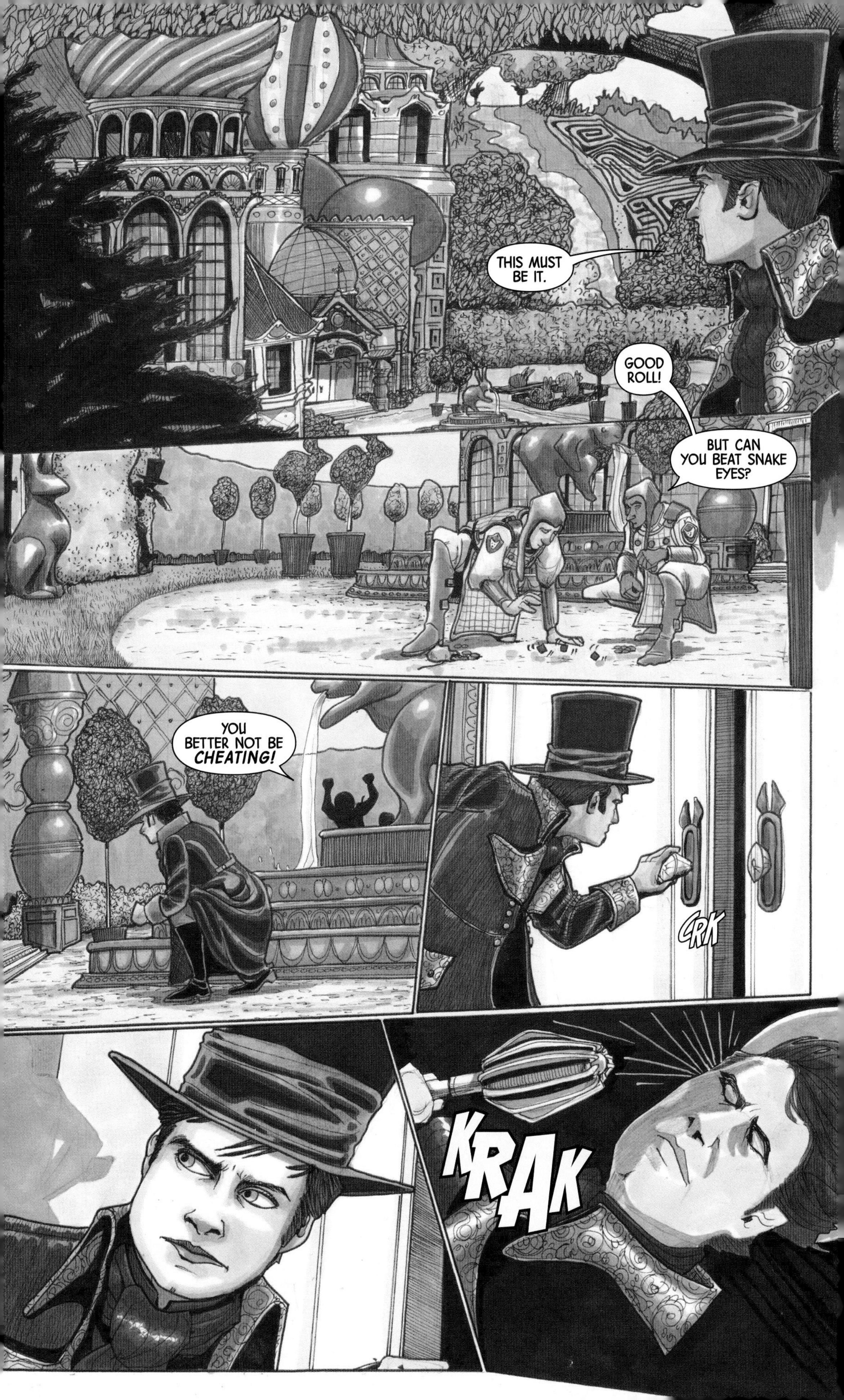
THIS MUST BE IT.
GOOD ROLL!
BUT CAN YOU BEAT SNAKE EYES?
YOU BETTER NOT BE CHEATING!
CRK
KRAK

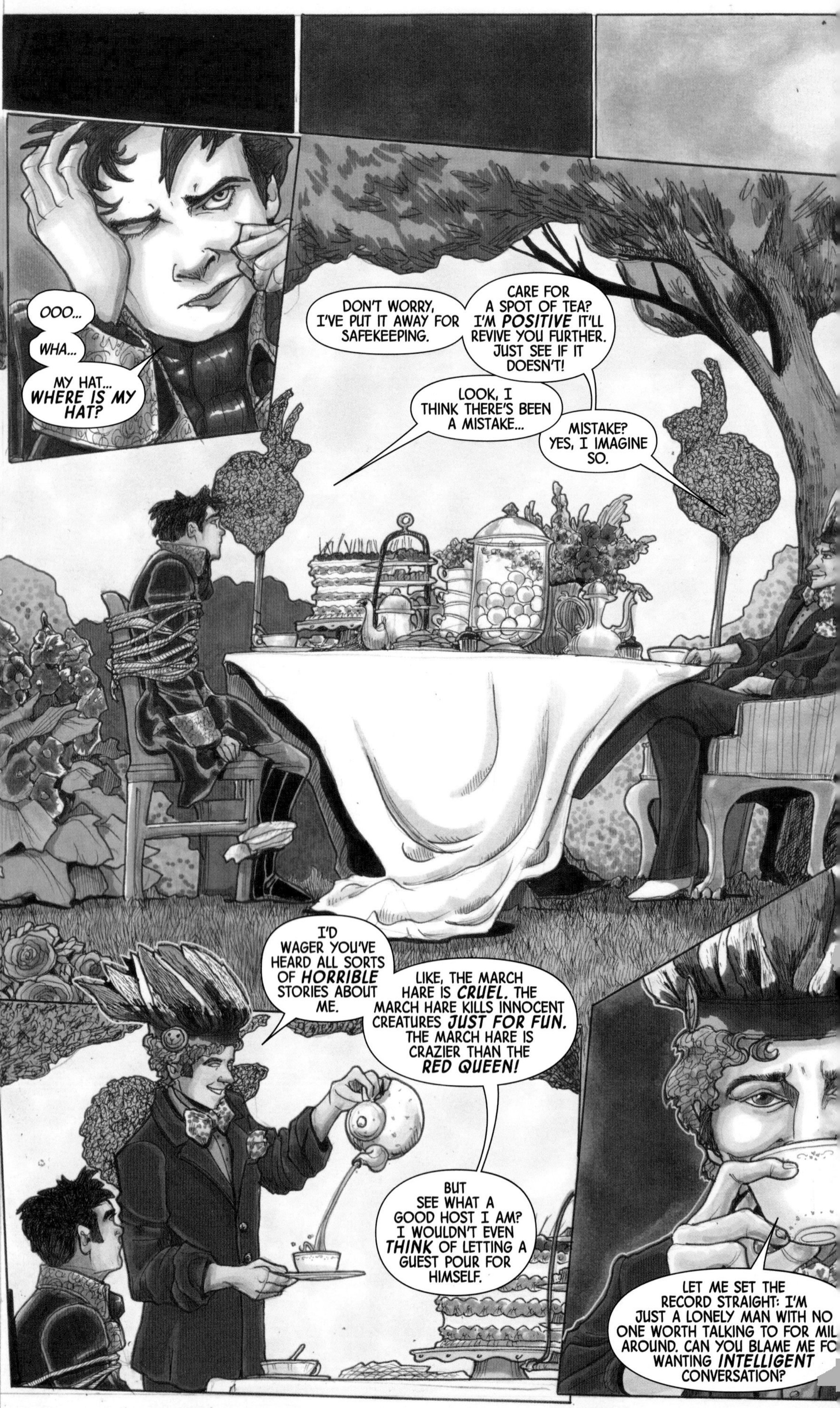

OOO...
WHA...
MY HAT... ***WHERE IS MY HAT?***
DON'T WORRY, I'VE PUT IT AWAY FOR SAFEKEEPING.
CARE FOR A SPOT OF TEA? I'M ***POSITIVE*** IT'LL REVIVE YOU FURTHER. JUST SEE IF IT DOESN'T!
LOOK, I THINK THERE'S BEEN A MISTAKE...
MISTAKE? YES, I IMAGINE SO.
I'D WAGER YOU'VE HEARD ALL SORTS OF ***HORRIBLE*** STORIES ABOUT ME.
LIKE, THE MARCH HARE IS ***CRUEL.*** THE MARCH HARE KILLS INNOCENT CREATURES ***JUST FOR FUN.*** THE MARCH HARE IS CRAZIER THAN THE ***RED QUEEN!***
BUT SEE WHAT A GOOD HOST I AM? I WOULDN'T EVEN ***THINK*** OF LETTING A GUEST POUR FOR HIMSELF.
LET ME SET THE RECORD STRAIGHT: I'M JUST A LONELY MAN WITH NO ONE WORTH TALKING TO FOR MIL AROUND. CAN YOU BLAME ME FO WANTING ***INTELLIGENT*** CONVERSATION?

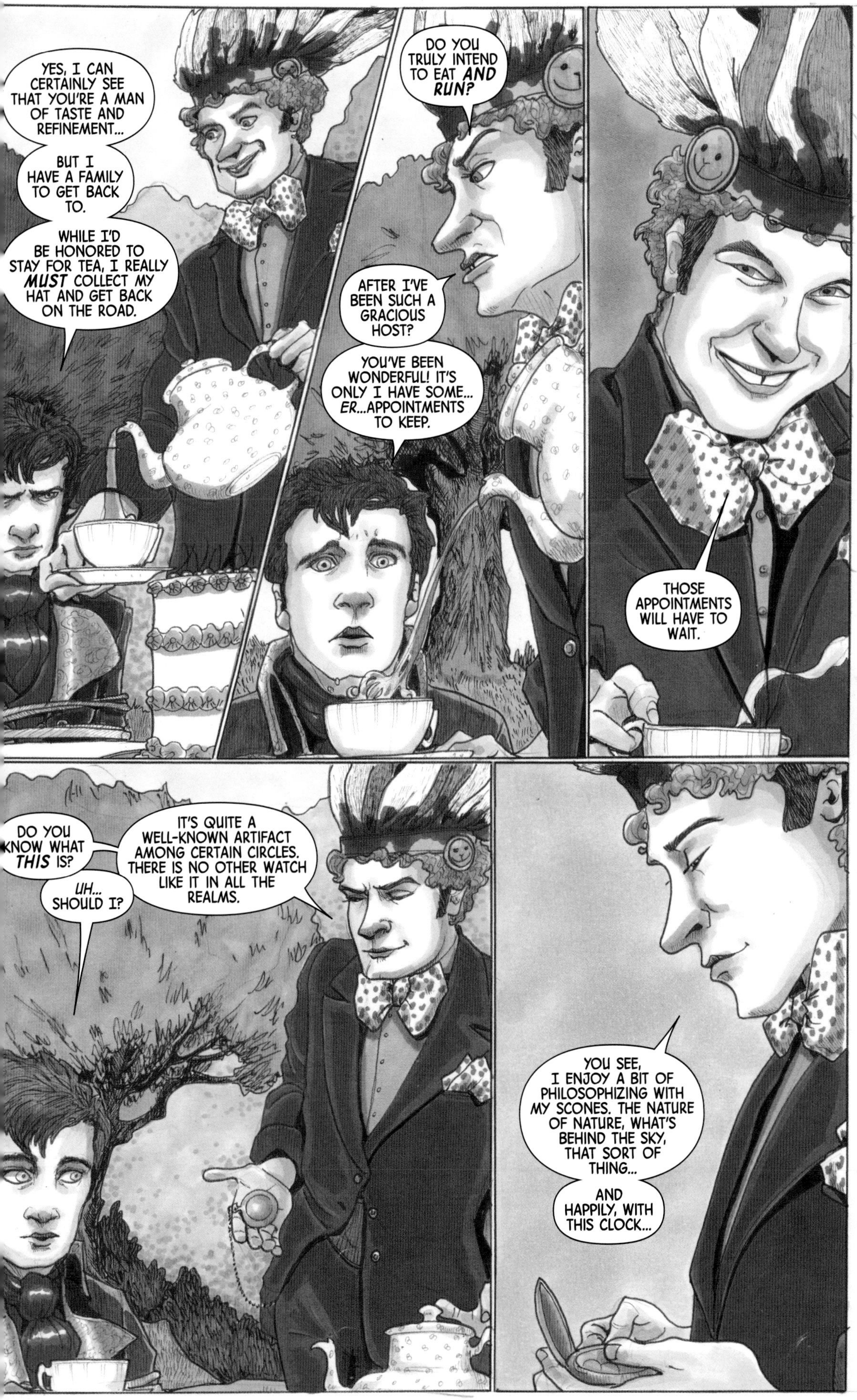

YES, I CAN CERTAINLY SEE THAT YOU'RE A MAN OF TASTE AND REFINEMENT...
BUT I HAVE A FAMILY TO GET BACK TO.
WHILE I'D BE HONORED TO STAY FOR TEA, I REALLY MUST COLLECT MY HAT AND GET BACK ON THE ROAD.
DO YOU TRULY INTEND TO EAT AND RUN?
AFTER I'VE BEEN SUCH A GRACIOUS HOST?
YOU'VE BEEN WONDERFUL! IT'S ONLY I HAVE SOME... ER...APPOINTMENTS TO KEEP.
THOSE APPOINTMENTS WILL HAVE TO WAIT.
DO YOU KNOW WHAT THIS IS?
UH... SHOULD I?
IT'S QUITE A WELL-KNOWN ARTIFACT AMONG CERTAIN CIRCLES. THERE IS NO OTHER WATCH LIKE IT IN ALL THE REALMS.
YOU SEE, I ENJOY A BIT OF PHILOSOPHIZING WITH MY SCONES. THE NATURE OF NATURE, WHAT'S BEHIND THE SKY, THAT SORT OF THING...
AND HAPPILY, WITH THIS CLOCK...

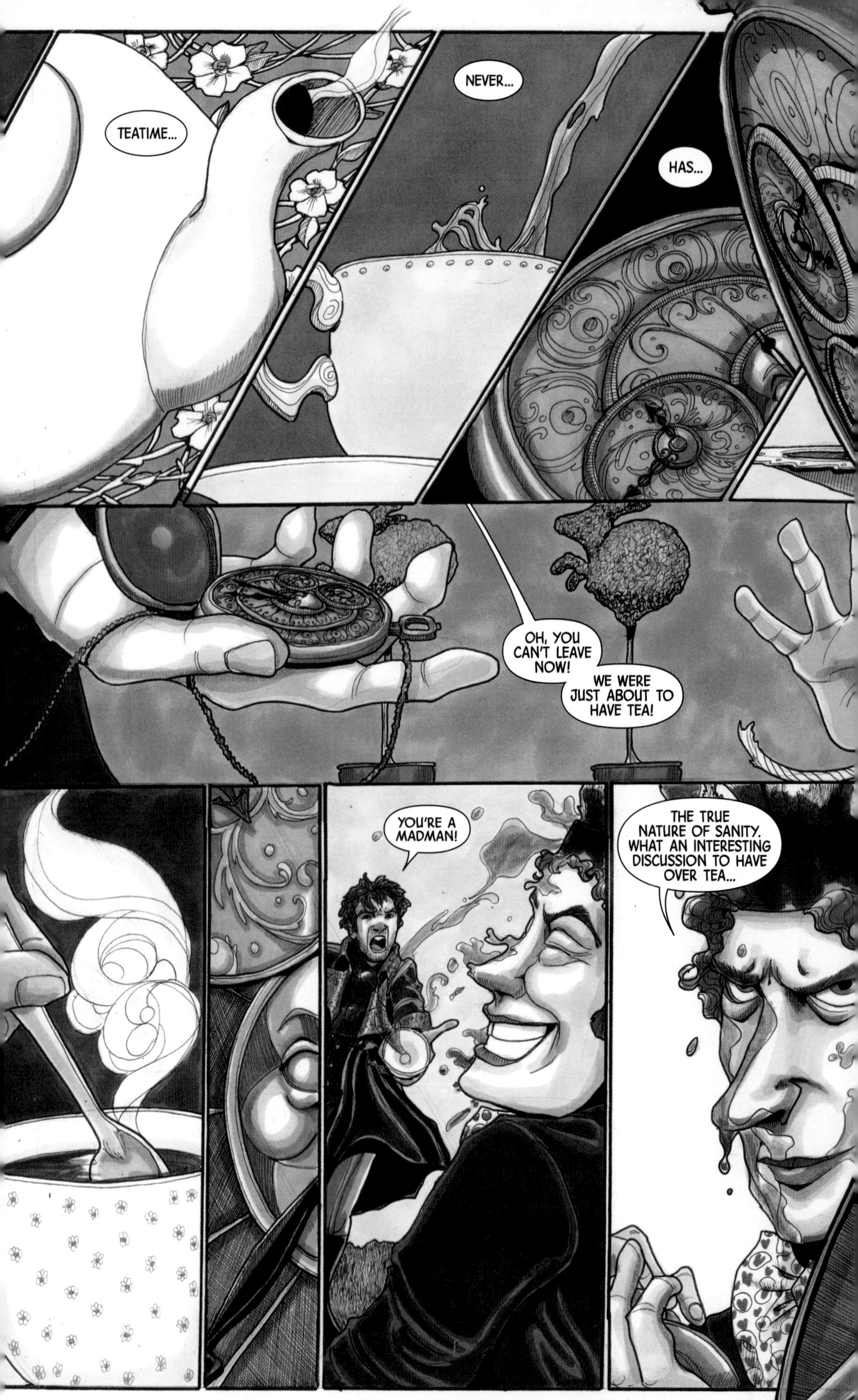
TEATIME...
NEVER...
HAS...
OH, YOU CAN'T LEAVE NOW!
WE WERE JUST ABOUT TO HAVE TEA!
YOU'RE A MADMAN!
THE TRUE NATURE OF SANITY. WHAT AN INTERESTING DISCUSSION TO HAVE OVER TEA...

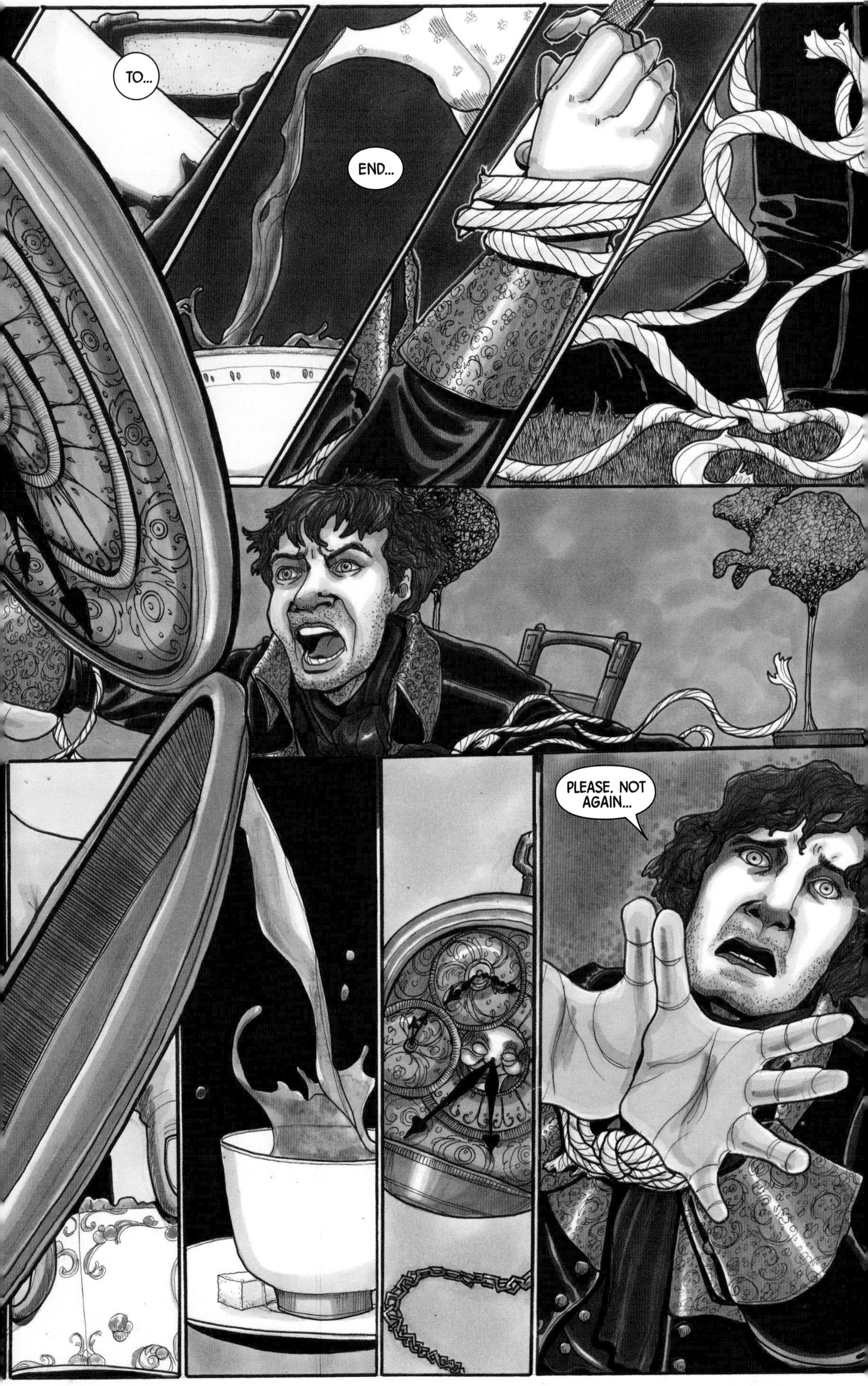
TO...
END...
PLEASE. NOT AGAIN...

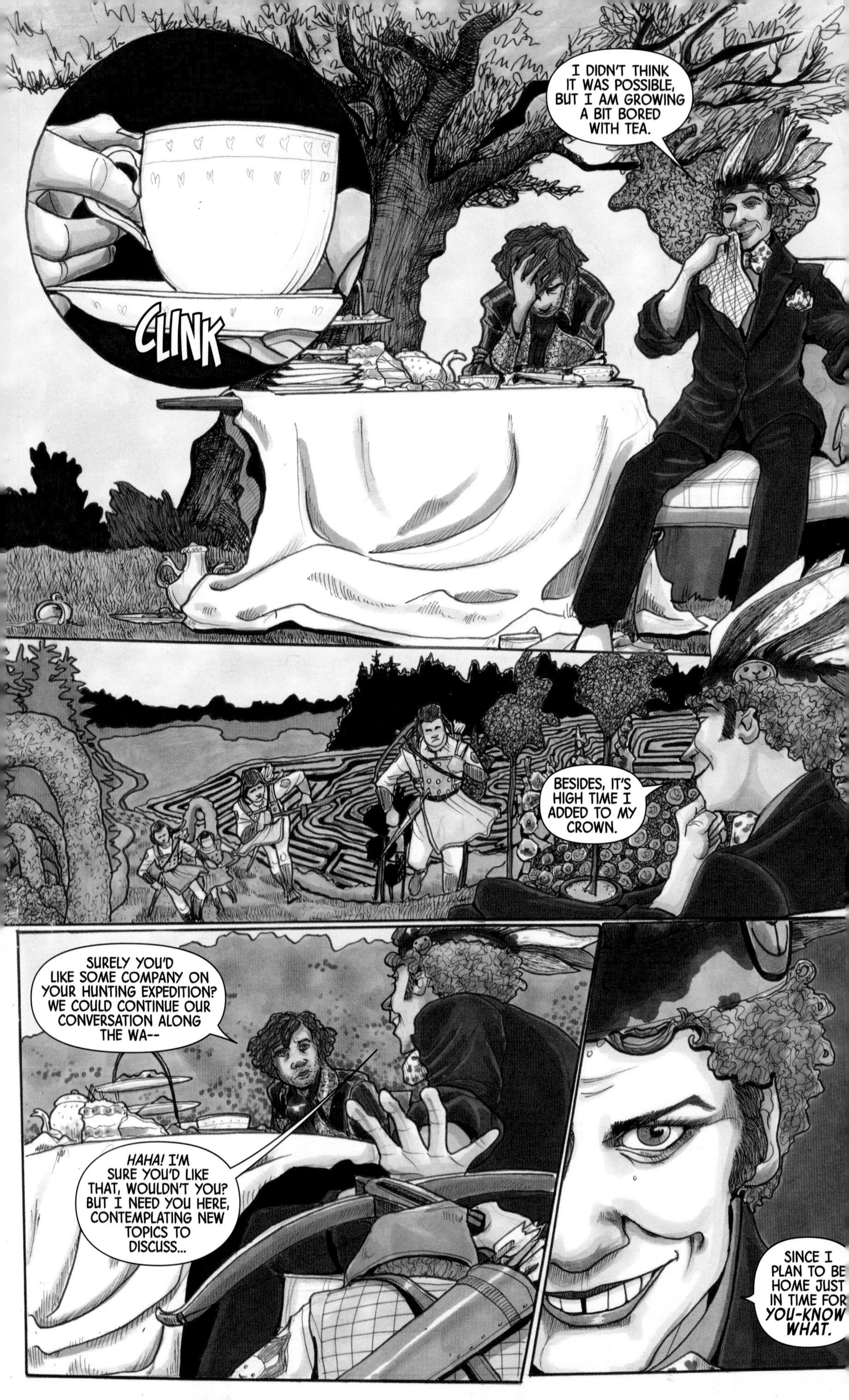
CLINK
I DIDN'T THINK IT WAS POSSIBLE, BUT I AM GROWING A BIT BORED WITH TEA.
BESIDES, IT'S HIGH TIME I ADDED TO MY CROWN.
SURELY YOU'D LIKE SOME COMPANY ON YOUR HUNTING EXPEDITION? WE COULD CONTINUE OUR CONVERSATION ALONG THE WA--
HAHA! I'M SURE YOU'D LIKE THAT, WOULDN'T YOU? BUT I NEED YOU HERE, CONTEMPLATING NEW TOPICS TO DISCUSS...
SINCE I PLAN TO BE HOME JUST IN TIME FOR YOU-KNOW WHAT.

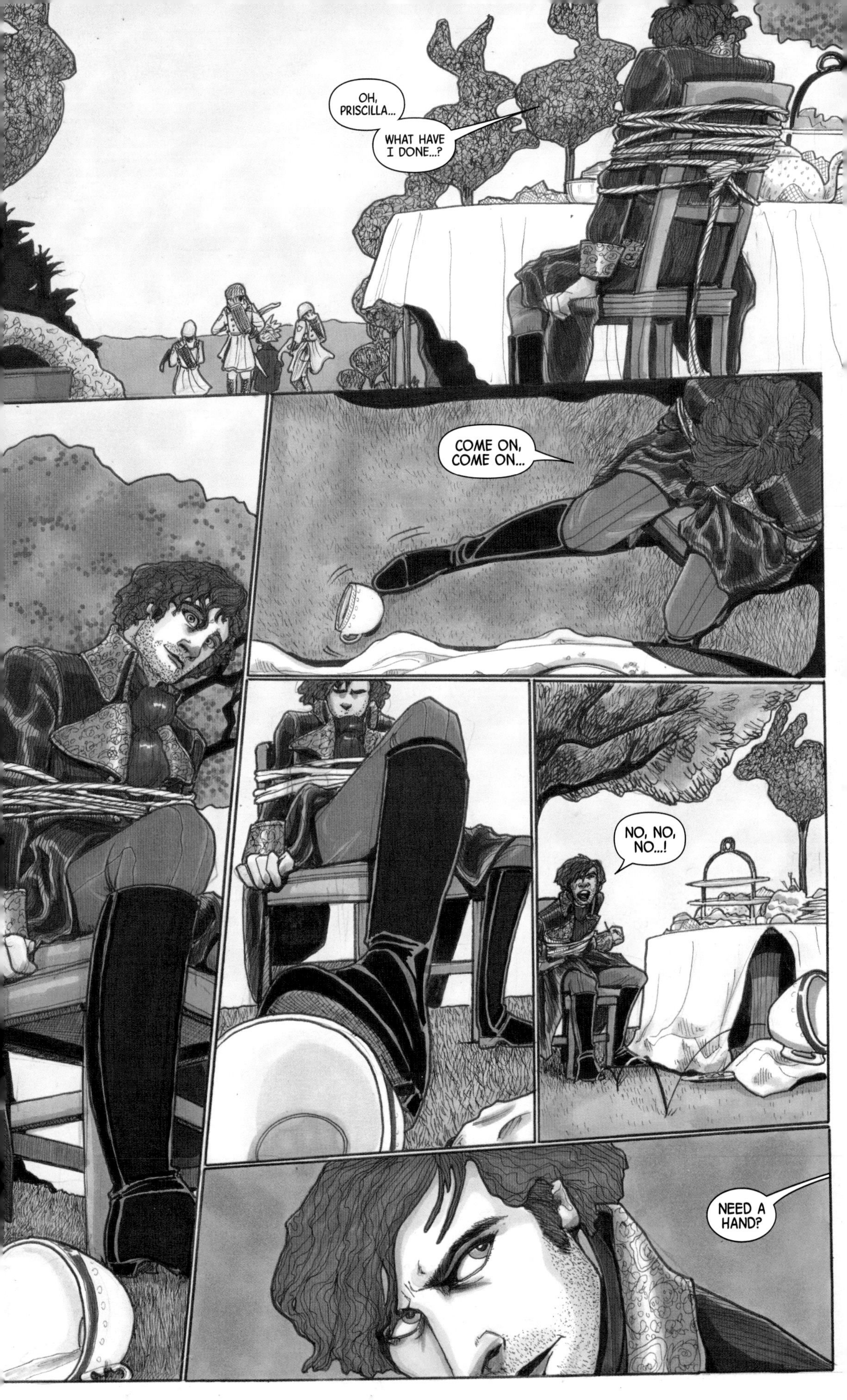
OH, PRISCILLA...
WHAT HAVE I DONE...?
COME ON, COME ON...
NO, NO, NO...!
NEED A HAND?

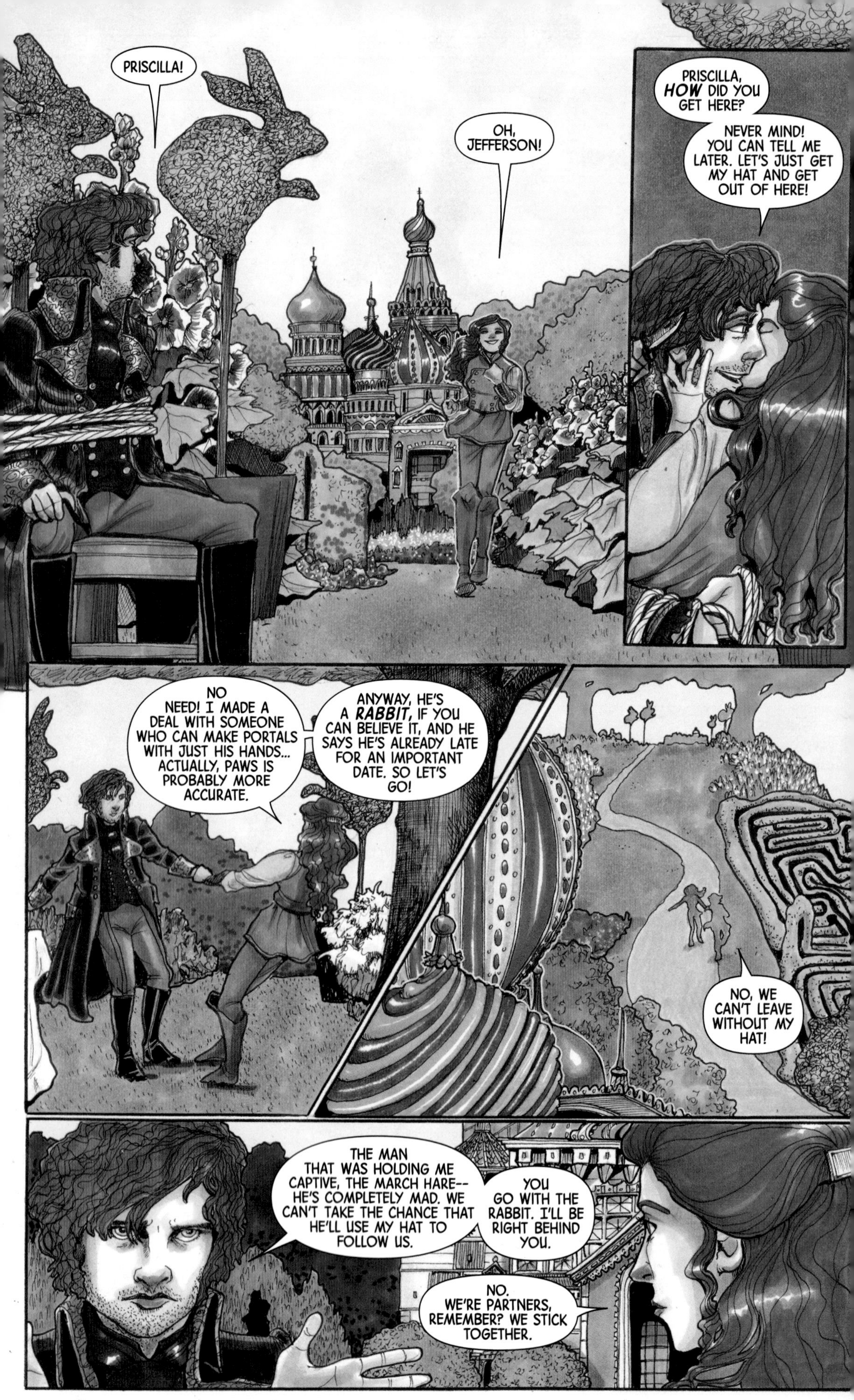
PRISCILLA!
OH, JEFFERSON!
PRISCILLA, HOW DID YOU GET HERE?
NEVER MIND! YOU CAN TELL ME LATER. LET'S JUST GET MY HAT AND GET OUT OF HERE!
NO NEED! I MADE A DEAL WITH SOMEONE WHO CAN MAKE PORTALS WITH JUST HIS HANDS... ACTUALLY, PAWS IS PROBABLY MORE ACCURATE.
ANYWAY, HE'S A RABBIT, IF YOU CAN BELIEVE IT, AND HE SAYS HE'S ALREADY LATE FOR AN IMPORTANT DATE. SO LET'S GO!
NO, WE CAN'T LEAVE WITHOUT MY HAT!
THE MAN THAT WAS HOLDING ME CAPTIVE, THE MARCH HARE-- HE'S COMPLETELY MAD. WE CAN'T TAKE THE CHANCE THAT HE'LL USE MY HAT TO FOLLOW US.
YOU GO WITH THE RABBIT. I'LL BE RIGHT BEHIND YOU.
NO. WE'RE PARTNERS, REMEMBER? WE STICK TOGETHER.

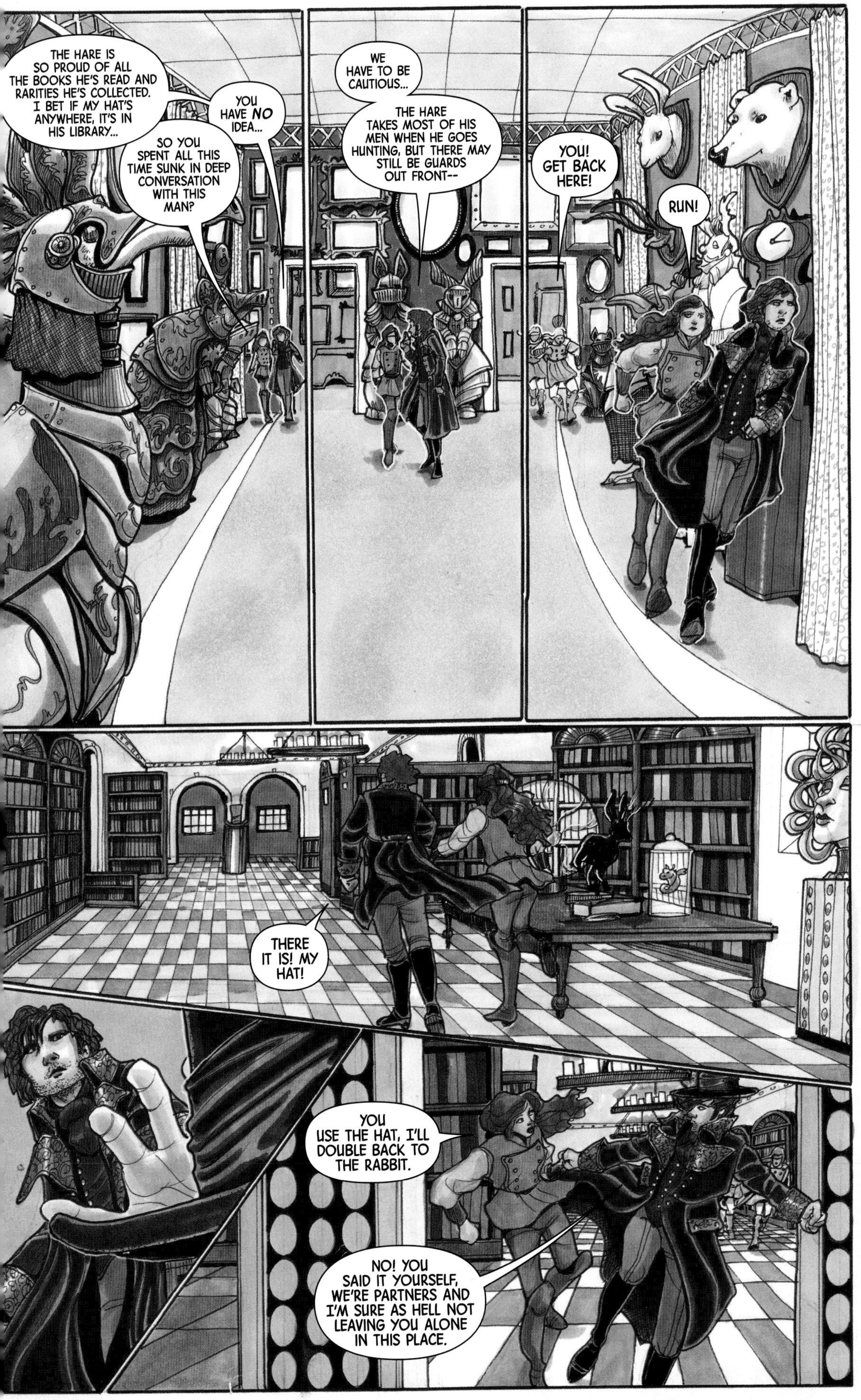
THE HARE IS SO PROUD OF ALL THE BOOKS HE'S READ AND RARITIES HE'S COLLECTED. I BET IF MY HAT'S ANYWHERE, IT'S IN HIS LIBRARY...
YOU HAVE NO IDEA...
SO YOU SPENT ALL THIS TIME SUNK IN DEEP CONVERSATION WITH THIS MAN?
WE HAVE TO BE CAUTIOUS...
THE HARE TAKES MOST OF HIS MEN WHEN HE GOES HUNTING, BUT THERE MAY STILL BE GUARDS OUT FRONT--
YOU! GET BACK HERE!
RUN!
THERE IT IS! MY HAT!
YOU USE THE HAT, I'LL DOUBLE BACK TO THE RABBIT.
NO! YOU SAID IT YOURSELF, WE'RE PARTNERS AND I'M SURE AS HELL NOT LEAVING YOU ALONE IN THIS PLACE.

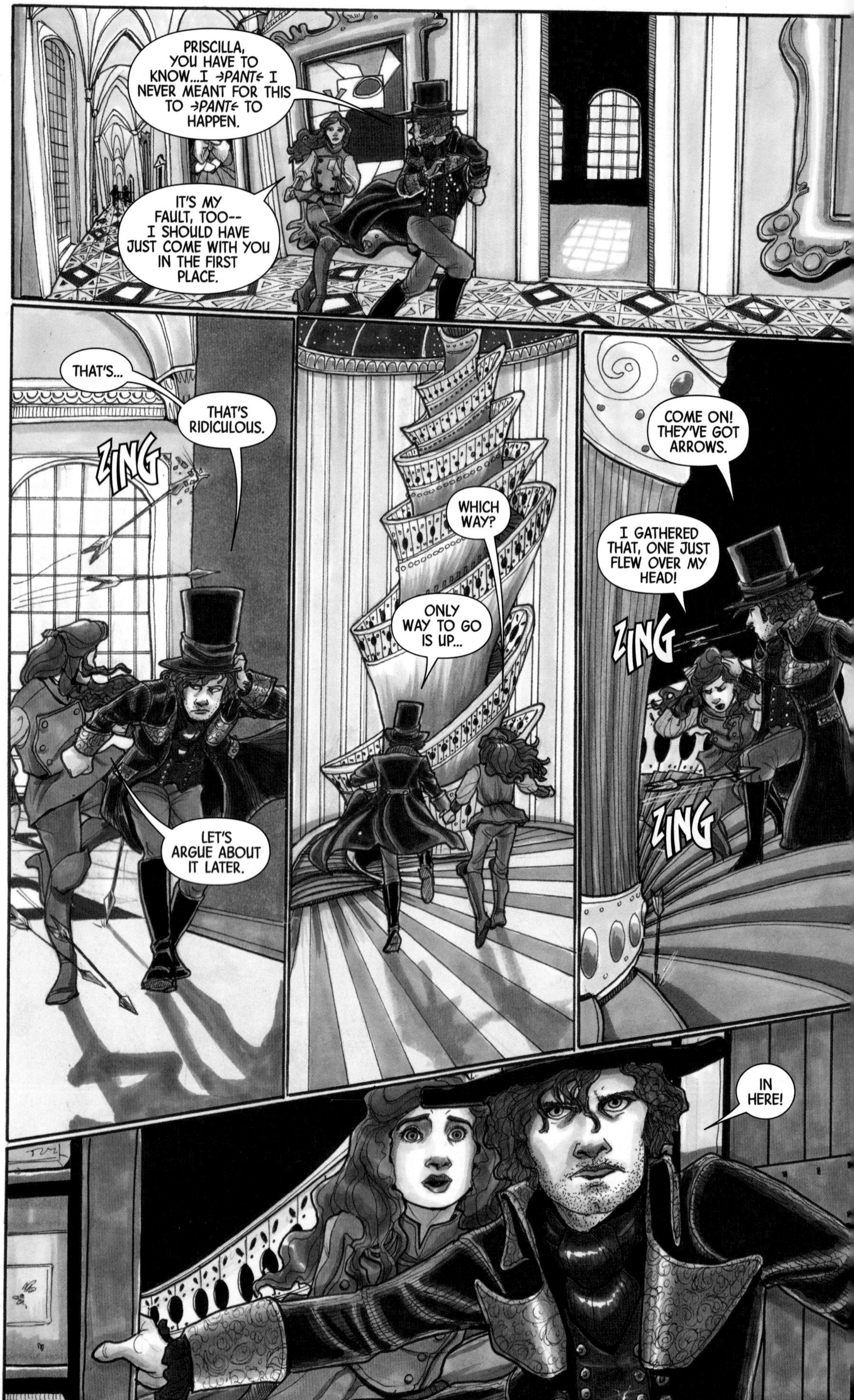
PRISCILLA, YOU HAVE TO KNOW...I →PANT← I NEVER MEANT FOR THIS TO →PANT← TO HAPPEN.
IT'S MY FAULT, TOO-- I SHOULD HAVE JUST COME WITH YOU IN THE FIRST PLACE.
THAT'S...
THAT'S RIDICULOUS.
ZING
LET'S ARGUE ABOUT IT LATER.
WHICH WAY?
ONLY WAY TO GO IS UP...
COME ON! THEY'VE GOT ARROWS.
I GATHERED THAT, ONE JUST FLEW OVER MY HEAD!
ZING
ZING
IN HERE!

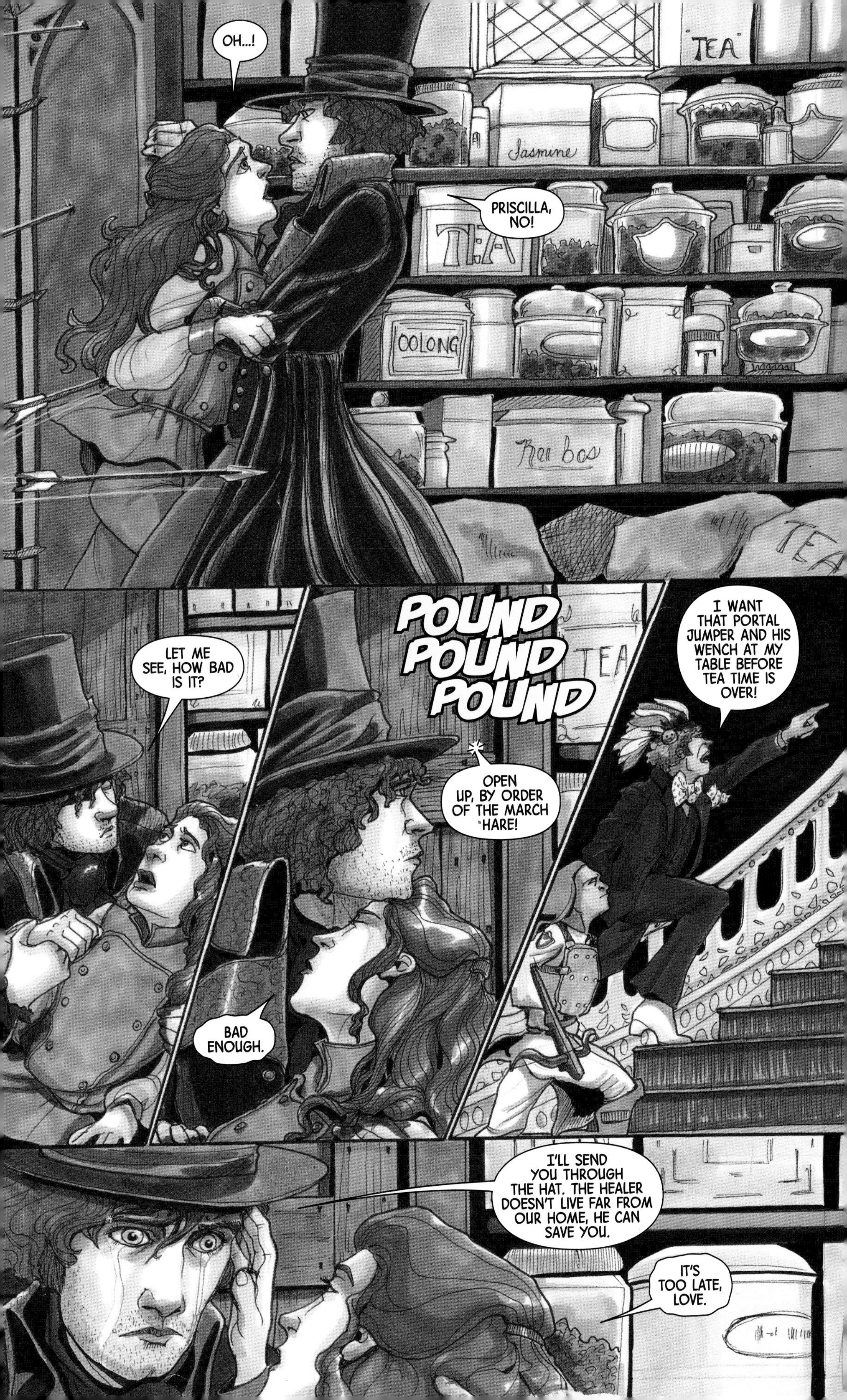
OH...!
PRISCILLA, NO!
LET ME SEE, HOW BAD IS IT?
BAD ENOUGH.
POUND POUND POUND
OPEN UP, BY ORDER OF THE MARCH HARE!
I WANT THAT PORTAL JUMPER AND HIS WENCH AT MY TABLE BEFORE TEA TIME IS OVER!
I'LL SEND YOU THROUGH THE HAT. THE HEALER DOESN'T LIVE FAR FROM OUR HOME, HE CAN SAVE YOU.
IT'S TOO LATE, LOVE.

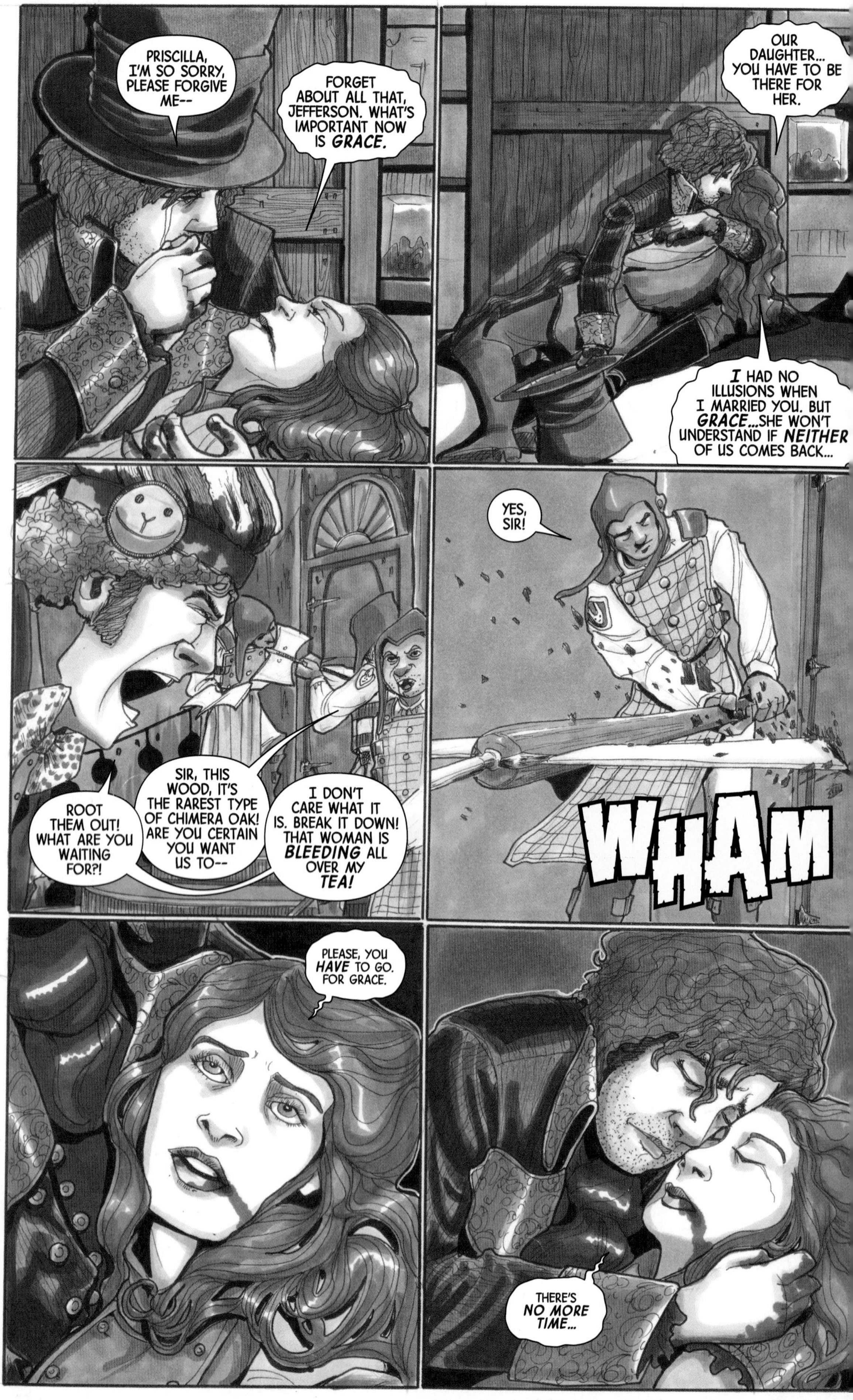
PRISCILLA, I'M SO SORRY, PLEASE FORGIVE ME--
FORGET ABOUT ALL THAT, JEFFERSON. WHAT'S IMPORTANT NOW IS GRACE.
OUR DAUGHTER... YOU HAVE TO BE THERE FOR HER.
I HAD NO ILLUSIONS WHEN I MARRIED YOU. BUT GRACE...SHE WON'T UNDERSTAND IF NEITHER OF US COMES BACK...
ROOT THEM OUT! WHAT ARE YOU WAITING FOR?!
SIR, THIS WOOD, IT'S THE RAREST TYPE OF CHIMERA OAK! ARE YOU CERTAIN YOU WANT US TO--
I DON'T CARE WHAT IT IS. BREAK IT DOWN! THAT WOMAN IS BLEEDING ALL OVER MY TEA!
YES, SIR!
WHAM
PLEASE, YOU HAVE TO GO. FOR GRACE.
THERE'S NO MORE TIME...

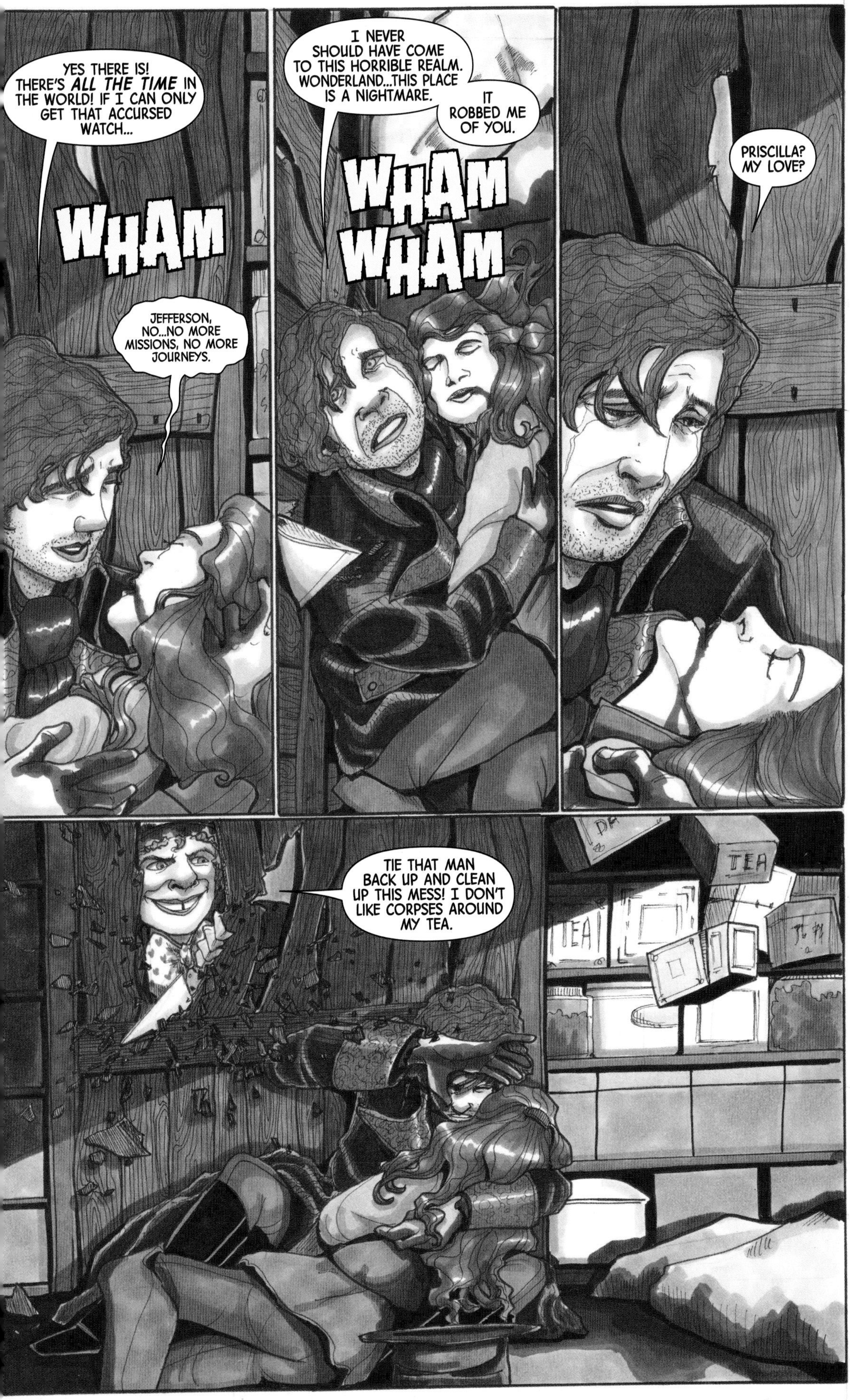
YES THERE IS! THERE'S ALL THE TIME IN THE WORLD! IF I CAN ONLY GET THAT ACCURSED WATCH...
WHAM
JEFFERSON, NO...NO MORE MISSIONS, NO MORE JOURNEYS.
I NEVER SHOULD HAVE COME TO THIS HORRIBLE REALM. WONDERLAND...THIS PLACE IS A NIGHTMARE.
IT ROBBED ME OF YOU.
WHAM WHAM
PRISCILLA? MY LOVE?
TIE THAT MAN BACK UP AND CLEAN UP THIS MESS! I DON'T LIKE CORPSES AROUND MY TEA.
TEA
TEA

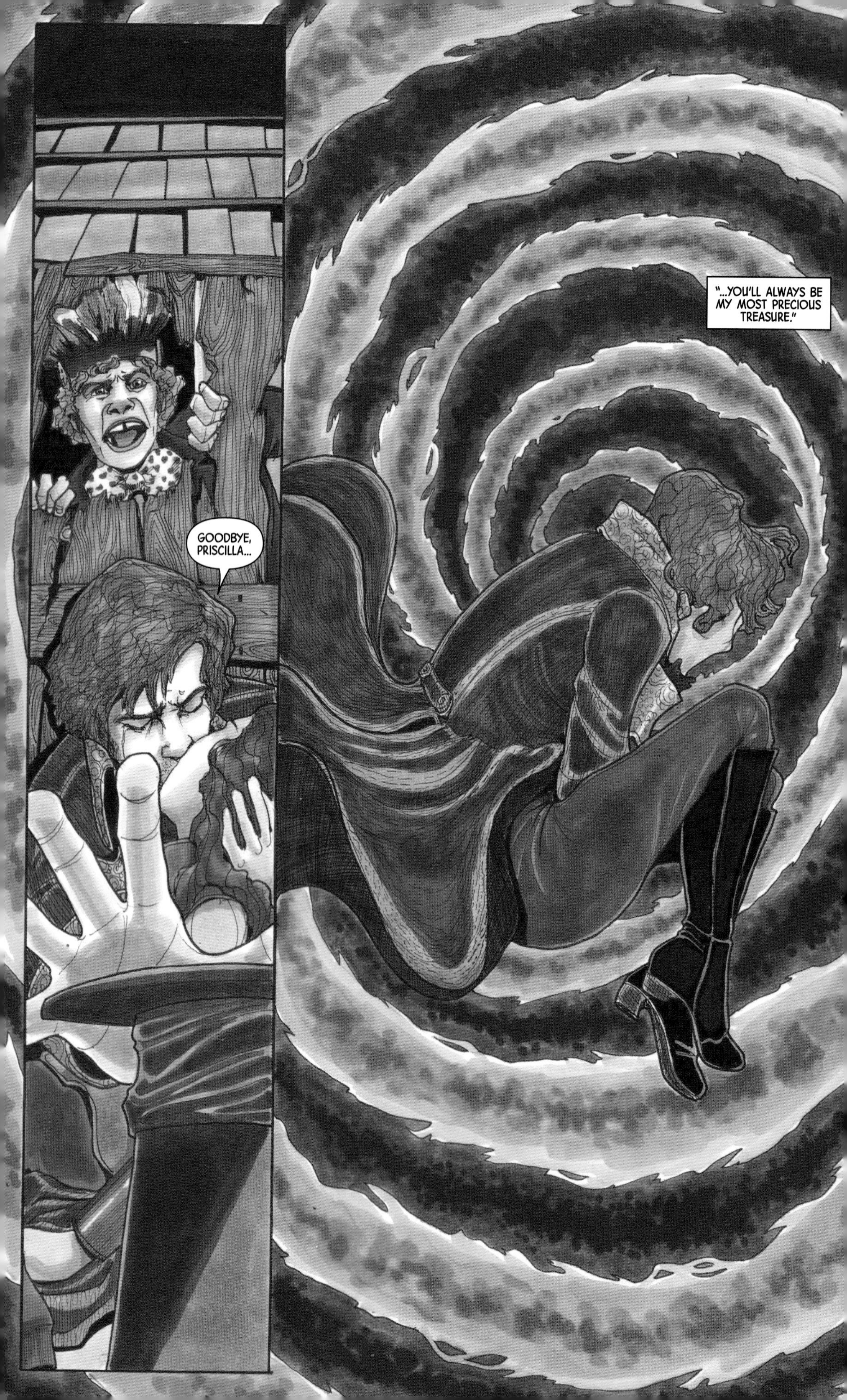
GOODBYE, PRISCILLA...
"...YOU'LL ALWAYS BE MY MOST PRECIOUS TREASURE."

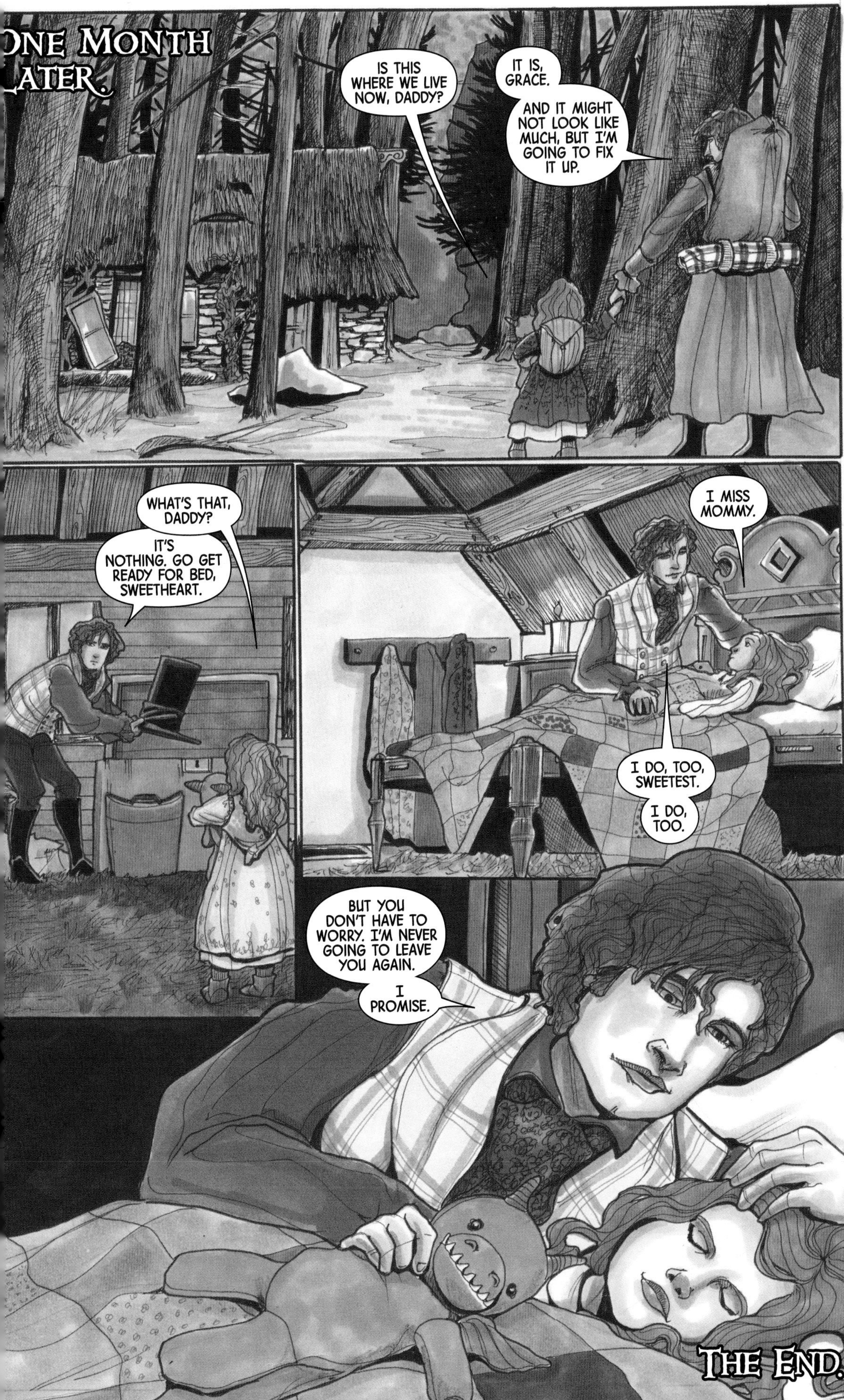
ONE MONTH LATER.
IS THIS WHERE WE LIVE NOW, DADDY?
IT IS, GRACE.
AND IT MIGHT NOT LOOK LIKE MUCH, BUT I'M GOING TO FIX IT UP.
WHAT'S THAT, DADDY?
IT'S NOTHING. GO GET READY FOR BED, SWEETHEART.
I MISS MOMMY.
I DO, TOO, SWEETEST.
I DO, TOO.
BUT YOU DON'T HAVE TO WORRY. I'M NEVER GOING TO LEAVE YOU AGAIN.
I PROMISE.
THE END.

BONUS

MATERIAL

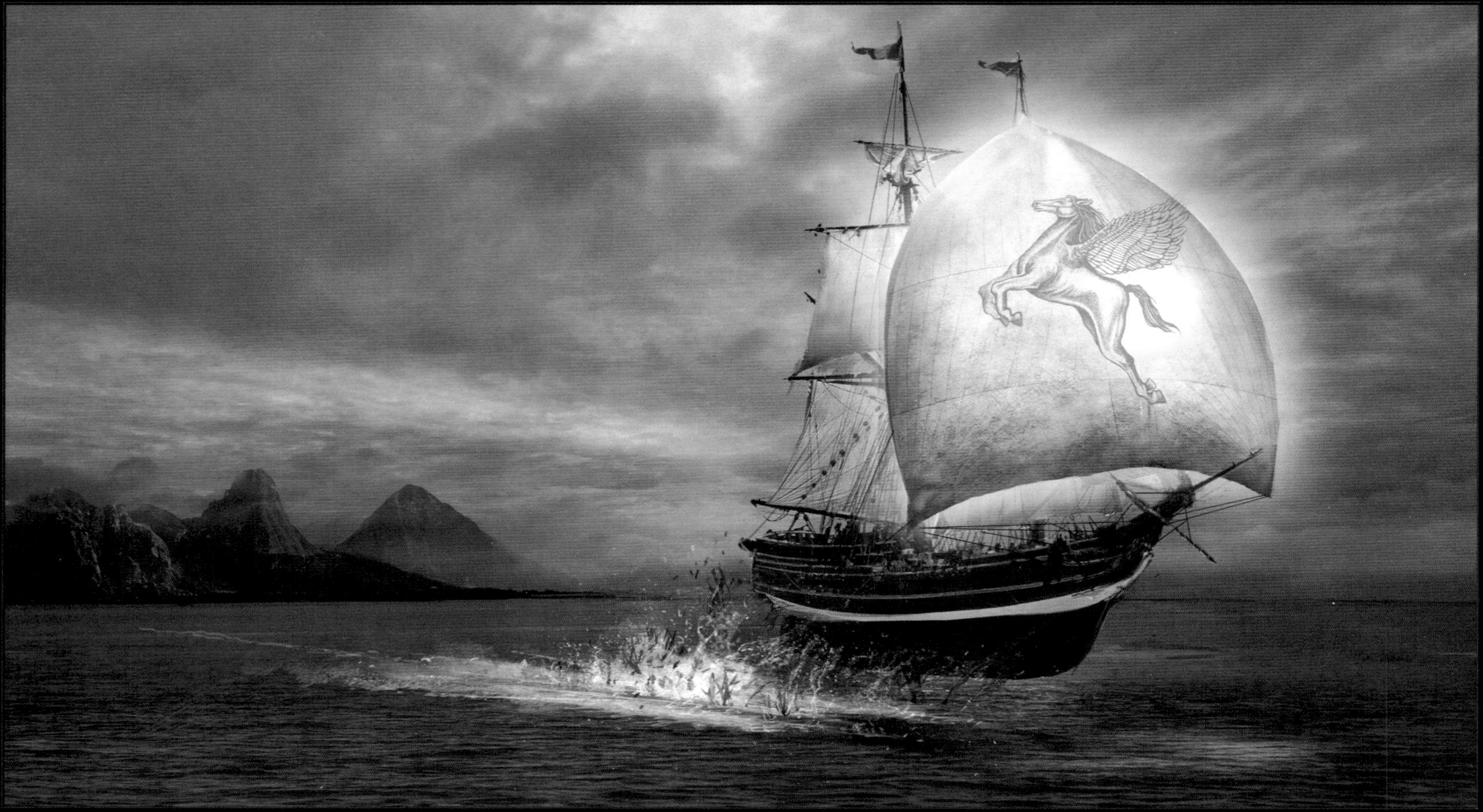

ONCE UPON A TIME SEASON THREE

EPISODE 305 "GOOD FORM"

JEWEL OF THE REALM FLYING

AUGUST 21st, 2013
EXECUTIVE PRODUCERS
EDWARD KITSIS, ADAM HOROWITZ, STEVE PEARLMAN

PRODUCTION DESIGNER: MICHAEL JOY
ILLUSTRATOR: JOHN GALLAGHER

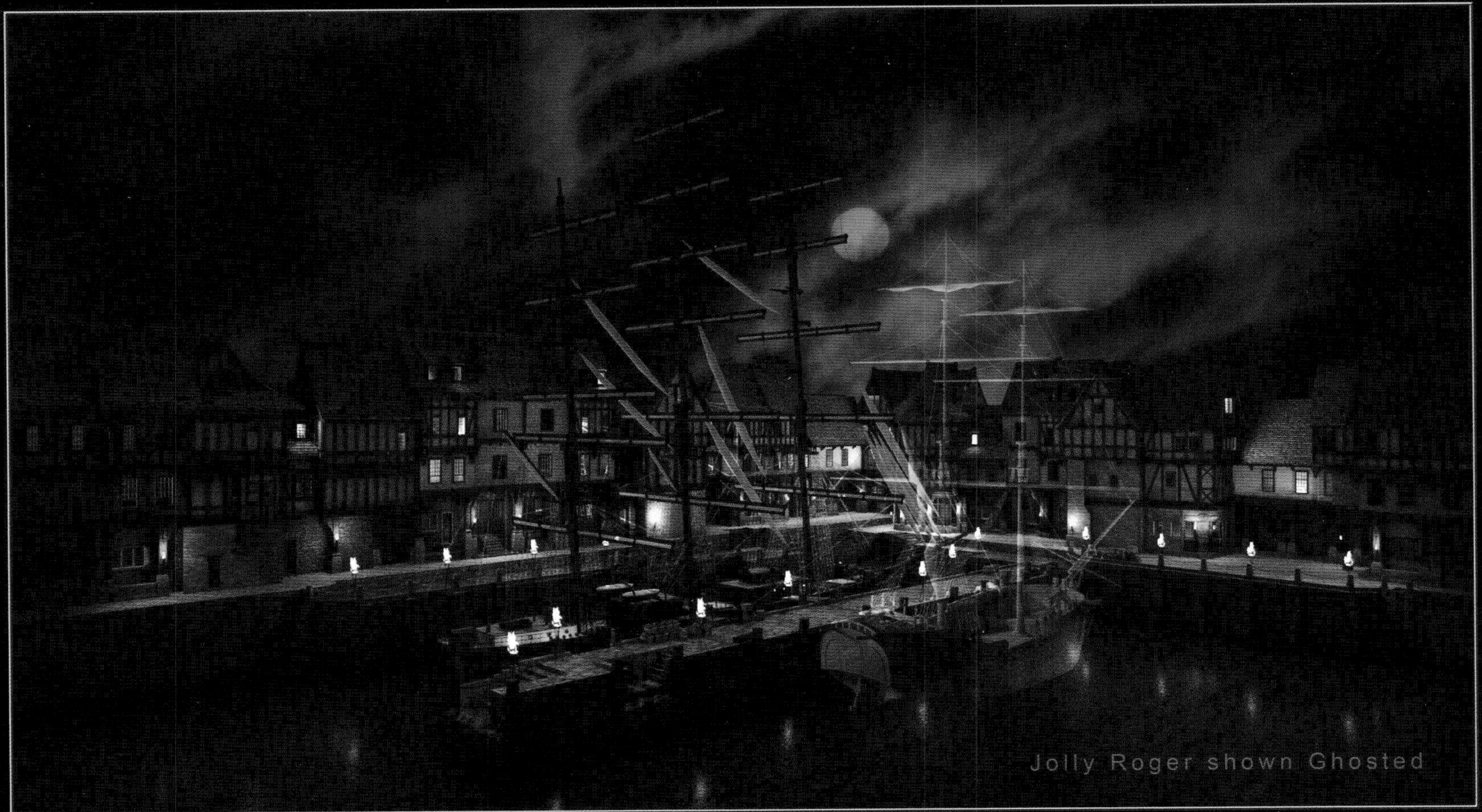
Jolly Roger shown Ghosted

EPISODE 317 "THE JOLLY ROGER"

ONCE UPON A TIME SEASON THREE

EXT - JOLLY ROGER & DOCK

JANUARY 28th, 2014
EXECUTIVE PRODUCERS
EDWARD KITSIS, ADAM HOROWITZ, STEVE PEARLMAN

PRODUCTION DESIGNER: MICHAEL JOY
ILLUSTRATOR: DOUGLAS MCLEAN

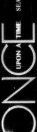

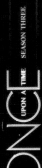

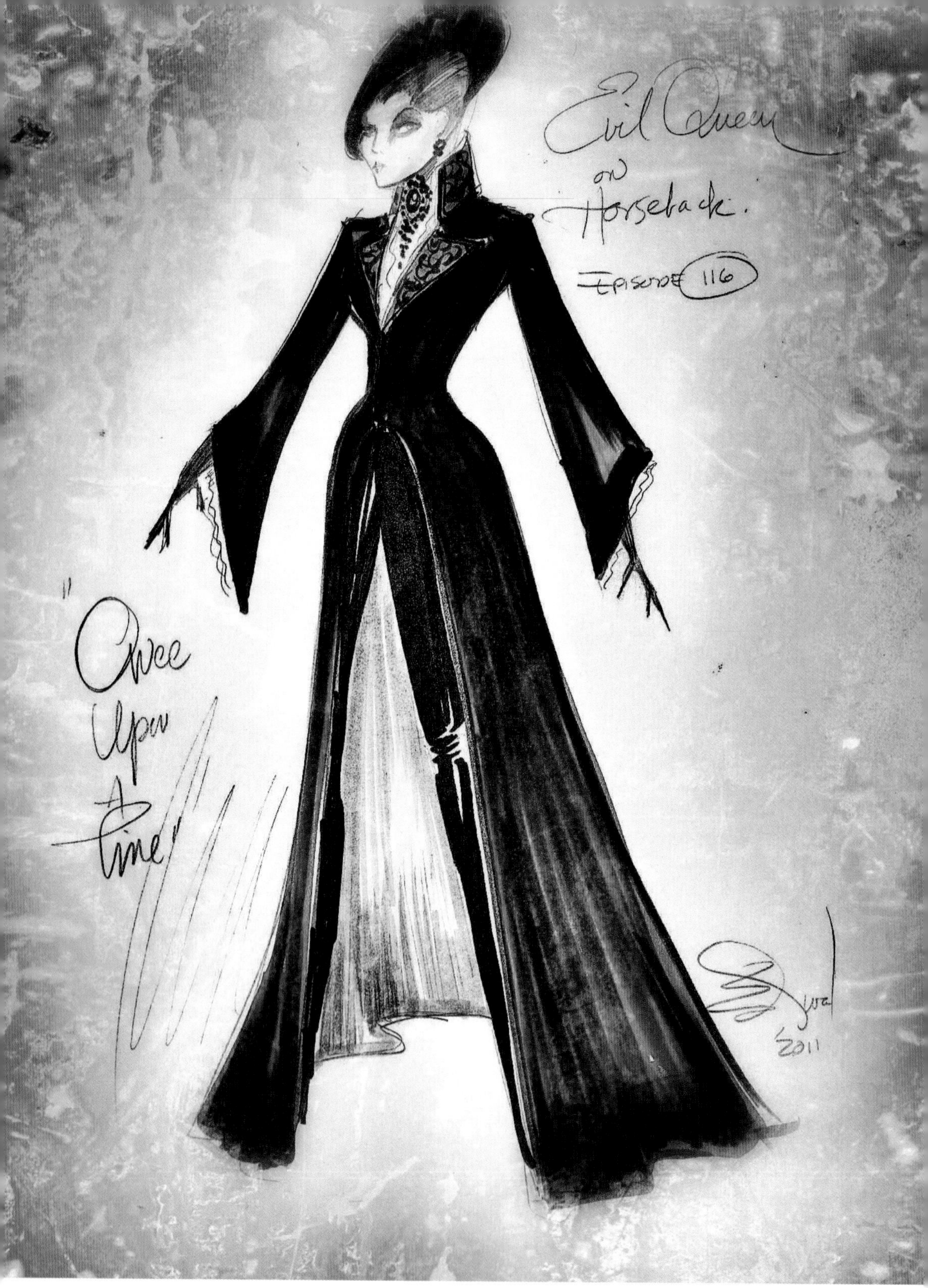
Evil Queen
on
Horseback.
Episode 116
"Once
Upon
A
Time"
2011

THE EVIL QUEEN

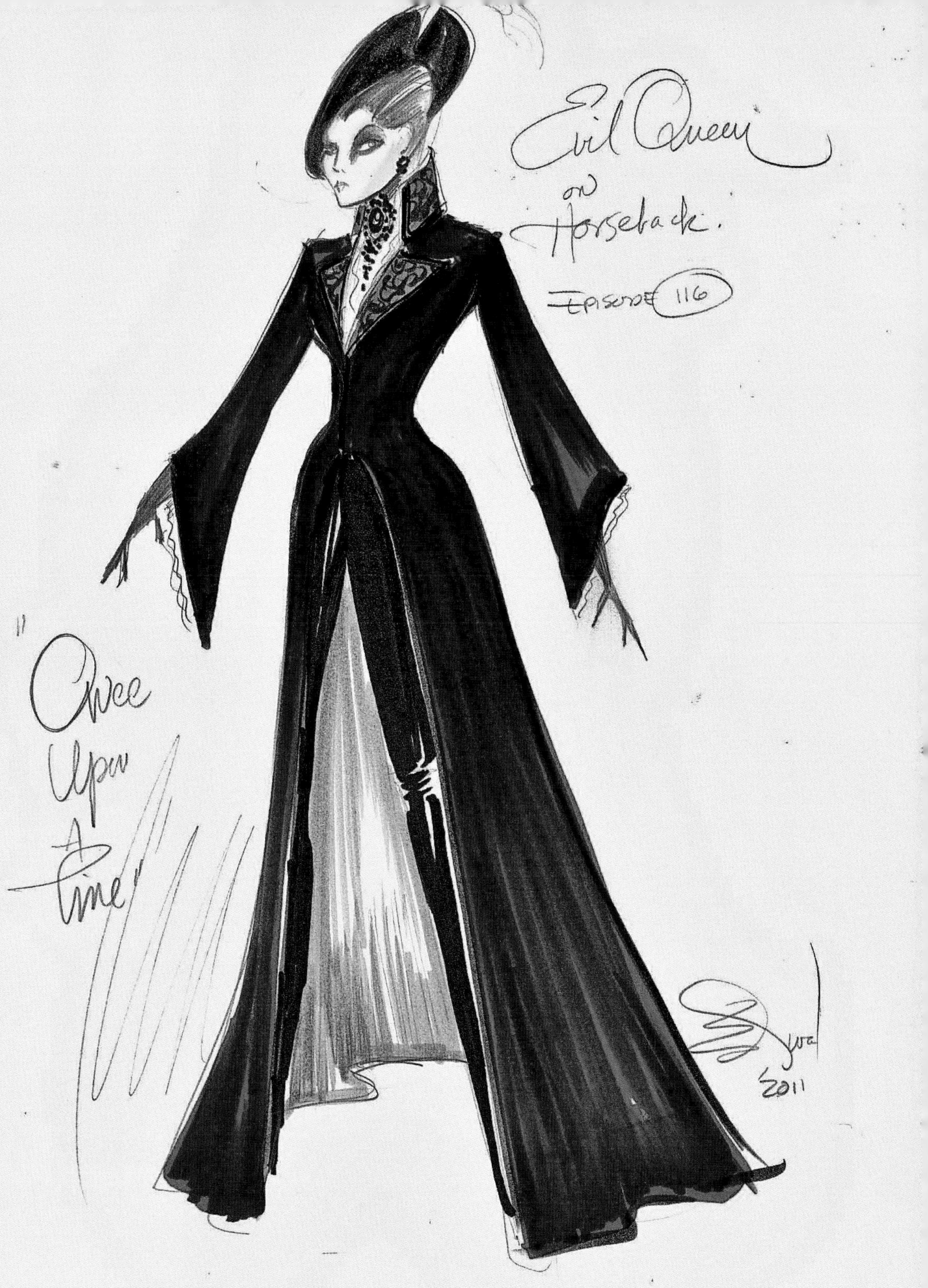
Evil Queen
on
Horseback.
Episode 116
"Once
Upon
A
Time"
2011

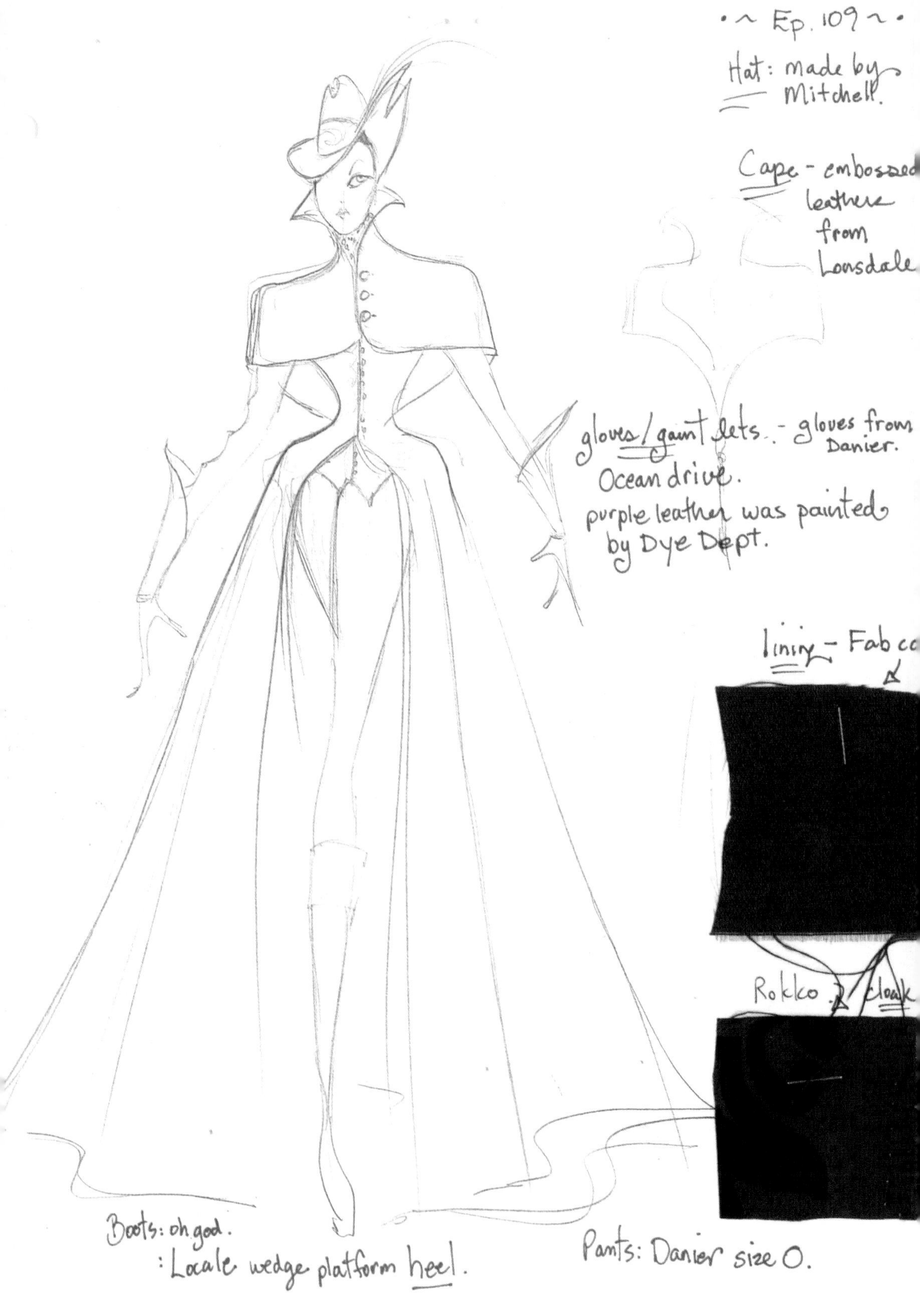
Ep. 109
Hat: made by Mitchell.
Cape - embossed leather from Lonsdale
gloves/gauntlets. - gloves from Danier.
Ocean drive.
purple leather was painted by Dye Dept.
lining - Fab co
Rokko
cloak
Boots: oh god.
: Locale wedge platform heel.
Pants: Danier size 0.

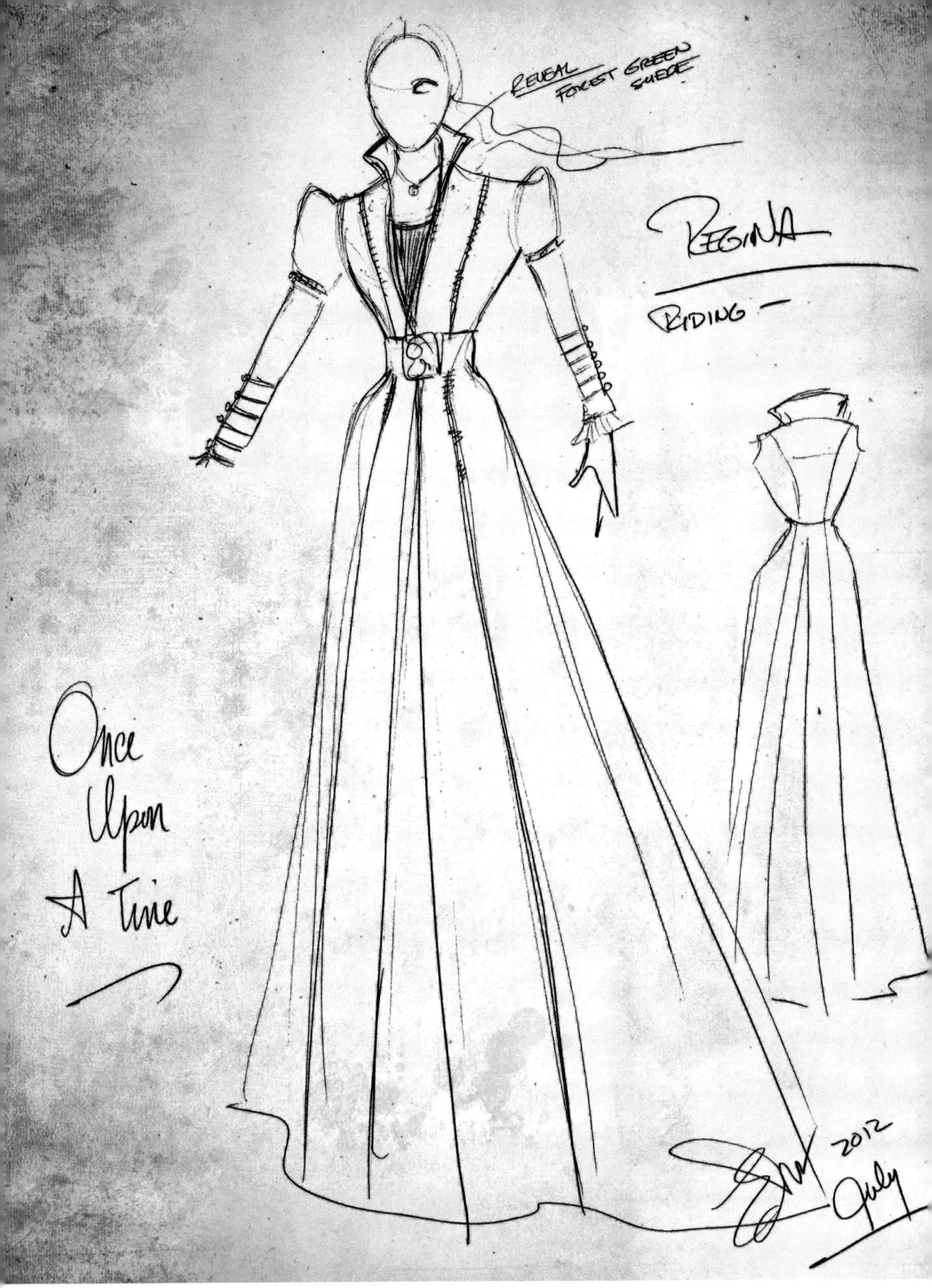
REVEAL
FOREST GREEN SUEDE
REGINA
RIDING
Once Upon A Time
2012 July

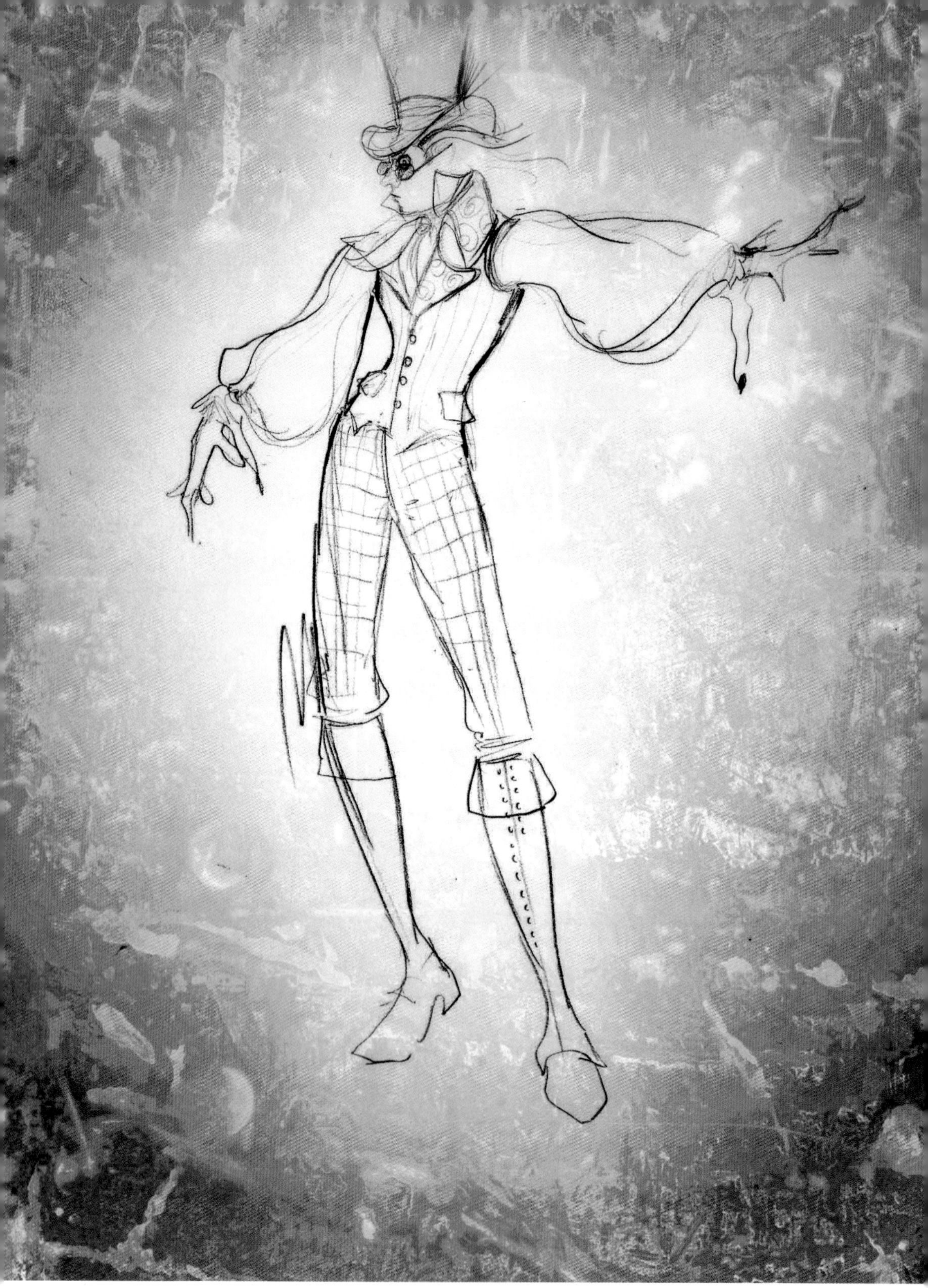

THE MAD HATTER

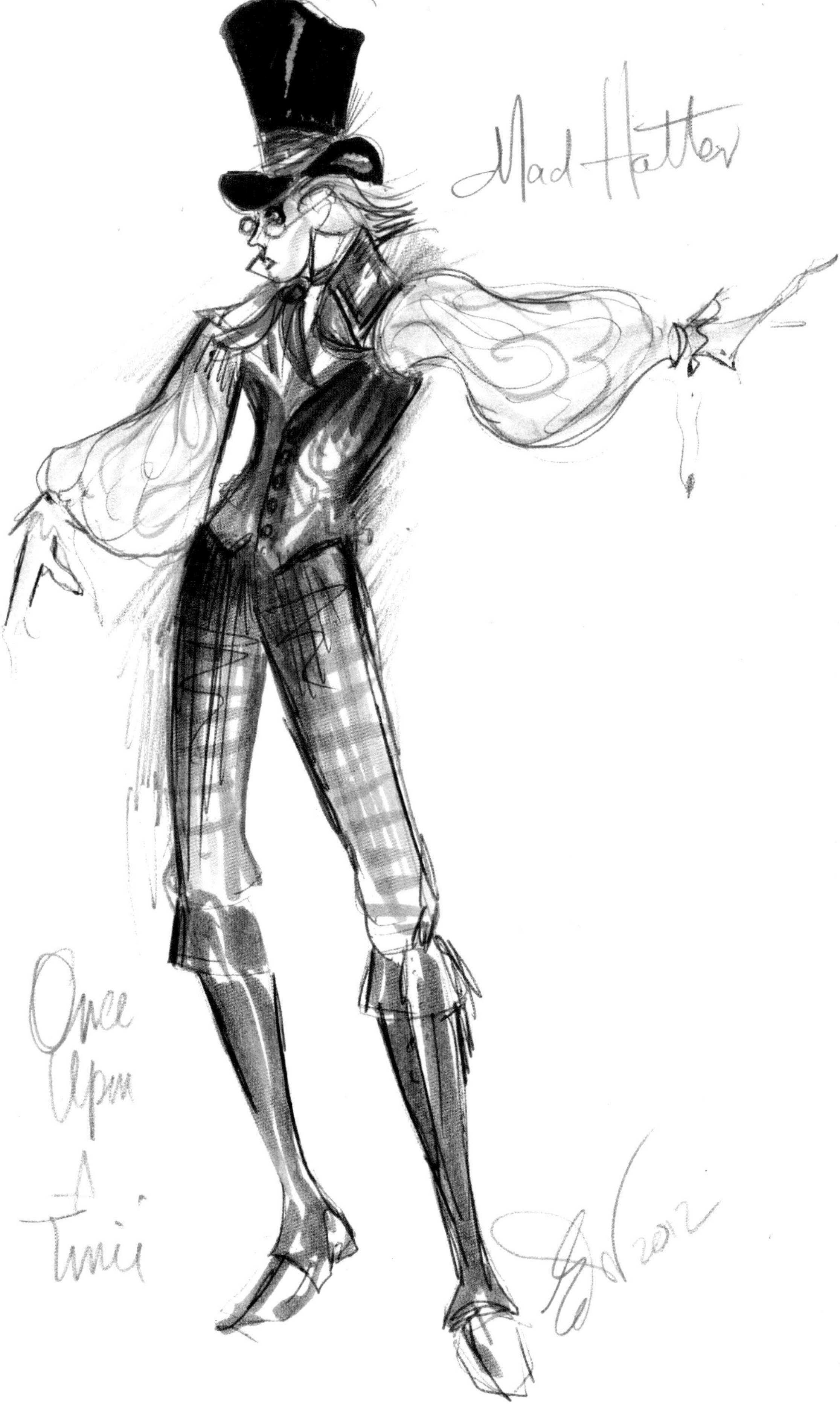
Mad Hatter
Once Upon A Time
2012

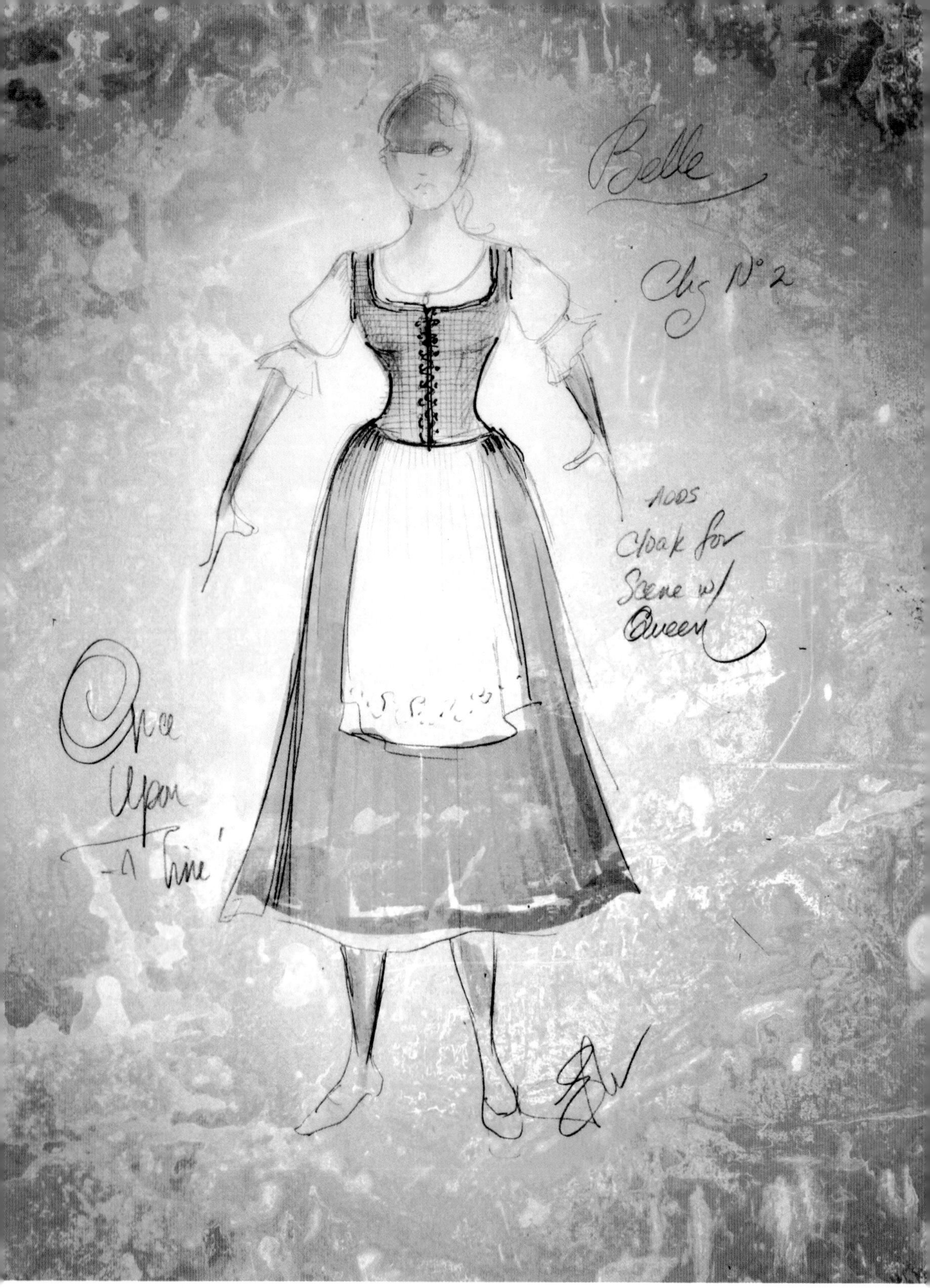
Belle
Chg N° 2
Adds Cloak for Scene w/ Queen
Once Upon A Time

BELLE

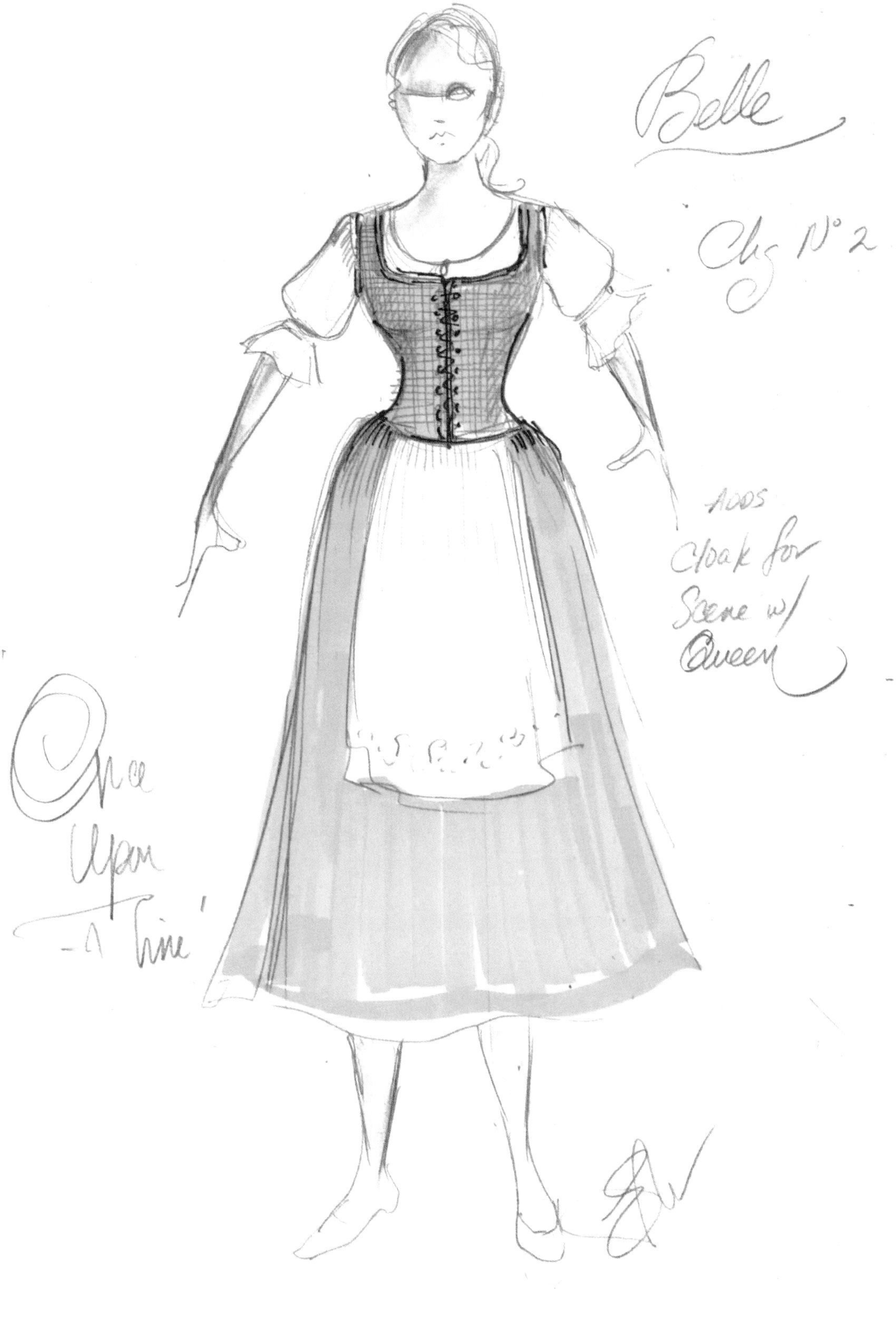
Belle
Chg N° 2
ADDS
Cloak for
Scene w/
Queen
Once
Upon
a Time

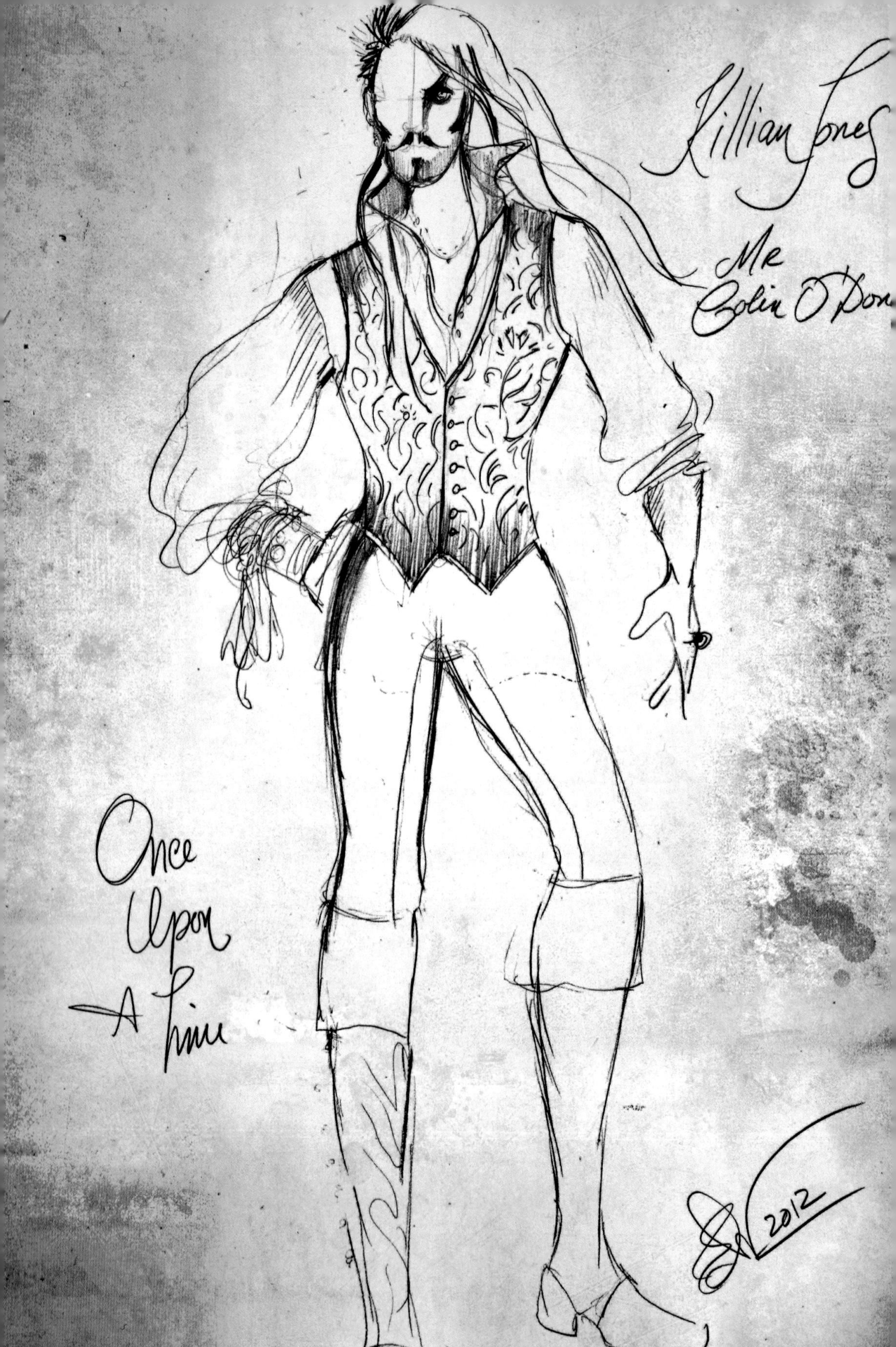

Killian Jones
Mr
Colin O'Don
Once
Upon
A Time
2012

KILLIAN

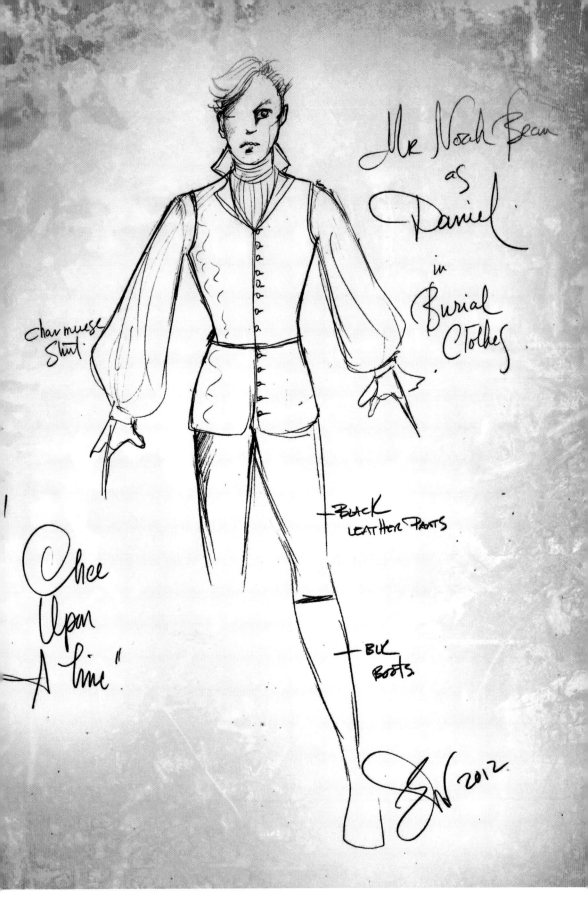

Mr Noah Bean as Daniel in Burial Clothes

Charmeuse Shirt.

Black Leather Pants

Blk Boots.

"Once Upon A Time"

SW 2012

DANIEL

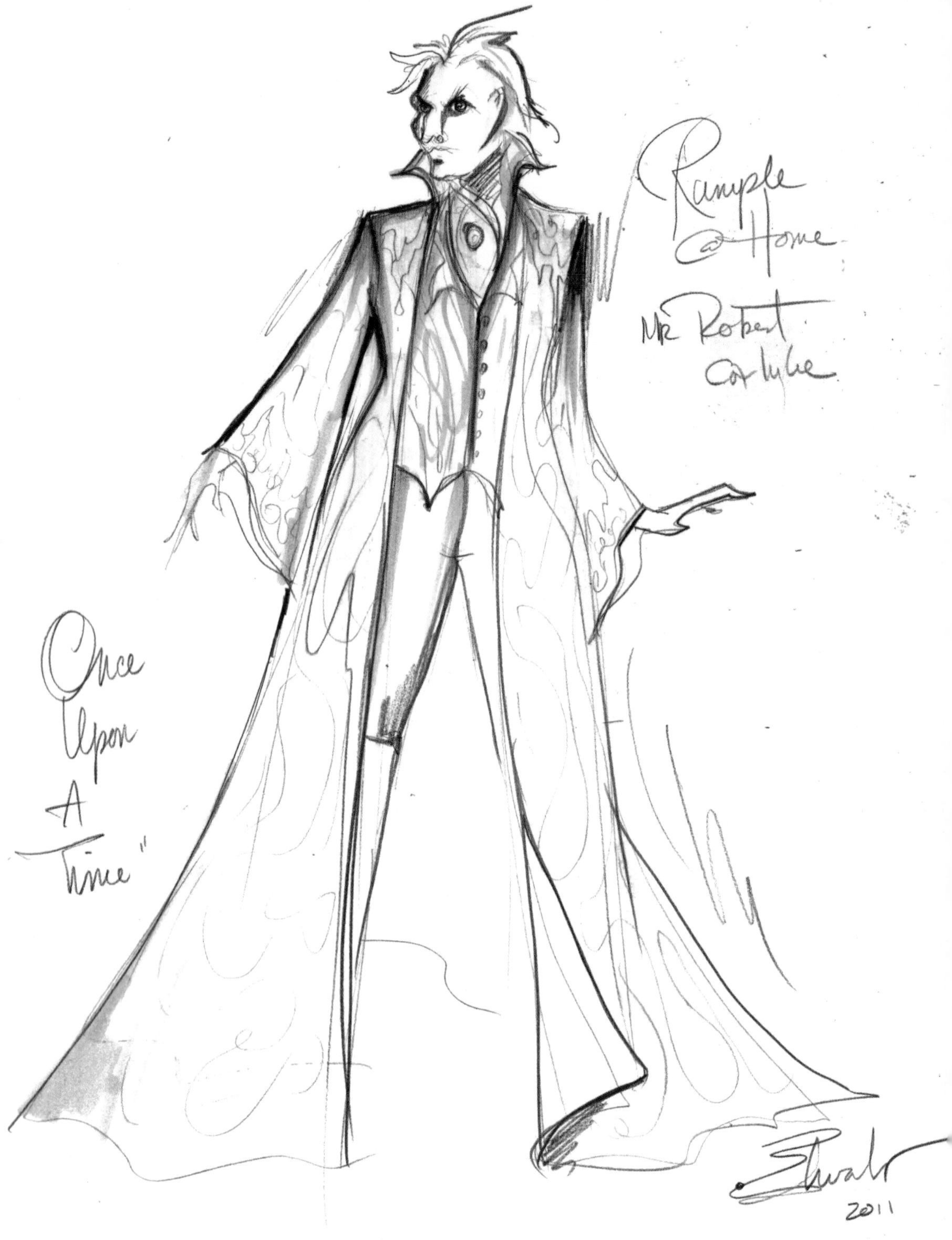
Rumple @ Home
Mr Robert Carlyle
Once Upon A Time"
2011

RUMPLESTILTSKIN

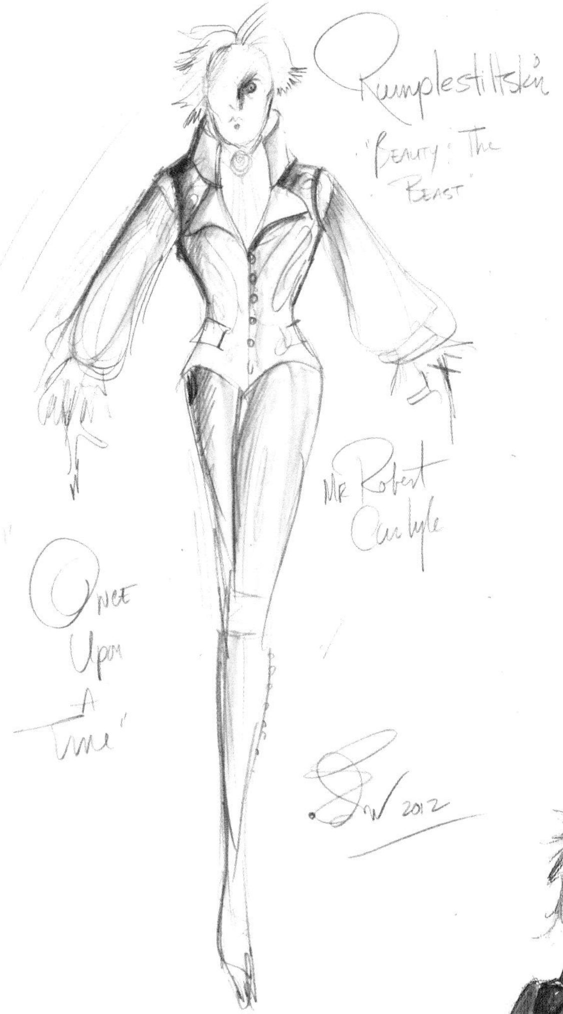

Rumplestiltskin
"Beauty & The Beast"
Mr Robert Carlyle
"Once Upon A Time"
2012

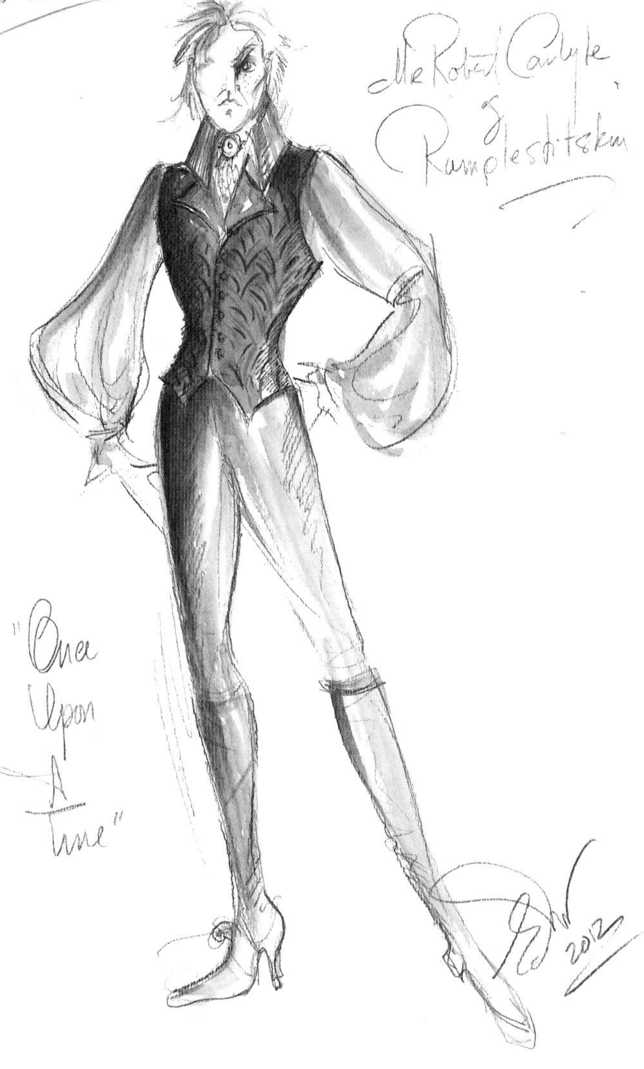

Mr Robert Carlyle as Rumplestiltskin
"Once Upon A Time"
2012